"*Future Jobs* lays out a roadmap to the best jobs and careers in America in the coming years. By also explaining the gaps between our educational system's current outputs and the different skill sets employers are increasingly seeking, Ed Gordon has done a service not just for students, their parents and educators, but most importantly, for the executives now losing the global talent search competition. Finally, by cataloging working examples of regional workforce development partnerships, Gordon shows there are solutions here today that can help deliver the technical training so key to our country's future prosperity."

—*William J. Bowe*
Executive Vice President, Encyclopædia Britannica, Inc.

"*Future Jobs* is the clearest, most incisive assessment of our job crisis I've seen. It's unique in getting beyond hand-wringing to real life solutions—an invaluable resource for individuals and communities."

—*Henry J. (Hank) Lindborg, Ph.D.*
Marian University
Past Chair, Career Workforce Policy Committee, IEEE

"*Future Jobs* puts the critical shortage of highly trained business, professional, and construction jobs into an extremely readable and understandable perspective. As a pioneer articulating this growing shortage of skilled professionals at a time of accelerated technical evolution, Gordon's book is a call to resolution that can be accomplished by America's business leaders, best equipped to resolve this problem."

—*Morris R. Beschloss*
Global Economist & Analyst, Business News Publishing

"You volunteer your time to education and employment initiatives. You donate resources. Read *Future Jobs: Solving the Employment and Skills Crisis* to know why your continued contributions will be absolutely essential to enlarging your community's future talent pool and keeping the U.S. an economic superpower."

—*Peggy Luce*
Vice President, Chicagoland Chamber of Commerce

"Everybody talks about the growing shortage of skilled workers, but nobody has done anything about it . . . until now. In *Future Jobs*, Ed Gordon documents the widening gap between the skills required by the 21st century workplace and the skills by the graduates of our 20th century schools. He also reports on the growing number of successful local initiatives to close the skills gap and accelerate economic growth. An open invitation to local activism! Just add leadership and stir!"

—*David Pearce Snyder*
Contributing Editor, *The Futurist* Magazine

"Dr. Gordon's book is a wake-up call to the world. The demographic and economic changes that have taken place in recent years not only in the US, but globally have changed things forever. The mismatch between the education our schools provide and the skills businesses need has never been greater. Our education system is ineffective, producing graduates with skills that are not needed and have no place in our society. At the same time businesses have numerous jobs that go unfilled because they cannot find individuals with the required skills and talent to fill them. His research and insights on the concept of Regional Talent Innovation Networks (RETAINs) may be the only way to re-sync our society and bring back the competitive advantage we have been known for."

—*George Vukotich, Ph.D.*
Dean, College of Business, Concordia University, Chicago

"If you care about the future of our economy for the next generation, read this book. Gordon delivers a wake-up call and it's time for us to wake up. *Future Jobs* provides all you need to know to get engaged—really engaged—in the single most important challenge we face as a nation: transforming our economy by investing in people and skills. With each of us taking small steps, our nation can make a huge leap. That's how it's done. That's how it's always been done."

—*Ed Morrison*
Regional Economic Development Advisor, Purdue University

"An amazing book that everyone needs to read! Dr. Gordon cites well-documented information about the mismatch of needed and available job skills, and he proposes solutions to the education-to-employment dilemma. He notes the success of many Regional Talent Innovation Networks in creating talent to meet the employment and skills crisis."

—*Pat Nellor Wickwire, Ph.D.*
President, American Association for Career Education

"A book every parent should read as soon as the first child joins high school. It will be a great help to make an informed decision about job opportunities and challenges our kids will encounter and how to help them in making the right choices."

—*Martin von Walterskirchen*
Regional Director, Americas Swiss Trade and Investment Promotion

"Ed Gordon pulls no punches in *Future Jobs*. He quickly identifies local, national, and international workforce challenges and provides us with a multitude of real solutions that will change lives, businesses and communities forever!"

—*Bob Zettler*
Workforce Consultant for Richland County
Commissioners Richland County, Ohio

"Ed Gordon, an expert on jobs and the people who do them, has zeroed in on a jobs crisis that should keep all of us—employers, educators, especially tomorrow's workers—awake at night. There's a "new job era" Gordon says, with a workplace that demands technological skills and education that most Americans don't have, and that schools aren't teaching. Our economy and our standard of living depend on solving this problem. In *Future Jobs*, Gordon shows the way."

—*Richard C. Longworth*
Senior Fellow, Chicago Council on Global Affairs

"Ed Gordon's *Future Jobs* offers a true reform and growth compass to educators, public officials, and business leaders facing skills and jobs mismatches in their communities. He focuses on regional public/private partnerships and presents careful research and pertinent case studies that offer practical guidance for reviving stalled economies."

—*Dale Ward*
Executive Director, High School Inc.

"Typical of Ed Gordon's in-your-face, call-to-arms style, *Future Jobs* does not disappoint. The book highlights contributions that education, government, business and American society have made to the talent crisis, as well as our collective responsibility for its resolution. Gordon provides well-researched, challenging perspectives and examples of real-life, real-time successes to spark much needed collective, cross-sector conversation. Unless we confront the mythologies we have created, identify the knowledge and best practices needed to revitalize our communities and their economies, provide freedom to public education to diversify, and sustain resources essential to supporting creativity and innovation, we will fail—again."

—*Judith A. Ponticell, Ph.D.*
Professor, Educational Leadership and Policy Studies, University of South Florida

"The United States is in serious danger of losing the global enterprise war. Not only will *Future Jobs* help you to understand how we got here, but it also shows critical ways you can support responding to this dire situation. The very survival of our country depends on people at all levels waking up to the perilous position to which our mismanaged priorities have brought us. This valuable book is the wake-up call this country needs."

—*Joyce Gioia*
CEO, The Herman Group

"Sustainable talent creation and attraction is the 'ground zero' of economic development. 'Talent-ready' has superseded 'shovel ready.' There is no quick fix to the decades of public-private disconnect and myopic perspective that have lead us all to this talent crisis. *Future Jobs* is an insightful blueprint for effective and immediate collaboration and an action imperative for individual and community survival."

—*Vicki L. Haugen*
President & CEO, Vermilion Advantage

"A wonderful book. Using RETAINs Ed Gordon solves today's employment and skills crisis."

—*Paul J. Miller*
Retired Partner, SNR Denton

"Ed Gordon hits the nail on the head! The alignment of workforce skills development and new 21st century jobs is the key to economic success."

—*Thomas Flavin*
CEO, Coachella Valley Economic Partnership (CVEP), Palm Springs, CA

"Everything you need to know about America's "good jobs" crisis, the growing work-skills gap and what we can do to fix the education to employment system is in this book. *Future Jobs* is a no-holds-barred wake-up call that every business person, employee, educator, parent and policy maker should read. Our future really is at stake."

—*Lynn E. Gresham*
Business Writer

"Addressing the skills shortage is one of the largest challenges we have faced in many years in our rural area. In *Future Jobs*, Ed Gordon once again explains the true problems, identifies the roadblocks and then offers a blueprint for sustaining our human capital and preserving jobs for the future. Through Ed's RETAINs (Regional Talent Innovation Networks), we have a chance to once again be a viable region."

—*Art Borum*
Executive Director, South Central Illinois Growth Alliance

"As a member of the post–baby boomer generation and a former state legislator, I am deeply concerned about the future of work and employment in America. Ed Gordon's research in *Future Jobs* is impeccable as always, and his policy and private-sector recommendations are actionable! Affecting change at local levels, through RETAINs, is a powerful workforce and economic development approach that is achievable in every community."

—*Jana M. Kemp*
Idaho Representative 2004–2006, 2010 Candidate for Idaho Governor

"This useful book offers important tools for those who seek or offer tomorrow's jobs. On the one hand, new career analysis techniques are invaluable for each hopeful employee and his or her family. On the other hand, an investment calculator allows businesses to consider new training programs in dollars and cents."

—*Fran Kellogg Smith Anderson, FASID*
Honorary Life Member Interior Design Educators Council

"There's certainly a skills gap. It's such a critical time with so many discussions about economic development. We need to act now."

—*Kithio Mwanzia*
Director of Policy & Government Relations, Greater Niagara Chamber of Commerce

"I have really enjoyed reading Ed Gordon's latest book as it has been most helpful in trying to keep jobs and draw businesses to our region. Business has to bring business and *Future Jobs* will be a wonderful help to me. This man does great research and is most insightful. Keep those books coming!"

—*George Darte*
Ontario, Canada
Past President, International Society of the Golden Rule

"Skill mismatches create opportunities to raise the skills, employment and earnings of American workers, but only by developing new policies that change the nation's thinking to attach more importance to occupational and employability skills. Edward Gordon's distinctive contribution points the way to this new thinking and, more importantly, offers constructive proposals for substantially improving the match between employer demand and worker skills."

—*Robert I. Lerman*
Professor of Economics, American University and Institute Fellow, Urban Institute

Future Jobs

Solving the Employment and Skills Crisis

Edward E. Gordon

Foreword by Kevin Hollenbeck

 PRAEGER™

An Imprint of ABC-CLIO, LLC

Santa Barbara, California • Denver, Colorado

Library of Congress Cataloging-in-Publication Data

Gordon, Edward E.
  Future jobs : solving the employment and skills crisis / Edward E. Gordon ; foreword by Kevin Hollenbeck.
     pages cm
  Includes bibliographical references and index.
  ISBN 978-1-4408-2933-8 (hardcopy : alk. paper) — ISBN 978-1-4408-2934-5 (ebook)
1. Labor market—United States.   2. Skilled labor—United States.   3. Occupations—United States—Forecasting.   4. Manpower policy—United States.   5. Education—United States.   I. Title.
   HD5724.G6373   2013
   331.10973—dc23   2013027612

ISBN: 978-1-4408-2933-8 (hardcover)
       978-1-4408-6365-3 (paperback)
       978-1-4408-2934-5 (ebook)

17   16   15   14   13   1   2   3   4   5

This book is also available on the World Wide Web as an eBook.
Visit www.abc-clio.com for details.

Praeger
An Imprint of ABC-CLIO, LLC

ABC-CLIO, LLC
130 Cremona Drive, P.O. Box 1911
Santa Barbara, California 93116-1911

This book is printed on acid-free paper ∞

Manufactured in the United States of America

To my beloved sister Marilyn, who is greatly missed.

Contents

Foreword

While reading Ed Gordon's panoramic, but sometimes frightening, review of the current and future state of the U.S. labor market, I was reminded of the adage about the frog in the pot. If you put a frog into a pot of boiling water, it will jump out. But if you put a frog in a pot of water and then boil it, the consequences will be dire for the frog. A dark interpretation of Gordon's analyses would suggest that we (workers, employers, policymakers, and politicians), like the frog, have not been alarmed enough by the signals of a widening skills gap, sluggish postrecession recovery, long-term trends in wages that are flat or downward sloping for most workers, rising inequality, and concerns about a failing educational system to jump to action, and now we face dire consequences in the form of a "talent cliff."

Ed is suggesting that a structural change has occurred. We have gone from the Computer Age to the Cyber-Mental Age. As a card-carrying member of the occupation that follows the dismal science, as economics is often referred to, I have been trained to think of the world in incremental terms. Change happens at the margin; not all at once in structural shifts. So, my view of the world is not so dramatic. Technological changes are causing the relative prices of skills to change, and the market will adjust. The turbulence that we are observing now is simply that of market adjustment. Of course, we marginalists have to confront the fact that structural changes have occurred—economies have transitioned from agrarian to industrial and from industrial to information technology based. At some point, we have to admit that the water is boiling, and we have to hop out of the pot.

Thankfully, this book is not a horror story. Ed provides us with a way to a happy ending, although he first disabuses us from the notion that importing talent will be a solution. While the importation of talent may be a (marginal) band-aid, he suggests that global competition and home country attraction will limit its effectiveness. Rather, Ed's policy prescription is in labor market intermediaries that he has dubbed RETAINs (Regional

Talent Innovation Networks). He provides several examples of these entities. Of course, sectoral- and regional-based labor market intermediaries
have been around for several years (see, for example, R. Giloth, 2004, *Workforce Intermediaries for the Twenty-First Century*, Temple University Press).
Although they are generally very difficult to evaluate, these intermediaries
are thought to be quite successful. The key question in my mind is the extent to which they meet the challenge of the third word in Ed's acronym,
that is, innovation. In my experience of observing and analyzing such intermediaries, I have found that new ideas and challenges have not been easily
accepted by these consortia of existing (dare I say, status quo) organizations. In some of Ed's descriptions of collaborative groups, however, I believe that he has hit the key ingredient that can inculcate innovation—that
ingredient is visionary leadership.

I have had the opportunity to study regional workforce development/
economic development consortia on a couple of occasions. In each study,
I have found that consortium success was almost perfectly correlated with
leadership talent. Using both objective and subjective measures of success,
consortia seem to thrive when there was an energetic leader who was well
respected by stakeholders, who was well organized, and who had excellent
communication skills.

Long a student of and a provider of corporate training, Ed has used the
forum of this book to once again advocate for a sensible and easily accomplished policy change that would begin to ameliorate the underinvestment
in skill development in this country. He argues that corporations should be
allowed to depreciate their investments in human capital just as they can
depreciate (physical) capital investments. The relentlessness of the pressure
to achieve positive quarterly financial performance incents companies to
minimize expenses to the extent that they can. Allowing training investments to depreciate over a reasonable time frame would improve quarterly
profits by spreading the direct costs of training and even the wage costs
of training participants over multiple quarters. This simple accounting
change would inculcate corporate attitudes of growing their own, rather
than poaching talent from competitors.

A final note of caution that I might offer to Ed and to readers is a concern about the homogeneity of populations and cultures. Several of the
praised examples in the volume have very little socioeconomic or cultural
diversity to confront: the economies of the state of North Dakota and the
country of Singapore, or the educational system in Finland, for example.
My hypothesis is that it is much more difficult to succeed when underlying talents, background, and ability are widely varying than when they are

more homogeneous. I would like to add some color to Ed's acronym, and make it REDTAINs (Regional Diverse Talent Innovation Networks).

Readers will find Ed's exposition from occupational choice to skills gap to talent cliff to educational reform to labor market intermediaries called RETAINs well written, well argued, and informative. Knowing Ed, I suspect he would also like to add the adjective provocative. I further suspect that he would be pleased if you are provoked incrementally or if you are provoked more profoundly. He just doesn't want you to wait until the water is boiling.

Kevin Hollenbeck
W. E. Upjohn Institute for Employment Research

Preface

A Job Market Tipping Point

Since 2013, when *Future Jobs* was originally published, the jobs-skills gap has continued to grow. As a result, the U.S. labor market is in turmoil. Millions of prime-age workers have given up even looking for employment. Their middle-class job woes greatly contributed to the chaos surrounding the 2016 populist election season.

However, 2017 marked a dramatic job-related tipping point. Business annual employee training investment rose from $70.6 billion to $93.6 billion (2017 Training Industry Report, *Training* magazine, December 2017). This one-year annual increase of $23 billion or 32.5 percent is unprecedented. It is by far the largest U.S. business increase in talent development expenditures since World War II. Most of this funding increase was in professional/industry-specific training of workers rather than executive/management development, which previously took the lion's share of training dollars. What motivated business to make this dramatic change?

With over 9 million vacant jobs across the U.S. economy at the end of 2017, companies are beginning to radically rethink their investments in worker training and education. As the December 8, 2017 issue of the *Kiplinger Letter* stated, "Businesses are turning to a new strategy: Train the workers they need themselves." The U.S. Chamber of Commerce estimates a loss of $26,000 per vacant job in profit or productivity for a business. This represents an overall $234 billion loss to the U.S. economy.

The U.S. Bureau of Labor Statistics reported that 6.5 million workers were unemployed in November 2017. However, an additional estimated 23 million trainable prime-age workers were not included in this number because they were discouraged from seeking employment since only 20 percent of U.S. businesses provided training programs to fill empty positions (Manpower, 2016). Yet if these company programs were expanded, the potential labor pool of U.S. workers would increase from 6.5 million to 29.5 million people.

The increasing financial pain from rising levels of job vacancies has caused businesses to dramatically increase their job training and reskilling programs. This, however, represents only half the battle for talent raging across the United States and the entire world. In survey after survey, American employers from large to small report that finding employees with requisite education and skill levels is their greatest problem. Respondents to a third-quarter 2017 Duke University/*CFO* magazine survey not only reported finding IT workers and managers difficult, but also indicated having problems finding rank-and-file employees with basic writing and math skills. Too few American adults have failed to master the critical skill of "learning how to learn."

The "Ah-ha" Moment

Edna, a young Hispanic student in the High School Inc. program at Valley High School in Santa Ana, California, was filmed as she gave a presentation on a greeting card company started in her career education program. As the camera rolled, she related how her student team worked with local volunteer professionals to successfully create and sell a new line of greeting cards. Her eyes brightened as she recounted the journey from the first day of class to meeting with mentors who encouraged her strive to her full capacity and then her success in becoming the president of the new student-run company.

Then in the course of her narrative, Edna's voice cracked, overwhelmed by a surge of pride. As her eyes filled with tears and her fingers fluttered, she had the courage to raise her voice and tell the world, "I learned how to do things I never thought I could do!" Edna had just experienced an important "ah-ha" moment that would influence the rest of her life. She realized she had attained the important ability of "learning how to learn." It is an ability that is essential in developing America's future workers (Jack E. Oakes, *Maximum Impact Education*, Rowman & Littlefield 2015, p. 51).

We need to develop more Ednas. "Learning how to learn" has become the essential skill set for workers. Businesses need more people who can easily adapt and learn new skills as job conditions and market demands rapidly change.

In 2018, only about one-third of the American workforce meets this standard, which is about the same proportion as in 1970. Over the past five decades, technology has raised the education bar for occupations paying a middle-class wage. The old high-wage/low-skill jobs of the past have permanently disappeared.

The U.S. Department of Education conducts a nationwide testing program, the National Assessment of Educational Progress (NAEP). In the latest round of testing, only 25 percent of 12th graders were proficient in math and 37 percent in reading. The alarmingly low skills levels of a significant proportion of U.S. students indicate they do not have the educational foundations that will equip them for success in higher education or today's labor market.

Lessons from the Past

We tend to forget that between 1890 and 1920 the United States experienced a similar automation/workforce crisis. The nation's economy shifted from being primarily agricultural to one based on industrial production. Urban areas swelled as factories and offices grew, and large numbers of immigrants came to the United States to find better economic opportunities. Public schooling in the cities took on the task of assimilating the newcomers and providing them with the ethos and education needed for jobs in offices and factories.

Even more importantly, children were removed from labor in factories and on farms and sent to school. For the first time, women attended high school in large numbers. This education revolution was triggered by the introduction of the new advanced technologies of that day: electricity, assembly lines, automobiles, tractors, telephones, radios, household appliances, and so forth.

Community, business, and political leaders came to see the links between supporting a new education-to-employment system and social progress. Samuel Gompers of the American Federation of Labor, newspaper publisher Henry George, industrialists Henry Ford and Andrew Carnegie, inventor Thomas Edison, and politicians such as Theodore Roosevelt and Woodrow Wilson all joined together in supporting and building mandatory, tax-supported public education.

This system fostered education and skills for this new age plus a work ethic that included punctuality, respect for authority, quality workmanship, and self-discipline. The United States was the first nation in history to attempt to create and support such an education-to-employment system.

For most of the 20th century (through two world wars; the rise of the U.S. middle class; and the collapse of the Soviet Union, ending the Cold War), this educational arrangement worked very well. It transformed the

United States from a rural, agricultural nation into the world's number one economic superpower. It was not a prefect system, but it was strengthened over the next decades by the GI Bill, vocational-technical programs, and much more. This system began failing in the 1970s as a new wave of technology was introduced and has now grown exponentially into the early 21st century.

Education Reform Is Crucial

Despite the enormity of the challenge, the United States and other nations must implement the massive socioeconomic changes required by the more demanding talent creation system of a 21st-century knowledge-driven, high-tech economy. Yet major components of our society such as businesses, unions, government, educators, and parents resist making major changes in schools, colleges and universities, technical and workplace training, and at home. This is happening because as a society we have failed to clearly provide a coherent picture of what sustains our modern standard of living. It explains much of the public's hostility to overhauling the largely outdated 20th-century education-to-employment system. This system is similar to running a high-performance race car on low-octane fuel! It is self-defeating for students/parents and workers/businesses.

Reforming the U.S. education-to-employment system needs to begin with stronger efforts to raise individual literacy, numeracy, and personal oral and written communications skills at the elementary and high school levels. Parents should be worried about their children's employment future. They can and should play a bigger part in preparing them for it—by fostering learning in the home and supporting more school options that promote learning how to learn through focusing on the development of each student's aptitudes and interests. In a rapidly changing world, every student needs to experience the "ah-ha" moment that connects learning to real life.

As *Future Jobs* advocates, career education needs to begin in elementary school and stronger career guidance should be provided in high school. A major objective of *Future Jobs* is to provide students and parents with guidance on preparing for careers and with information on the career areas that have the most promise for growth.

Inside every business, innovation occurs only when properly educated and skilled workers can utilize advanced technologies that increase performance, productivity, and profits. For this to happen, businesses must make both short- and long-term investments in training and education. The United States requires dynamic local business leaders who get this message.

They need to broadly participate in updating education and training and spearhead a culture change that acknowledges the real impact of learning on the American economy.

The Promise of Regional Collaboration

Substantive socioeconomic change requires a buy-in by major sectors of a community. *Future Jobs* focuses on how regional cross-sector collaborative efforts are solving the skills-jobs disconnect in their local communities. These Regional Talent Innovation Networks (RETAINs) have many local brand names such as High School Inc. (Santa Ana, CA), the Vermilion Advantage (Danville, IL), or the New North (18 counties in northeastern Wisconsin). These and over 1,000 other RETAINs are advancing their region's economic growth through collaboratively linking diverse community sectors. In *Future Jobs,* you will learn how in the short term they are coordinating training programs for current workers, while in the long term they are rebuilding the education-to-employment pipeline by effectively linking educational institutions and local business sectors.

Identity politics is threatening to divide America into warring groups demanding individual privileges instead of supporting the greater community's needs through personal civic engagement. A RETAIN offers a forum that unites rather than divides, rebuilds rather than defends the status quo.

Acknowledgments

There are many individuals who have supported this research in important ways that I wish to gratefully acknowledge, especially the following: Nicki Askov, Carolyn and James Ausman, Morris Beschloss, Ronald Bird, Michael Bloom, George Darte, Anne Edmunds, Isaac Eliachar, Thomas Flavin, Tom Frisbie, Joyce Gioia, Dianne Glass, Joanna Greene, Larry Guzzetta, Vicki Haugen, Jana Kemp, Joan Klaus, DeBorah Lenchard, Richard Longworth, Henry Lindborg, Peggy Luce, Jim McShane, Paul J. Miller, Ronald R. Morgan, Ed Morrison, Harry Moser, Tapan Munroe, Robert M. Naiman, Richard Oliphant, Charles J. O'Malley, Vin O'Neill, Boyd Owens, James Parker, Frances Ryan, Jennifer Schramm, Patty Shortt, Ed Skonezny, David Pearce Snyder, William Strauss, Dan Swinney, Andrea Taylor, Pat Tucker, Martin von Walterskirchen, Dale Ward, Pat Nellor Wickwire, Robert J. Witchger, Ira Wolf, Beth Zander, Mike Zenanko, and Robert Zettler.

I also thank Brian Romer, who while at Praeger/ABC-CLIO agreed to take on this book, and Hilary Claggett, senior editor for Business, Economics and Finance, for her support throughout this book's production.

John Willig, my literary agent, deserves a great deal of credit for teaching me about the difficult world of publishing. Without his continuing advice and encouragement, this book would never have been written.

Kevin Hollenbeck at the W. E. Upjohn Institute for Employment Research for many years has coached and worked with me on multiple training and employment issues. I am profoundly grateful for his invaluable professional assistance and insightful foreword.

Valerie Collier has once again risen to the challenge of remaining an indispensable part of our editorial team. Her diligent, outstanding work was indispensable in helping prepare the manuscript.

Above all others, my wife and partner, Elaine Gordon, has contributed much blood, sweat, and tears on the research and editing of this work. Her insights, suggestions, and rewrites have made it a far better book.

For any errors or omissions in this book, I take full responsibility. But the enjoyment of writing comes from hearing back from all of you readers on your own thoughts, comment, and suggestions.

Edward E. Gordon
Chicago, Illinois

Introduction
The Jobs Revolution

The vision of the future should shape the agenda for the present.[1]
—Shimon Peres, Nobel Peace Prize Speech, 1994

During the past two decades, I have written about and worked with business, government, and educational institutions facing a widening skills-jobs disconnect. The jobs revolution is not going away. It now looms ominously over all Americans and the global economy.

Here are some snapshots from workers and businesses.

Jan is a recent college graduate with a degree in communications. Now, she can't find a job that matches her education.

Ben dropped out of high school to become a construction worker but was let go in the housing recession. There are few good paying jobs for people like Ben with no skills or little education.

After finishing high school, Cody worked hard for a decade and became an office manager. Then, in 2010, the company went out of business. Though she took some college business courses, Cody finds companies have little interest in hiring her.

For the past 20 years, José has been an IT programmer. Now, he is unemployed but lacks the latest software knowledge to fill current computer positions.

Robert is a production manager at an aerospace facility. His company has back orders for aircraft stretching to the end of the decade. He can't find additional aerospace technicians to meet increased customer demands or even to replace his baby boomer workers who are retiring. Worse yet, Robert's parts subcontractors are also having difficulty finding skilled technical workers. These companies are often unable to supply vital components to meet his production needs.

As the client services vice president of a major fund management company, Betty needs to hire large numbers of personal financial advisors. They will assist baby boomers in evaluating distribution plans for their retirement accounts. However, she is experiencing increasing difficulty in recruiting recent college finance graduates. Most candidates seem to lack the oral and written communication skills or personal motivation for conducting counseling sessions with clients.

These snapshots illustrate a gap that has been growing since the 1980s between worker qualifications and the skills employers are seeking. Technology and global business practices have continuously raised the employee knowledge bar for most jobs. Yet the education-to-employment system has remained the same. We have failed to respond to the challenge of creating a larger talent pool of skilled people in our communities.

Also, a major demographic shift is underway. Every day, 10,000 baby boomers are retiring; 70 million will retire between 2010 and 2020. Their technical skills are increasingly found to be in short supply as employers struggle to find replacement workers.

Society has been in denial. If a major economic event doesn't have a personal impact, most people will not change their cultural outlook. Public opinion will only begin to shift as the majority of people become directly caught up in this unfolding jobs revolution.

But now we have reached an employment tipping point. The broad requirements of the U.S. job market can no longer be supplied simply by maintaining the current failing system. This talent shambles is set to worsen.

The United States and the world are locked into a structural labor market race between advanced technology on one side and demographics and education on the other. Too few Americans are prepared to run in this race. By the end of this decade, many businesses will no longer have the talent they need to sustain themselves.

Around the world, workers and businesses are caught up in a transitional labor market era. The ready availability of skilled talent, not location, is now the primary factor in determining local employment. In this new era, the success or failure of individual businesses and of regional or national economies will largely be determined by their ability to provide more people who can meet labor market requirements with the right skills at the right time.

Instead of the needed systemic overhaul, many leaders in business, government, and education still think they can make the old system well again. "We all think that we know certain things to be true beyond doubt, but these things often then turn out to be false, and until we unlearn them, they get in the way of new understanding," stated Matt Ridley, author of *The Rational Optimist* (2011).[2]

Many still fail to grasp that technological progress is occurring too fast for labor markets and current talent creation systems to meaningfully adjust. These talent problems are structural. They also are systemic. U.S. businesses will make big gains as they find better ways to use new technologies, but only if they relearn the importance of investing in the education and training that workers and students need for this new jobs era.[3]

Until recently, U.S. businesses have bridged this skills deficit by using the twin talent safety valves of importing educated workers or exporting overseas high-pay/high-skills jobs wherever they could find a skilled talent pool. These talent safety valves are beginning to fail in part because this is also an international jobs–talent issue. The World Economic Forum (2011) predicts that this disconnect will persist for decades and the worst global talent shortages are yet to come.[4]

The demand for talent and the supply of workers with the desired skills are out of balance all over the world. The populations of Japan, South Korea, and many European nations are in decline. India and China are moving into more sophisticated high-tech manufacturing or IT services. They both are now encountering severe shortages of engineers, scientists, and technicians with the requisite educational preparation due to their deficient public education systems and the inadequate standards of institutions of higher learning.

A major structural change also is occurring in the U.S. labor market. Though the GDP has risen, unemployment has not fallen in a way consistent with the number of jobs openings. Why?

U.S. productivity is increasing. In manufacturing and most other business sectors, it's not just advanced machines. It's increasingly evident that many new advanced technologies are digitizing the whole economy.

Past history shows that today's surge in U.S. productivity will create tomorrow's jobs and raise living standards. New jobs will come from rising efficiencies in production and innovative technologies spawning new products and services throughout the entire economy.

The flip side to these breakthroughs is that today's and tomorrow's jobs require advanced technical skill levels. A workplace may need fewer people, but they must be better educated and able to work with advanced computer systems. This has become the new normal for employment whether it is in an office, production facility, hospital, law firm, or service business.

These digitized jobs present a new problem. The consensus among employers is that people need to be reskilled for the new workplace. The urgent need to create more skilled workers is now a central political and economic concern in communities across America.

A new U.S. job era has arrived. The availability of better educated talent with up-to-date career skills now largely determines where businesses will locate in the United States or anywhere in the world. Those communities that break down the structural barriers between businesses, education, and community groups and that collaborate to renew their talent creation and economic systems will attract new businesses and retain current ones. Those that don't will wither and die.

The Great Recession has accelerated an ongoing labor market shift that was masked by the many low- or semi-skilled jobs created during the housing/financial bubble. In today's labor market, employment for low- or semi-skilled workers has fallen dramatically. Even middle-skilled professionals have seen a steady decline in jobs because of automation. In general, the job opportunities are brighter for high-skilled people who have kept their knowledge and applicable certifications up-to-date and who can relocate to where jobs exist.

The American education-to-employment system is largely failing to prepare more people with the required skills to compete in this new labor market era. Laid-off workers often lack the skills to move into jobs in growing sectors of the economy. Businesses and government job training programs are largely inconsistent, short term, or too generic.

As a direct result over this decade, the United States is at real risk of an expanding poverty cycle as talent deficits spread across the entire economy. Systemic change will not be easy. However, holding onto the job-skills status quo portends an economic disaster.

At present, America is unilaterally ceding its global leadership in technology and innovation to other nations. The economic advantages gained from U.S. educational exceptionalism in the 20th century have disappeared. Too many younger workers lack both the general education and specialized career skills, let alone a strong work ethic, to sustain a middle class standard of living. They are now adding to the growing American underclass.

In 2013, over 89 million Americans of working age were not part of the U.S. labor market. The number of people looking for work (labor participation rate) was near the historic low of 63.6 percent, while the average duration of unemployment remained near historic highs. Why are so many Americans sitting on the job sidelines, while over six million jobs are vacant across the United States?

How can we bring these people back into the job market? What can be done locally and regionally to restructure the talent creation system? How can we rebuild the jobs pipeline that connects local businesses to the skilled talent needed to remain competitive and survive?

Future Jobs: Solving the Employment and Skills Crisis offers answers to this jobs and skills disconnect and other pressing employment questions. Its foremost objective is to give people and businesses alike renewed hope for a better future workforce and confidence about meeting the challenges that stand in the way.

Future Jobs explores the concept behind Regional Talent Innovation Networks (RETAINs) and their credibility as a major labor market change engine. RETAINs are community intermediaries. They act as hubs for cross-sector partnerships engaged in a systemic redesign that matches skills and jobs to regional economic development. RETAINs facilitate broader civic engagement by forging links between businesses, educators, community leaders, and ordinary citizens.

Future Jobs presents a problem and solution format in four parts:

Part I: What will be the hot jobs over the next decade? How can individuals find the career areas that best suit them? What are the best ways of preparing for these careers?

Part II: What stands in the way of rebuilding the jobs pipeline? How has our culture blindsided businesses and people from recognizing the necessity for updating the education-to-employment system?

Part III: What makes RETAINs a flexible and powerful employment solution? Where have RETAIN breakthroughs begun to rebuild the talent creation system?

Part IV: How can future business and government policy changes help bring RETAINs to scale across the United States and around the globe? What are future potential scenarios for U.S. job market and the economy?

The U.S. federal and state budgets now face an indefinite period of reduced government resources. Private sector employers will be the main source of job creation and innovation. They will hire people to support innovation and business expansion, but not until they again recognize the tremendous potential of investing in the American workforce.[5] We are lagging behind many of our competitors who are more effectively investing in their own workforces, because much of U.S. business culture remains at the mercy of Wall Street's fixation on short-term profit.

As a result of all these converging issues, we have found ourselves in a profound watershed era of economic change. "We're at one of those extraordinary moments in history when each of us gets the opportunity to play an important role in not only transitioning to a new world, but also designing it," stated John L. Petersen, president of the Arlington Institute.[6] This requires a renewed level of civic engagement from all of us, as part of a pro-jobs, pro-growth agenda addressing the employment and skills crisis and downplaying short-term profit taking.

This author's ultimate objective is to help everyone reconsider the choices we will need to make in the journey through the employment crossroads. The time for action is today, before other skilled foreign competitors take away our future.

Part I
Jobs and Careers

Chapter 1

The "Good Jobs"

The wealth of a country is its working people.[1]

—Theodor Herzl

New Job Era Arrives

The on-going U.S. employment crisis has left many people believing there is no tomorrow and for good reason. Since mid-2008, six million jobs have vanished, many permanently.

Somehow, since 2001, America's gross domestic product (GDP) almost doubled to over $15 trillion. How did this happen? The answer—U.S. productivity is increasing. Advanced machinery requiring fewer workers produces more goods. People with advanced skills are using new advanced technologies to digitalize the whole economy. Exports of these goods and services have reached an all-time high.

More than 30 million Americans are now unemployed, underemployed, or have given up looking for a job. It may seem a fantasy, yet a rising tide of employers now report over six million job vacancies. In many legitimate instances, these employers lament that they are unable to find workers with the requisite skills for vacant jobs. It is becoming increasingly clear that workers need both a better general education and specific career preparation to fill most of these jobs. This has now become the new normal for employment, whether it is in an office, production facility, construction site, law firm, or service business.

U.S. labor market's supply and demand are clearly out of sync with workplace realities. There is an increasing gap between what people are prepared to do versus what businesses want. Each of us has to face a new job era.

There is a silver lining to the current employment thunderclouds. The U.S. Bureau of Labor Statistics forecasts that 54.7 million jobs will have to

TABLE 1.1 New vs. Replacement Jobs 2010–2020 (Selective List)

Job Area	New Job Growth	Replacement Jobs	Total Job Openings
All Jobs	20.5M	33.7M	54.7M
1. Graphic Design	37,000	87,000	124,000
2. Media and Communication	106,000	219,000	325,000
3. Construction Trades	1M	1M	2M
4. Auto Technicians	157,000	229,000	386,000
5. Technical Repair and Maintenance	409,000	570,000	979,000
6. Bus Drivers	83,000	125,000	208,000
7. Fast Food Workers	425,000	1.1M	1.5M
8. Waiters/Waitresses	196,000	1.1M	1.3M
9. Retail Clerks	1.0M	3.0M	4.0M
10. Building/Grounds Occupations	664,000	1.0M	1.6M
11. Farming, Fishing, Foresting	–	290,000	290,000
12. Production Workers	357,000	1.8M	2.2M
13. Hairdressers/Barbers	103,000	131,000	234,000
14. Sales Occupations	1.8M	4.6M	6.4M
15. Engineers	160,000	366,000	526,000
16. Artists	16,000	47,000	63,000
17. Actors	3,000	17,000	20,000
18. Health Care Practitioners	2M	1.6M	3.6M
Career Areas			
Physicians	168,000	137,000	305,000
Dentists	32,000	46,000	78,000
Dental Hygienists	69,000	36,000	105,000
Therapists	190,000	108,000	298,000
Registered Nurses	712,000	495,000	1.2M
Dietitians	13,000	22,000	35,000
Pharmacists	70,000	70,000	140,000
19. Home Health Aides	706,000	131,000	837,000
20. Health Care Technicians	720,000	580,000	1.3M
21. Lawyers	74,000	138,000	212,000
22. Postsecondary Teachers	306,000	280,000	586,000
23. Reporters/Correspondents	–	18,000	18,000

Sources: Data from Bureau of Labor Statistics, "Table 1.2 Employment by Detailed Occupation, 2010 and Projected 2020," last modified February 1, 2012, http://www.bls.gov/emp/ep_table_102.htm; Bureau of Labor Statistics, "Estimating Occupational Replacement Needs," last modified February 1, 2012, http://www.bls.gov/emp/ep_replacements.htm.

be filled by 2020. Of these, 33.7 million (62%) are replacement positions for exiting baby boomers and 20.5 million are new jobs (see Table 1.1).

Between 2010 and 2030, the exodus of about 79 million baby boomers from the workforce will offer many job and career opportunities. (For more about the impact of baby boomer retirements on the labor market, see Chapter 3.) This will even be true in occupations that are forecast to shrink or not grow significantly, such as positions for reporters and correspondents or jobs in farming, fishing, and forestry.

The major question remains—what types of good jobs are currently going unfilled and are projected to be growth areas in the future? A good job is defined here as employment with ample benefits that financially supports a family.

The Hot Occupations

The first consideration is what career sectors will be in demand between now and 2020. Occupational projections and surveys by government, universities, and business research organizations point to five general growth areas that are part of almost every U.S. industry: (1) research and development, (2) information technology, (3) operations, (4) management, and (5) sales.

Science, technology, engineering, and mathematics (STEM)-related occupations will experience significant growth. By the end of this decade, employment in core tech occupations will have increased by almost 20 percent to about 800,000 jobs.

Many of these STEM jobs are driven by exports to booming overseas markets. This includes IT, aerospace, industrial equipment, pharmaceuticals, chemical, and agriculture products. Thirteen percent (12.8%) of all U.S. output is being exported. This is the highest level ever recorded by the U.S. Commerce Department and represents 10 percent of America's GDP.[2]

Most of these STEM jobs will require postsecondary education. Sixty-five percent demand at least a bachelor's degree. Only health care and education occupations have more education-intensive requirements (see Table 1.2).

TABLE 1.2   Education Distribution of Job Growth Due to New and Replacement STEM Jobs 2018

Level of Education	Computer Occupations	Engineers & Engineering Technicians	Life & Physical Science Occupations	Architects Surveyors & Technicians	Mathematical Science Occupations	Total STEM
High School Dropout	10,100	1,600	—	300	—	12,000
High School Graduate	85,000	130,800	6,100	4,000	700	226,600
Some College	184,600	98,100	3,300	4,600	4,400	295,000
Associate's Degree	121,400	175,500	—	8,300	1,700	306,900
Bachelor's Degree	563,400	182,400	129,900	79,400	23,900	979,000
Master's Degree	221,900	72,600	85,000	40,100	11,600	431,200
Professional Degree	8,700	5,300	8,700	2,300	1,900	26,900
Doctorate	24,600	9,500	69,200	3,700	4,600	111,600
Total	1,219,700	675,800	302,200	142,700	48,800	2,389,200*

*Numbers may differ slightly due to rounding.

Source: Georgetown University Center on Education and the Workforce, Forecast of Occupational Growth through 2018, as cited in Anthony P. Carnevale, Nicole Smith, and Michelle Melton, "STEM," Georgetown University Center on Education and the Workforce, 2011. Used by permission.

The Hot Jobs

The second consideration is how does all this translate into specific jobs. The Manpower Group talent shortage surveys of employers from 2007 to 2012 listed the jobs shown in Table 1.3 as the most difficult to fill.

The most consistent shortages in these surveys were for sales representatives, followed by skilled trades, engineers, drivers, and machinists/machine operators. Prior to 2011, technicians were consistently on this list. Surveys conducted by the Society for Human Resource Management in 2011 and 2012 also confirm shortages of engineers, sales representatives, accounting, and finance staff. High-skilled technical positions and scientists also occupied top spots in these surveys. Other sources point to growing shortages for health care professionals and management staff in biomedical and life science areas due to the aging of the large baby boomer cohort.[3]

According to the Bureau of Labor Statistics, 7 of the top 10 occupations expected to see the largest job growth are low-wage or very low-wage jobs (see Table 1.4). Four of the five occupations with very low pay on this list may not require a high school diploma, but these workers will most likely be condemned to staying in low-paying jobs for life if they do not obtain further education. Also, the 2012 Georgetown University Center on Education and the Workforce study, "The College Advantage," indicates that during the Great

TABLE 1.3   Hardest to Fill Jobs in the United States

	2007	2008	2009	2010	2011	2012
Skilled Trades	*	3	3	1	1	1
Engineers	*	1	1	8	3	2
IT Staff	*	9	8	*	6	3
Sales Representatives	1	5	5	2	2	4
Accounting & Finance Staff	8	6	*	*	5	5
Drivers	6	*	7	5	4	6
Mechanics	3	7	*	*	*	7
Nurses	*	*	2	3	*	8
Machinists/Machine Operators	10	2	10	*	10	9
Teachers	2	*	4	*	8	10

*Did not appear in top 10 jobs cited by employers.

Sources: Author's analysis of Manpower Group, *Talent Shortage Survey Results*, 2007–2012.

TABLE 1.4   Ten Fastest Growing (Number of Jobs) Occupational Areas 2010–2020 Projections

Ten Occupations with Most New Jobs	Projected Job Growth 2010–2020	Median 2010 Annual Wage
1. Registered Nurse	711K	Very High
2. Retail Salespersons	706K	Very Low
3. Home Health Aides	706K	Very Low
4. Personal Care Aides	607K	Very Low
5. Office Clerks, General	489K	Low
6. Food Prep & Serving Workers	398K	Very Low
7. Customer Service Reps	338K	Low
8. Heavy Truckers & Tractor-Trailer Truck Drivers	330K	Moderate
9. Laborers & Freight Stock & Material Movers	319K	Very Low
10. Postsecondary Teachers	305K	Very High

Source: Author analysis of Bureau of Labor Statistics, "Employment Projections—2010–20," Table 6, last modified February 1, 2012, http://bls.gov.news.release/pdf/ecopro.pdf.

Recession job losses were far higher for those with less schooling than for those with a four-year degree or higher.[4]

If you are looking for a job, what career areas will be in demand during this decade? A close look at hiring trends offers this composite list:

1. Teachers in health specialties
2. Computer network architects
3. Civil engineers
4. Medical scientists
5. Environmental engineers
6. Software engineers and web developers
7. Mobile media designers, engineers, and editors
8. Product management in high growth industries such as cloud computing, e-commerce, mobile devices, consumer web
9. Marketing (online, new media)
10. Network systems and data communication analysts
11. Accountants (CPAs)
12. Machinists (experienced fabricators, CNC operators)
13. Health care workers (low skill/pay home care aides to higher skill/pay nurses, lab technicians)
14. Biomedical engineers (medical devices)
15. Industrial hygienists (toxic substance removal)

16. Geoscientists (energy exploration and extraction)
17. Embedded engineers (software for microprocessors)
18. Data occupations (network and data software analysts ABAP, SOA, ETL, Weblogic, JDBC, UAL, JBoss, WebSphere)
19. Occupational health and safety workers (specialists in safety equipment technologies)
20. English teaching positions (English taught overseas as the international language)
21. Skilled craft and technical workers (skilled trades, tech applied to manufacturing and industrial jobs)
22. Teachers/Professors (elementary—higher education)[5]

Current popular culture insists that a four-year college degree is the only path for securing a good job. In fact, there are many in-demand career areas for those with two-year degrees (see Table 1.5).

Those who complete a four-year college degree will find that their field of study will have a significant impact on employment opportunities and

TABLE 1.5   Occupations with High Projected Growth Typically Requiring a Two-Year Degree at the Entry Level

Occupation	2010 Median Pay ($)	% Increase 2010–2020	Numeric Growth 2010–2020
Construction Managers	83,860	17%	86,600
Nuclear Medicine Technicians	68,560	19%	4,100
Dental Hygienists	68,250	38%	68,500
Nuclear Technicians	68,090	14%	4,100
Registered Nurses	64,690	26%	711,900
Diagnostic Medical Sonographers	64,380	44%	23,400
Radiologic Technicians	54,340	28%	61,000
Respiratory Therapists	54,280	28%	31,200
Geological & Petroleum Technicians	54,020	15%	2,100
Cardiovascular Technicians	49,410	29%	14,500
Paralegals & Legal Assistants	46,680	18%	46,900
Medical Equipment Repairers	44,490	31%	11,900
Environmental Engineering Technicians	43,390	24%	4,600
Physical Therapy Assistants	37,710	45%	51,100
Veterinary Technicians	29,710	52%	41,700

Source: Data from the Bureau of Labor Statistics, *Occupational Outlook Handbook, 2012–13,* last modified April 26, 2012, http://www.bls.gov/ooh.

TABLE 1.6   Best Paid College Degrees

Degree	Starting Median Pay	Mid-Career Median Pay
Petroleum Engineering	$98,000	$163,000
Aerospace Engineering	$62,500	$118,000
Actuarial Mathematics	$56,100	$112,000
Chemical Engineering	$67,500	$111,000
Nuclear Engineering	$66,800	$107,000
Electrical Engineering	$63,400	$106,000
Computer Engineering	$62,700	$105,000
Applied Mathematics	$50,800	$102,000
Computer Science	$58,400	$100,000
Statistics	$49,300	$99,500

Source: "2012–2013 PayScale College Salary Report," PayScale.com, accessed April 17, 2013, http://www.payscale.com/college-salary-report-2013/majors-that-pay-you-back. Used by permission.

salary levels. Currently, degrees in STEM areas largely command the highest pay (see Table 1.6).

The Hot Jobs Analysis

As we have seen between 2010 and 2020, the U.S. Labor Department projects that 20.5 million new jobs and over 33 million replacement jobs will need to be filled. However, several important factors make this decade a major job change era:

1. Most of the fastest growing and good paying jobs will be in occupations that require some form of postsecondary education/training. This includes apprenticeships and occupational certificates, as well as two/four-year degrees and graduate/professional degrees.
2. The fastest growing occupations are related to health care, personal care, community, and social sciences. Also, greatly increased demand will exist for jobs at all levels of complexity in the science, technology, engineering, and mathematical occupational areas.
3. Low-skill jobs will still account for the greatest number of job openings, but they are not high-paying jobs.
4. A combination of economic and demographic forces will also affect job openings. Due to the exit from employment of the baby-boom generation, replacements will generate more job openings than new job creation, as illustrated in Table 1.1.

A New Jobs Era

Without doubt, this is not your father's or mother's workplace anymore. We have entered a watershed era in which the very nature of work is being transformed. This is not an unprecedented occurrence. There have been at least four previous labor market eras over the course of human history (see Table 1.7).

As is true today, the transition periods between these historic eras were often marked by social and economic turmoil due to the changing nature of workplaces and jobs. Currently, many workers are faced with the necessity of making the transition to a labor marketplace dominated by digital technology. The good-paying, low-skill jobs of the Industrial and Computer Eras are now being replaced by the new high-skill occupations of this Cyber-Mental Era. Today's good jobs require workers to have the knowledge and preparation for creating, implementing, or using these new technologies and the information they produce. In short, today's labor market requires many more workers to have completed both a good to great liberal arts general education plus the specific career education required for a technical or professional occupation.

While an accurate understanding of future job opportunities is very useful, this is only the first step for finding a good job. The next chapter will focus on key career issues that both younger and older workers need to explore on the road to a lifetime of successful employment.

TABLE 1.7 The Progress of Labor Market Eras

	I	II	III	IV	V
Era	Prehistory	Agricultural Age	Industrial Age	Computer Age	Cyber-Mental Age Digital Technology
Time	100,000– 5,000 BC	5,000 BC– AD1850	1850– 1970	1970– 2006	2006–?
Focus	Survival	Food	Machines	Automation	Innovations
Result	Hunting- Gathering	Farming	Mass Production	Data/ Robotics	Intelligent Machines
People	Subsistence Work	Manual Work	Semi-Skilled Work	Information Work	Knowledge Work

Chapter 2

Career versus Jobs
What Are the Issues?

You never achieve real success unless you like what you are doing.[1]

—Dale Carnegie

Now, you can see that the U.S. job market does have a tomorrow. But what career areas offer you the most desirable occupation? Getting an accurate answer is of fundamental importance, whether you are just starting to work, unemployed, or thinking about changing jobs. You will need honest answers to some basic questions about the job market and yourself. This has never been easy and has become more complicated during this change era for jobs.

Generational Challenges

Young people have been especially hard hit during the Great Recession. Unemployment rates for those aged 16–24 have been well above other age groups.

For recent high school grads, finding a full-time job has never been harder. In January 2013, the unemployment rate for those aged 16–19 was 23.4 percent and for 20–24, 14.2 percent. Simply put—most entry-level jobs now require more than a high school diploma (see Table 2.1).

In 2012, half of recent college graduates were either jobless or under-employed. This was the fifth consecutive year that newly minted graduates faced such a tough labor market. Ten percent of younger adults have moved back in with their parents. For 26-year-olds, this reached 20 percent, almost double the figure in 1970.

Success in the job market seems to be driven largely by your field of study. Contrary to prevailing popular culture, a four-year college degree

TABLE 2.1   Changes in Educational Requirements for U.S. Jobs—1973, 2010, and 2020

Level	Percent Share of Jobs		
	1973	2010	2020
Master's Degree or More	7%	11%	11%
Bachelor's Degree	9%	21%	24%
Associate's Degree	12%	10%	12%
Some College or Occupational Certificates	—	17%	18%
High School Diploma	40%	30%	24%
Less than High School	32%	11%	12%

Source: Data from Anthony P. Carnevale, Tamara Jayasundera, and Andrew R. Hanson, "Career and Technical Education: Five Ways that Pay," Georgetown University Center on Education and the Workforce, September 2012, 2.

may not be the magic key to job success for everyone. Even those college graduates with degrees in math, science, or technology often discover that precise specialized certifications or relevant experience are required for good positions.[2]

Workers over the age of 55 are facing a different set of challenges. While the unemployment rate for this age group has been lower than the overall national average, it has increased sharply since the recession's beginning, rising to 7.3 percent in July 2011. A year later, the figure was 6.5 percent. About four million Americans between the ages of 55 and 64 lack a full-time job (one in six). The unemployed over 55, however, do experience greater difficulty in finding new jobs. About half have been unemployed longer than 27 weeks, and those who do find jobs often take a significant pay cut.[3]

"The age bias hasn't been solved yet, but attitudes do seem to be improving," stated SaraRix, senior strategic advisor with the Public Policy Institute of American Association of Retired Persons.[4] A growing number of companies are recognizing that the baby boomers have knowledge and work experiences that can fill in their widening talent gaps.

The labor force participation rate of those over the age of 55 has risen, in part due to declines in the value of their assets and savings and employer shifts to defined contribution retirement plans. However, a late 2011 MetLife survey of the oldest baby boomers (those then aged 65) showed 59 percent were at least partially retired, 45 percent fully retired, and 14 percent retired with a part-time job.[5]

In February 2012, two million people in the U.S. workforce resigned or retired. This was the highest number of job turnovers since the recession began. This is good news for both younger workers and boomers still seeking employment.

All the above generational challenges raise a fundamental issue for contemporary America. Who is to blame for this major generational and jobs and skills disconnect? The United States needs to better prepare both younger and older Americans to fill a rising tide of higher skilled jobs across all business sectors. Part II will provide an in-depth analysis of the cultural, economic, and educational disconnect behind this long-term talent crisis.

Questions for the Career Game

Today, most American high school students plan to be professionals. The majority expect to complete a bachelor's degree. Surveys show that teenagers' career expectations are increasingly out of line with what is possible. Sociological studies indicate that many students have set their goals "on highly ambitious and improbable careers in the professional sports or entertainment industries regardless of their capacity."[6]

Most teenagers greatly underestimate the education needed for an occupation. Once in college, students soon discover that an academic major often does not bestow specific career job skills that will lead directly to a career. This occurs because there are poor channels of communication between educational institutions and businesses in most local communities.

High unemployment rates among recent high school and college graduates helped to spawn the Occupy Wall Street Movement across the United States. Some students and parents are beginning to have doubts that a postsecondary education is worth the price.

No matter what phase you are at in your personal career, it is worthwhile for you to consider 10 core issues before you make major decisions about your future career/job goals:

1. What personal career skills have you developed or want to build on?
2. What are your strongest academic skills?
3. List some of your greatest personal interests and experiences in life (e.g., hobbies, volunteer activities, internships, part-time jobs, etc.).
4. How might you apply all of the above strengths and interests to potential jobs and careers? Today? Five years from now? Ten years?
5. Why are you motivated to consider this occupation(s)?
6. Who has inspired you to think about this career area for yourself? Why?

7. What skills, education, and experience do you already possess that can be used successfully for this career?

8. What new career preparation will you need to acquire for this career through education, training, and experience?

9. How strong are job opportunities in this career area in your city, state, or region? Today? In five years? Ten years? Are you willing to relocate for this career?

10. Where can you find accurate information to answer these questions on occupational requirements and the short-term/long-term job outlook in a specific occupation?

Answers for the Career Game

Our current educational system often does little to help most students or adult workers develop answers to these core career issues. The curricula of the majority of U.S. elementary and secondary schools are still based on the assumption that all students are equally endowed with the same aptitudes, interests, and intellectual capacities. This has given too many students a blinkered view of their career options.

People possess a wide mix of natural talents and innate abilities. There are at least seven specific human ability areas that education can tap for job/career development for any individual (see Table 2.2).

Individuals usually possess a mixture of these abilities, with several clearly dominating. We have long understood that schooling can help develop about 50 percent of the population's ability for abstract reasoning and advanced problem solving, and about 50 percent of their abilities to solve the practical challenges of everyday life.

Though innate abilities tend to run in families, frequently the final career choices of individual family members are quite different. My father was a carpenter, contractor, and a great athlete. He had strong logical mathematical, spatial, motor, and interpersonal abilities. In contrast, I can't drive a nail straight and have limited depth perception, making me a terrible athlete. Yet, I did inherit many of his logical, interpersonal skills, and added stronger linguistic and intrapersonal abilities.

I have other ancestors who were ship captains, engineers, and preachers, from whom I may have inherited some of my abilities. Also, each generation's educational/cultural/social opportunities nurture or discourage the abilities and skills growth of each person.

Your own career preferences are, therefore, made up of four components: natural talents, personality traits, the type of work that gives you

TABLE 2.2   Human Abilities/Skills/Careers

Abilities	Skills	Career Potential
1. Linguistic	Reading a book, writing a report, giving an extemporaneous talk.	Communications, Educational, Public Relations, Sales, Marketing
2. Logical-Mathematical	Solving math problems, providing a logical theorem.	Scientific, Health Care, Finance, Math Teachers, Engineering, IT, Accounting
3. Spatial	Traveling through unfamiliar areas with ease; figuring out how to fit suitcases into the trunk of a car; playing right field well.	Skilled Trades, IT, Engineering, Scientific
4. Musical	Remembering a tune; singing a song; composing or playing music.	Musician, IT, Communications, Advertising
5. Bodily-Fine Gross Motor	Used in playing golf or tennis; performing gymnastics or ballet.	Surgeon, Skilled Trades, Athlete, Skilled Manufacturing
6. Interpersonal	Used in deducing what other people mean from what they say; understanding body language, facial expressions.	Sales/Marketing, Medical, Communications, Retail, Journalism, Hotel, Advertising, Leisure, Educational
7. Intrapersonal	Understanding why someone is sometimes overconfident; takes rejection so poorly; or fails to achieve an important goal.	Counseling, Medical, Pastoral, Educational, Managerial, Advertising

Source: Adapted from Robert J. Sternberg, "What Should We Ask about Intelligence?" *Network News and Views,* May 1996, 25.

a sense of purpose and meaning, and a potential career that arouses your feelings, passions, and a sense of personal mission. How can you find a clear set of answers to all of the above questions we have raised?

The best way is by using a local career assessment center. Many post-secondary institutions offer career testing, including community colleges, four-year colleges, and universities. Career assessments will help you identify personal strengths and preferences and match them to potential career and job opportunities.[7]

TABLE 2.3 Health Science Career Cluster in Illinois

Occupation	SOC Code	Interests	Minimum Education	Growth Outlook	Current Workers	Salary Entry	Salary All
Ambulance Drivers & Attendants, Emergency Medical Technicians	53-3011.00	SRE	Mod. OJT	1.92	1,034	$17,880	$25,270
Anesthesio-logists	29-1061.00	IRS	Profess.	1.97	2,729	$157,190	$220,710
Athletic Trainers	29-9091.00	SREI	Bachelor	*	*	$32,190	$45,440
Cardiovascular Technologists & Technicians	29-2031.00	IRS	Associate	2.14	2,115	$27,460	$48,600
Chiropractors	29-2011.00	IRSAE	Profess.	2.08	2,767	$30,720	$77,240
Clinical, Counseling & School Psychologists	19-3031.00	IS	Doctorate	1.02	5,640	$37,130	$71,730
Dental Assistants	31-9091.00	SRE	Mod. OJT	2.92	12,401	$23,600	$33,270
Dental Hygienists	29-2021.00	SCRE	Associate	2.97	7,357	$34,760	$61,110
Dental Laboratory Technicians	51-9081.00	RI	Long OJT	-0.96	1,340	$18,500	$37,140
Dentists, All Other Specialists	29-1029.00	*	Profess.	*	*	$104,610	$141,970
Dentists, General	29-1021.00	IRS	Profess.	1.18	5,317	$47,590	$135,070

Interests key: A=artistic; C=conventional: E=enterprising; I=investigative; R=realistic; S=social. See endnote 7 for further explanation of these terms.

Source: "Career Outlook in the US," http://www.careeroutlook.us (accessed June 28, 2012). Used by permission.

More importantly, you need to seek an institution that will offer you a more personalized holistic explanation of your career assessment results. You need to better understand your inner talents and how they can be developed for lifetime career opportunities. Harvard University psychologist Howard Gardner stated, "The single most important contribution education can make to a person's development is to help them toward a field where their talent best suits them, where they will be satisfied and competent."[8]

After identifying your personal strengths and potential career alternatives, the next step is to look at the current and future outlook for jobs and careers within a specified area of the United States. You need up-to-date accurate information about specific jobs and career areas, including educational requirements, growth potential, current employed workers, entry salary, and average salary.

A good source for obtaining such information is the "Career Outlook in the US" website, http://www.careeroutlook.us. (See Table 2.3 for an example of the information it provides.) "Career Outlook" gives you the ability to obtain and sort various types of labor market information by individual states. You can select from a list of 16 career clusters, or from 6 career interest categories, or cross-reference the two.

"Career Outlook" was developed by Chris Droessler at the North Carolina Department of Instruction and by educators in the School-to-Work Section of the Association for Career and Technical Education. The information is derived from multiple data tables of the U.S. Department of Labor and is updated annually.

An additional valuable job tool available at "Career Outlook" is the "Interest Profiler," an online career assessment resource. It helps individuals find out what their interests are and how they relate to specific occupations. The "Interest Profiler" ranks a person's personality preferences around six broad career interest areas: realistic, investigative, artistic, social, enterprising, and conventional.[9] You can, then, use this information to better select specific jobs listed in the occupational cluster data you have selected.

Recalibrating Your Job Search

Personal career information is great, but what do you do with it? The job future looks bleak for too many in the current generation of young people. As mentioned earlier, many are living with parents or relatives. Less than 20 percent have full-time employment. Most (72%) think they need additional career education. Yet, only half are enrolling in formal education programs.

A 2013 Pew Charitable Trust analysis found that college enrollment had slightly declined among people aged 21–24 between 2007 and 2011.[10]

By 2009, the U.S. Census Bureau found that Americans aged 18 and older had the following education credentials:

10.9%—technical/career certificate
8.2%—associate degree
17.1%—bachelor's degree
9.2%—advanced degree[11]

Although a four-year degree improves the employment prospects of recent college graduates, about 9 percent remained unemployed. As the college major of graduates substantially affects their employment prospects, pursuing a career credential may be the best option for many until the U.S. economy recovers and when baby boomer retirements, later in this decade, will offer soaring numbers of replacement jobs.

About 33 percent of U.S. adults have returned to school in the last five years for more training. Of those surveyed in a 2012 *New York Times* poll, 80 percent were currently employed and 10 percent unemployed. Most did not have a four-year college degree and were under the age of 45.[12]

Many of the adults pursuing additional education are seeking specialized degrees or certificates in response to this job market. "It's not that we don't need engineers and Ph.D.'s and research scientists," states Joe Arnold, a government affairs manager with BASF, a chemical company. "We do, but that's not all we need. We need skilled craftsmen. We need operators."[13]

Across the United States, local technical colleges are now enrolling in such programs students who already hold bachelor's or master's degrees. "We know what our employers want in employees," asserts Chris Matheny, vice president of instructional services at Fox Valley Technical College in Wisconsin. "We design our curriculum around the type of things that are going to get people employed or promoted or on to the next stage of their career."[14]

National movements, such as the Campaign for Young America, are also focusing on better aligning postsecondary programs with the needs of local employers.[15]

This doesn't mean that everyone should be a science, technology, engineering, or math major. In a Duke and Harvard University survey of 652 U.S.-born CEOs and heads of production engineering at 502 technology companies, only 37 percent held degrees in IT or engineering and 2 percent in math. The rest had education and training in business, accounting, finance, health care, and even the arts and humanities.

The business world today needs tech heads. But humanities majors may provide important insights on how technology can be made easier to use. Because they have learned more about people, liberal arts majors often can make better project or product managers if they receive additional job training from their employers.[16] A generation ago, this was common in the business world, and the trend is now building to restart job training programs as more companies experience difficulty in filling vacant positions.

Many individuals may never find the ideal career fit. Most people just need to discover what they might enjoy doing, a manageable work fit, and available jobs that meet these needs.

You could devote your entire life to teaching, Wall Street, or technology, and in the end feel you have been a total failure or a hero. The key lesson is that society's cultural attitude regarding desirable careers or hot jobs will change over your lifetime.[17]

The world is now in a major career transition era. Many will experience major unhappiness during this adjustment phase. A Rutgers University survey asked recent college graduates what they would have done differently to be better prepared for today and tomorrow's workplace. They offered some good advice, including:

1. Be more careful about selecting a major or minor.
2. Do more internships or part-time work in a field related to your studies.
3. Take more classes to prepare for a career.
4. Take greater care in selecting a college, university, or technical school program.[18]

Whether you now are a student, a recent graduate, already in the workforce, or now unemployed, personal ongoing career education will be increasingly important in order to find, hold, or advance your career. The unrelenting pace of technological change in every business sector makes this a necessity and not an option. If possible, seek out employers that place a high priority on the ongoing development of their employees' skills. (In Appendix I, you will find a "Career Analysis Scorecard" to help you consider the job road ahead.)

The next three chapters will analyze the current barriers to filling jobs in the United States and around the world. They will consider, in turn, the challenges facing both employers and employees in this fast-paced Cyber-Mental Age. Many components in this employment disconnect have been building for many decades and require new thinking about a system-wide change.

Part II

The Roadblocks

Chapter 3

The Widening Job-Skills Gap

Finding sufficient skilled talent has become something like searching for a needle in a haystack.[1]

—Booz & Co.

Once in a Lifetime

The United States and much of the world is caught in a watershed era of permanent and fundamental labor market changes. "What we're witnessing is the breakdown of the great American jobs machine," says Mortimer Zuckerman, editor-in-chief of *U.S. News and World Report*.[2]

The Computer Age began in 1951 when John von Neumann built Maniac (mathematical and numerical integration and computer) in Princeton, New Jersey. Maniac became the prototype for computer processors ever since.[3]

Next, in 1957, Russia's launch of its Sputnik triggered the Cold War's space and arms race that spurred huge investments in science and technology. Then came personal computers. Entrepreneurs, such as Microsoft's Bill Gates and Apple's Steve Jobs, launched software and hardware advances that made personal computers a fixture of homes, offices, and factories around the world.

Without most of us really noticing, as businesses took advantage of the exponential increase in computing power to do more with fewer people, the United States moved from the Computer Age to the Cyber-Mental Age. Heavy equipment manufacturer, John Deere in Moline, Illinois, exemplifies what happened. Half of Deere's salaried employees are engineers. But it needs hundreds of technicians who know about satellite guidance, artificial intelligence, telematics, and other pervasive digital technology.

These processes spread throughout Deere's entire organization. Engineering know-how is still important, but now all of Deere's production people, not just the managers, also need to know how to collaborate and work on problem-solving as a team.[4]

Thirty years ago, 80 percent of American manufacturing workers were unskilled. In today's new Cyber-Mental Age, this has been reduced to 12 percent, as digital technology is now embedded throughout most organizations. Middle jobs in offices are also shrinking. Today's more complex 21st-century jobs require critical thinking and higher levels of communication (reading, writing, mathematics). As Edward Rust, Jr., State Farm Mutual's chief executive, has stated, "the U.S. needs workers with verbal and written communication skills, people who can think critically and possess intellectual curiosity."[5]

These are the demands of the future jobs growing across the United States and world economy. Highly technical fields have seen an upsurge in specialization requiring precise skill sets. The next wave of technological advances will only further increase these trends.

Technologies of the Future

America is at the beginning of its third great technological revolution. "The next wave of transformational innovation" is either underway or will begin within two years, says an Economist Intelligence Unit report from KPMG International.[6] Here are some of the major breakthroughs that will produce new employment opportunities:

Big Data

"Cloud" service centers mobilize the computing capacities of thousands of PCs to simultaneously meet the needs of millions of users. Crunching data faster and cheaper will lead to tens of thousands of personalized applications across science, business, medicine, government, and so forth for both industry and consumers.

Nanoscience

Extreme miniaturization at the molecular level is creating a new class of electronic and structural materials, such as graphene. Breakthroughs are beginning in medicine, genetic research, and molecular electronic applications. The impact of nano will be so widespread that it compares to the 20th-century invention of the transistor or silicon computer chip.

3-D Printing

Additive manufacturing or 3-D printing is a process that makes solid objects from a digital model by adding layer upon layer of materials. A wide variety of materials can be used, including plastics, polymers, metals, ceramics, and even living tissues. Additive manufacturing printing greatly simplifies the production of industrial prototypes and customized objects, such as dental crowns. A host of medical and industrial applications for this process are now being developed.

Advanced Robotics

Robots are being married to advanced artificial intelligence. We can now remotely control the movement and manipulation of objects. Robotics can assemble smart phones, transport hospital supplies, prepare and track medications, and fly drone aircraft. Robotic applications exist across industrial, manufacturing, service, and agricultural business sectors.

All these technology discoveries will create hundreds of thousands to eventually millions of new jobs in programming, technical maintenance, management, manufacturing, and health care. The challenge will be finding the talent with the required education and skills for these occupations.[7]

Bye-Bye Baby Boomers

In 2010, the generation who got their name from the U.S. birthrate surge after World War II began to leave the workforce. Seventy-nine million will retire in the next 20 years. That is about 10,000 a day for two decades.

The entire world is now in the midst of a demographic upheaval. By 2050, most developed countries in East Asia and Europe will turn into de facto retirement homes as 33 percent or more of their people will break the age 65 barrier. According to the United Nations, the population of the European Union (EU) is set to shrink from 496 million in 2010 to 452 million in 2025. The EU's workforce will also shrink, losing about one million people a year. German statisticians estimate that the proportion of their workforce over the age of 50 will rise from 25 percent today to 45 percent in 2020.

In Asia, Japan's population is shrinking by 100,000 people each year. The rate of annual population loss in South Korea is 50,000. China will be short 10 million workers by 2020.

Between July 2010 and July 2011, the U.S. Census Bureau recorded the slowest population growth since 1940 and a steep drop in the birthrate. Only

40 million Generation Xers will be available in America to replace those retiring. Even if the U.S. birthrate remains at replacement rate (which is increasingly doubtful), there will be a considerable shrinkage in the worker pool of those aged 25–46. The Congressional Budget Office (CBO) also predicts a continued decline in the labor participation rate. The real threat from these demographics is that only one-fourth of U.S. organizations have done any serious planning on how to cope with an expanding talent crisis.

Despite the conventional wisdom that the baby boomers have saved little for retirement or will work forever, a MetLife Study (2012) showed they are retiring in droves. Many have left the workforce for health reasons or were laid off. About half say they are on track or have achieved their retirement savings goals.

A flood of U.S. public sector employees have also begun to retire. In some states, this has been a planned outcome to reduce budget deficits. But many of these aging workers are retiring to take advantage of public pension benefits.[8]

The U.S. Labor Department found that in the prior Veteran or Silent Generation (born from 1928 to 1945) one in nine men over the age of 75 was still at work. This is a record. Since life expectancy has risen, some of the healthier boomers indicate they want to stay active, and at least work part-time. We need them. In order to bridge the job-skills disconnect, America requires at least 25 percent of its skilled boomers to remain at work until 2025. As Neil Roden, HR consulting partner at PricewaterhouseCoopers, asks, "If organizations can keep a worker with skills that the market can't replace, why wouldn't they?"[9]

The challenges posed by the exodus of the baby boomers from the workforce are not confined to a decline in numbers, but in education and skill levels, as well. Throughout the history of the United States, each succeeding generation has been better educated and more skilled for future careers than the proceeding generation. Unfortunately, this record has ended with the baby boomers.

Due to the Cold War and the Space Race with the former Soviet Union, the National Defense Act (1957) funded a variety of math and science programs in elementary and secondary schools, as well as higher education student scholarships. This helped to stimulate a major expansion of advanced technology across the U.S. economy. President John Kennedy's pledge to land a man on the moon was realized in 1969. The Apollo space program spurred further scientific breakthroughs.

However, by the late 1970s, much of America's emphasis on basic scientific research and technological innovations began to recede. The emphasis on math and science education also waned during the 1980s and 1990s in U.S. schools. The boomers generation in 1972 attained an 82 percent national high school graduation rate, an all-time high; in the following decades, this declined among the Gen Xers and Millennials bottoming out at 72 percent in 2011. "The segment of today's workforce nearing retirement is much more highly educated than past retirees. As a result, we are very likely to be adding many more less-educated workers than we lose to retirement," says economist Robert I. Lerman at the American University and the Urban Institute.[10]

Other analysts also expect that this boomer stampede to the job exits will leave the United States facing huge skills gaps. Anthony Carnevale at Georgetown University has projected that by 2018 Americans will produce three million fewer college graduates and 4.7 million fewer postsecondary certificate graduates than demanded by the economy. He also has stated that the United States needs to produce 20 million workers with postsecondary credentials by 2025 for sustained economic growth.[11]

Researchers at the National Bureau of Economic Research believe that the size of the baby boomer retirement, coupled with their higher education levels, could lead to skill shortage, particularly in those states and cities with large and growing Hispanic populations. This ethnic group has the lowest level of high school completion and college graduation. States that fit this profile include California, Arizona, Nevada, New Mexico, Colorado, Texas, and Florida. This author would also add urban areas in other states, such as Chicago and New York. A growing nationwide skills-job disconnect is more likely as the rising tide of boomer retirements continues to 2030.[12]

We cannot wish away the demographic changes that are now occurring around the world. They are real. The results will be frightening.

Skills Structure Collapses

Is this skills and jobs mismatch a new problem? A large body of economic, business, and educational research on this issue stretches back decades. Yet, some researchers at the Federal Reserve Bank of Chicago, the University of California at Berkeley, and at the Wharton School believe that "the research is far from certain."[13] I disagree.

In 1991, I authored *Closing the Literacy Gap in American Business*. It focused on steps U.S. businesses could take to counter the decline in their workers' reading and math abilities. By 2000, severe shortages of American workers with the skills needed for advanced technologies prompted me to write *Skill Wars: Winning the Battle for Productivity and Profit*. Yet the demand for more knowledge in the workplace continued to rise world-wide. *The 2010 Meltdown* (2005) and *Winning the Global Talent Showdown* (2009) spotlighted business' growing needs for additional thinking and problem-solving talent in the United States and overseas. This talent beat continues today. Yet, baby boomers' talent is not being adequately replaced.

Over the past 20 years, the problems associated with talent declines in the workplace have only grown in size and complexity. They are now clearly having an adverse impact on technological innovation and business sustainability. Yet, too many leaders in business, academe, and government have chosen to ignore or marginalize their importance. Developing more talented people does not fit into their vision of how the world functions in a culture dominated by short-term results and the defense of the status quo. This broad cultural disconnect has brought the United States and much of the world to the point of a critical skills structure collapse across their economies.

U.S. unemployment has been high since 2008. However, the true extent of the employment contraction of the U.S. economy has been obscured because millions of workers have left the job market. By the end of 2012, 89 million Americans of working age were not part of the labor market often because they lack skills for 21st-century jobs. The Center on Education and the Workforce at Georgetown University has reported that, since the recession began, 5.6 million workers with a high school diploma or less have lost their jobs. The U.S. labor force has shrunk by over 4 percent. Almost 25 percent of all households have at least one person now unemployed and looking for work, according to TechnoMetrica Market Intelligence (June, 2012).[14]

Yet an estimated 6.8 million vacant jobs exist across the economy. While it seems that skilled talent abounds, in reality, knowledge workers are at a premium.

"The mismatch between the skills in demand by firms today and the skills available in the U.S. labor force suggests that unless a significant retooling of the U.S. labor force takes place, there will be an elevated rate of unemployment for an extended period," stated John E. Silvia, chief economist at Wells Fargo. "Thus, the key difference between our view on the economy through 2023 and the CBO's is that there are more than cyclical factors that need to be overcome to return to a more robust pace of economic growth."[15]

There is widespread agreement supporting this viewpoint. Dana Saporta, an economist with Credit Swiss, estimated that the gap between jobs and skills in the labor market has added 1.5 percent to the U.S. unemployment rate. This translates to at least one and a half million jobs that could have been filled, according to economist Harry Holzer at Georgetown University. The International Monetary Fund (IMF) sees a much broader skills-job disconnect. Prakash Loungani, an IMF economist, estimates that 25 percent of U.S. unemployment is structural. That is equivalent to over three million jobs.[16]

The McKinsey Global Institute (2011) found that over 30 percent of U.S. firms had vacant positions open for six months or longer because of a lack of qualified candidates. A 2012 Towers Watson survey canvassed 278 U.S. companies. Over 60 percent of these employers reported difficulty recruiting critical skill employees. This level of recruiting difficulty was nearly the same as in 2005–2006 when the economy was booming and unemployment was very low.[17]

The Society for Human Resource Management (SHRM) is the world's largest human resources association. Between January 2010 and July 2012, SHRM's monthly Lending Indicators of National Employment Survey showed an overall steady increase in both vacant positions and in recruiting difficulty. This was true for both salaried and hourly workers across manufacturing and service sector companies.[18]

In an October 2011 analysis, Jennifer Schramm, SHRM's manager of workplace trends and forecasting, stated that "HR professionals are reporting that, despite the high rate of unemployment, it is becoming more difficult to find the right candidates for a range of skilled positions." She added that these persistent talent shortages have made it necessary for organizations of all sizes to develop the workers they will need for the future. "Those that have a late start may be at a disadvantage."[19]

World on the Brink

The jobs and skills mismatch is not simply escalating in the United States, but across the globe as well. Reports on this crisis have grown increasingly dire.

In 2009 and 2011, the Economist Intelligence Unit was commissioned by Lloyd's of London to conduct surveys of global corporate executives on the top risks they face. "The risk of talent and skill shortages rose from a relatively lowly 22nd-ranked priority in 2009 to 2nd in 2011," stated the report on the 2011 survey, "and companies feel relatively less able to manage this risk."[20]

The global talent crisis has begun to worry CEOs even more than the recession. A Met/Life/Maxis Global Benefits Network survey (2012) found that nearly 60 percent of executives ". . . cite a growing global shortage of talent as a factor that could limit their entry into both developed and emerging markets, more so than economic weaknesses, or even political instability."[21]

Despite high unemployment rates, global talent shortages are growing. The World Economic Forum found in 2011 that 70 percent of German employers reported having difficulties recruiting the right people. This included Siemens that had 12,000 unfilled positions worldwide. At the same time, 80 percent of Japanese companies reported difficulty filling positions. A 2010 Canadian study projected that this nation needed to train, retrain, or recruit an additional 4.2 million postsecondary skilled workers (168,000 per year) over the next 25 years to keep the Canadian economy growing.[22]

In 2011, Manpower, one of the world's largest staffing firms, stated that "the world stands on the brink of a global employability crisis."[23] Then, in 2012, it warned that for the seventh year in a row the world continued to face an acute talent mismatch. Yet, only 25 percent of employers were addressing skill shortages through employee training and education.[24]

"If employers don't think leaving important positions unfilled is a problem now," warned Jeff Joerres, Manpower's chairman and CEO, "they will in the future as unemployment rates fall and skilled talent is harder to come by." He further advised, "Employers today must proactively develop a workforce recruitment and development strategy if remaining competitive and achieving the desired results are the goal."[25]

U.S. Students Are Ill-Prepared for Employment

A 2012 McKinsey report on the education-to-employment system found that "Fewer than half of youth and employers . . . believe that new graduates are adequately prepared for entry-level positions."[26]

Many young adults are bitter over the efforts made by their high school to prepare them for postsecondary education or a career. A 2011 *Associated Press* survey of 18- to 24-year-olds reported that most high schools offered weak help to students in choosing a field of study for a future career or even in helping them find the right postsecondary program. Young people also gave high schools failing marks on providing instruction on the latest technology in their future field of study and gaining work/internship experiences.[27]

At the other end of the education-to-employment food chain, employers from the manufacturing, IT, service, and other business sectors see U.S. students lagging behind the rest of the world. Six out of every 10 applicants for basic tech jobs don't qualify because they lack a basic liberal arts education in reading, writing, math, and science, contended Doug Oberdelman, chief executive of Caterpillar. "We are customers to that education system that we see failing in this country and other competitors around the world are exceeding in their education system."[28]

In Oregon, Intel's new $6 billion facility near Portland will add 1,000 new employees. But most will come from outside the state. "Oregon is 49th in the percent of high school students who go to college," stated Renee James, an Intel senior vice president, at a 2011 Portland Business Alliance meeting. "We can do better than that."[29] James contended that change must begin in the state's elementary schools where students and their parents need to be taught the importance of a postsecondary education for their future careers. If Oregon does not act on Intel's cry for talent, perhaps another state will when another production facility is planned.

It's the same story all across the United States. The number of college graduates and technicians with postsecondary credentials in science, technology, engineering, and math (STEM) had flattened to about 225,000 by 2010. This is far short of the estimated 400,000 people needed by 2015 estimates the Business-Higher Education Forum, a coalition of business leaders, postsecondary institution presidents, and foundation leaders.[30]

Service sector employers also fault American education on developing critical skills. Edward Rust, Jr., State Farm Mutual Insurance chief executive, believes that America needs employees with good verbal and written communication skills who are critical thinkers and intellectually curious. "The consequences of not addressing this are much greater than they appear today," says Rust. "We cannot pass this problem on to the next generation. Today's human capital must be educated for the challenges of our present time."[31]

Falling Off the Talent Cliff

Imagine what will happen to our businesses and society if we wake up one day and discover we had fallen off the talent cliff. What if there weren't enough plumbers to fix broken pipes, dentists to fill cavities, financial counselors to advise boomers on their retirement accounts, or technicians to perform mammograms, repair a car's computer, or an airplane's engine, or fix the technical glitches at the New York Stock Exchange?

This is no longer idle speculation. That day has arrived. We are now critically short of what Peter Drucker called "knowledge technologists," people with the analytical ability and special technical skills to correctly use old and newer technologies.

A large portion of this shortfall will be in STEM-related occupations. The U.S. Commerce Department estimates that by 2018 STEM employment will grow by 17 percent, compared to 9.8 percent for other occupations. STEM skills are required in more than 50 occupational areas ranging from the computer/math fields to engineering, physical/life science, and managerial jobs.[32]

According to Anthony P. Carnevale, of Georgetown University's Center on Education and the Workforce, the vast majority of these jobs will require some form of postsecondary education or training. He lists these requirements as follows:

- Almost two-thirds Bachelor's degrees and above.
- 35 percent sub-baccalaureate education or training including at least:
  - One million associate degrees.
  - 745,000 certificates.
  - 760,000 industry-based certifications.[33]

The bottom line: Unless we adopt proactive talent creation policies now, we will face a world in which there will be a lot of people without jobs and, at the same time, a growing number of jobs without people. This is not a future anyone wants or needs.

Four Sectors in the Talent Spotlight

There are four sectors of the U.S. economy in which the skills crisis is particularly acute. Each has its own special problems and needs.

1. Health Care

Help wanted: Doctors, nurses, pharmacists, lab technicians, therapists, dentists, and just about anyone who is trained in a broad array of health care occupations to cope with a rapidly aging population. The Bureau of Labor Statistics (BLS) estimates that by 2020 jobs in this field will grow by over 20 percent. Let's review a few examples.

The Association of American Medical Colleges (ACA) expects a shortage of 63,000 doctors by 2015, 91,000 by 2020, and reaching 130,000 by 2025. These projected shortages are due both to increasing patient numbers and an estimate that one-third of all U.S. doctors will retire by 2020. Already, the ACA reports a shortage of at least 16,000 primary care physicians across America.

To reduce these shortages, nearly two dozen new medical schools have reopened or are planned across the country. However, it will take considerable time for the dearth of physicians to be filled. At present, at least 17 states lack at least one doctor in one of the 13 medical subspecialties. Susan Salka, chief executive of AMN Healthcare Services Inc.—the largest U.S. health care staffing company—states that there is a growing demand across all areas of medicine, including pediatric and geriatric specialists, oncologists, emergency medicine doctors, and surgeons.[34]

When doctors are scarce on the ground, nurse practitioners help pick up the load. With over 100,000 nursing positions already unfilled, this does not look like a near-term solution for U.S. regions caught short of health care professionals.

By 2020, the BLS projects the need for 1.2 million additional nurses. The good news is that nursing schools are expanding. Unfortunately, over 75,000 applicants were still turned away due to a shortage of faculty, classrooms, and clinical teaching sites, or because of state budget cuts. As a result, the United States may still face a shortage of 400,000 nurses by 2020. Current projections are that U.S. nursing education programs will not produce the needed number of graduates until 2030.[35]

In Kansas the health care crisis revolves around teeth. Almost half the 105 counties in Kansas have two or fewer dentists. Fifteen counties have no dentists.

Today, across America nearly 4,500 areas, mostly in rural locations, are short of dentists. The Institute of Medicine estimates that 9,600 additional dentists are needed. These shortages will increase as boomer dentists retire.[36]

2. IT

Microsoft's Redmond, Washington, campus employs 40,500 people. Yet, in 2012, its unfilled jobs rose from 4,000 to almost 5,000 with over 6,000 jobs vacant across the United States. Google was also trying to increase its workforce by 25 percent to 6,300 jobs (2011).[37] Other tech companies are increasingly short of IT workers. Accenture needed 5,000 people in the United States out of the 66,000 positions it was seeking to fill globally (2011). AT&T had openings for about 2,800 employees in IT operations, architecture, network engineering, and tech labs positions (2011). All these vacant positions are projected to increase due to future growth and rising retirements.[38]

These companies only represent the tip of an IT talent war raging across this industry, from the giants to the start-ups. Over 80,000 new IT jobs were created in 2010–2011. In 2011, CareerBuilder.com posted 30,000 open tech jobs. Many of these positions, however, required specialized skills of five or more years of IT experience. Gartner, a technology research company, expects 1.9 million IT jobs to be created in the United States between 2012 and 2015.[39]

Companies are attempting to alleviate these shortages by raising salaries and retraining. Some are looking further to the future. In 2012, Microsoft and Boeing each contributed $25 million for scholarships in science and technology fields at Washington's state universities.

3. Aerospace

As airlines seek more fuel-efficient planes, they have placed a record number of orders for Boeing's new 787 Dreamliner and the European Airbus 380. Boeing was on track to build about 600 planes in 2012. However, both companies now face a significant worker shortages.[40]

"This is a global circumstance," stated Jim McNerney, Boeing's president, chairman, and chief executive. ". . . no single nation can produce enough creativity, talent or knowledge to meet today's marketplace challenges alone. . . . many seasoned and skilled workers are close to retiring and insufficient numbers of capable workers are being prepared to replace them."[41]

The acute nature of Boeing's position can be judged by the fact that, by 2015, 40 percent of its workforce may be gone. "That's some 60,000 employees eligible to retire in five years [2010–2015]," indicated Rick Stephens, senior vice president of human resources at Boeing. "We just don't see the [recruitment] pipeline meeting our needs."[42] This includes about 8,700 machinists (2012).

A record order backlog has been building at both Boeing and Airbus. Bernstein Research estimated (2011) that it might take Airbus and Boeing between seven and eight years to work through their backlogs.[43]

In the 1990s, Boeing was also behind in aircraft production, paying out billions in late penalty fees to the airlines. Boeing initiated a career education program of secondary and postsecondary education that provided over 500 Boeing internships. It also pursued a joint effort with the International Association of Machinists and Aerospace Workers of voluntary worker retraining at Boeing's Everett, Washington, and Wichita assembly plants. These programs did not meet Boeing's skilled worker needs.[44]

In 2003, Boeing tried another strategy. It outsourced its new 787 Dreamliner to over 25 major aerospace contractors and numerous subcontractors around the world. Boeing hoped that this outsourcing strategy would help them overcome potential U.S. production worker shortages.

Unfortunately, Boeing's outsourcing strategy proved a disaster. The new Boeing 787 is far more sophisticated than prior models requiring the integration of composite structures, digital technologies, and advanced computers. Many contractors failed to deliver components on time and many of the delivered parts did not fit together. Jim McNerney admitted that this plan had been, "overly ambitious . . . we've seen more of the bleeding edge of innovation than we'd ever care to see again."[45]

Boeing has adjusted its Dreamliner production program by bringing much of the work back to its Everett assembly plant. It has also added a 787 manufacturing site in Charleston, South Carolina, through its purchase of a previous contractor, Vought Global Aeronautica.

Rick Stephens stated Boeing spends about $80 million annually on worker training (2011). Boeing is hiring thousands of new employees and implementing more extensive training programs for new aerospace technicians. Boeing now has a 13-week training program for entry-level employees that was previously only 7 weeks long. Deficiencies in problem solving and communication skills led to this change; all this is part of an overall effort to ramp up production.[46]

It is clear that aerospace industry faces a critical shortage of skilled workers. In 2011, Jim McNerney warned that "without a strong pipeline of future talent, companies won't have the capacity to pursue new opportunities."[47] A 2012 World Economic Forum survey found that 72 percent of U.S. aircraft manufacturers reported major shortages of skilled production and other technical personnel.[48]

4. Manufacturing

U.S. manufacturing accounts for about 12 percent overall of U.S. gross domestic product. It employs over 11 million Americans. Manufacturing supports almost another seven million jobs in related industries. Over 60 percent of U.S. exports come from this sector. Advanced automation has continued to raise productivity from 1987 to 2010 by 4 percent each year. But nearly 2.7 million U.S. manufacturing employees were age 55 or older in 2011.[49]

To continue to raise American productivity, both current and newly hired workers must know how to use the latest advanced equipment. "People have to be retrained for the new machinery," is a common refrain among U.S. employers. This is the key investment for continuing improvement in productivity and U.S. competitiveness.

America revolutionized agriculture in the 20th century through its technological productivity. In the 21st century, the same American worker productivity is beginning to revolutionize manufacturing. For example, the manufacturing sector in New Jersey illustrates this transformation. In the mid-1940s, over 50 percent of its workforce was in manufacturing. Today it is around 7 percent. Yet, in 2012, the dollar value of goods manufactured in the United States was about $1.9 trillion—an all-time high. This astounding growth in productivity results from fewer highly skilled people using complex automated equipment.[50]

A steady drumbeat of reports and studies, however, indicate that skills deficits are hampering the growth of manufacturing. A 2011 Advanced Technology Services (ATS)/Nielsen survey found that 32 percent of the large American manufacturers polled had 15 or more job openings for skilled workers.[51] Wanted Analytics reported that in the United States there were more than 184,000 online job advertisements for engineers in September 2012; this was a 27 percent increase over the same period in 2010.[52] In the United States, as many as 600,000 skilled technical positions in manufacturing were vacant, according to a Manufacturing Institute and Deloitte Consulting 2011 study.[53] A Boston Consulting Group study warns that at the end of the decade this shortage could rise to over 875,000 highly skilled U.S. workers.[54]

The National Tooling and Machining Association (2012) reported that 80 percent of America's 5,800 tool and die firms were seeking one to five technicians. The demand for skilled computer numerically controlled (CNC) operators is also significantly outpacing the supply. In high-tech manufacturing, they control the computerized equipment that makes parts or forms match. The United States needs an additional 25,000 CNC technicians each year, as automation and boomer retirements expand. America is now only producing 8,000 new operators annually. This net yearly loss of 17,000 CNC machinists will in the immediate future undermine America's high-tech manufacturing potential.[55]

This skilled worker deficit is largely due to the fact that manufacturing has become part rocket science. Running tech-driven machines now requires a basic understanding of metallurgy, physics, chemistry, pneumatics, electrical wiring, and computer code. Moreover, tech workers need thinking skills to problem solve when a machine malfunctions.[56]

Both large and small U.S. businesses are suffering from this skill and jobs disconnect. A *Wall Street Journal* and Vistage International survey (2012) found that 41 percent of small manufacturing firms couldn't find applicants with the required skills or experience.[57] This includes Bertrand Products, Inc., which makes transmission parts for helicopters. Bertrand has plenty of orders for its South Bend, Indiana, factory. "The biggest challenge we face is a skilled labor force," says Paul Bonin, president of Bertrand Products. "I can't take the work because I can't find the workforce."[58]

Rebuilding the pipeline for skilled manufacturing workers won't be cheap. An ATS/Nielsen survey found that many larger industrial companies expect skill shortages to increase training costs by at least $100 million between 2011 and 2016. Two-thirds of the smaller firms expect to invest $50 million to develop a new workforce.[59]

"Reverse Globalization": Reshoring

The possibility that U.S. manufacturing may be on the verge of a significant renaissance makes solving the skills crisis of even greater importance. A reshoring trend, says Boston Consulting, is likely to bring up to three million manufacturing jobs back to the U.S. from overseas by 2020. China and other low-wage countries are at a tipping point. It appears from their research that more products will be "Made in America, Again."[60]

Harry Moser, president of Reshoring Initiatives, thinks that "Labor costs were the number one factor companies considered in relocating or sourcing manufacturing to supply the U.S. market." Chinese wages have been increasing at 18 percent annually for the last 10 years. Much of that cost savings is now gone. Other factors in this reshoring trend that Moser cites include "a desire to get products to market faster, and a more rapid response to customer orders; savings from reduced transportation and warehousing; improved quality; reduced theft of trade secrets, and the elimination of bribes paid to corrupt foreign officials."[61]

The decision of Douglas Oberhelman, chief executive officer of Caterpillar, to open a new Caterpillar plant in Victoria, Texas, is a confirmation of Moser's observations. The decision to move back to the United States was based on wanting to be closer to equipment buyers, lower freight costs, reduced shipping time from Asia, and the size of the local skilled workforce.[62] Other industry leaders agree. "This new trend of moving more supply closer to demand location appears to be a new shift for many manufacturers," concluded a 2011 Accenture reshoring study.[63]

Two other studies provide further information on the scope of reshoring. A Massachusetts Institute of Technology survey of over 100 multinational companies found that 14 percent of those surveyed said they planned to reshore.[64] A Hackett Group research study (2012) found that the cost gap between the United States and China has shrunk by nearly 50 percent over the past eight years, and is expected to stand at only 16 percent by 2013. "As the cost gap falls below 15 percent," says David P. Siervers, Principal, Strategy and Operations Leader, the Hackett Group, "the economic opportunity will require more companies to rebalance their supply chains and move capacity back closer to customers in the U.S."[65]

"There is a great potential for the reshoring of manufacturing to the US," stated Eric Spiegel, chief executive of Siemens in America. "But if companies have problems finding qualified people, a lot of it won't happen."[66]

The next wave of breakthrough technologies, outlined earlier in this chapter, will produce a cascade of new product and service jobs. The United States can expand the growth of a higher paying labor economy if it closes the skills and job disconnect.

So, why have we waited until now? Across the United States, there is a clear need to boost the education and career skills of both younger and older workers. Making such reforms is time consuming, unglamorous, and unpopular. Though the evidence we have reviewed seems overwhelming, there are deep cultural biases that fight changing the system. In the following chapter, we will consider how American popular culture has shaped the employment perspectives of our society.

Chapter 4

Career Culture— Business Culture Fantasies

Technology is easy to develop, developing a new attitude, moving the culture from one mental model to another, that's the difficult part.[1]
—Dean KamenSegway Inventor

Career Culture Fantasies

Today's career culture problem is what we might call science friction. In 1959, a Cambridge University chemist, Charles Percy Snow, saw the world being divided into two cultures at war over the scientific revolution. The split was between literary people on one side and scientists on the other. (I might now add a third group of underskilled people in between.) There were scientists who had not read Dickens, but humanities (and today business) graduates who were scientifically illiterate. The latter was more important because these people were to be in charge of society.

This ruling class of business-humanities graduates Snow thought was indifferent, if not actually antagonistic, to understanding science. He saw this cultural fallout as not just an obstacle to scientific progress, but a real threat to the future of 21st-century society.

Other experts agree with Snow. "I think science is still misunderstood by most people. Sensationalist news reporting, and an inadequate education system means that both young and old consider science to be either dull or dangerous, nerdy or pointless," explains popular math author Simon Singh (*Fermat's Last Theorem*, 2002).[2] In most elementary and secondary schools, little effort is made to teach science as applied technology or to better integrate scientific understanding into the students' general curriculum.

Boosting the image of science and technology among women is particularly crucial. In 2010, women received 57 percent of the undergraduate degrees awarded by U.S. colleges and universities. However, only 18 percent of bachelor's degrees in engineering and 18 percent of undergraduate degrees in computer science were awarded to women. Moreover, the percent of women earning degrees in computer science declined from 2004 to 2009. Women hold less than 25 percent of U.S. science, technology, engineering, and mathematics (STEM)-related jobs.[3]

"It is a question of good PR," says Alica Navarro, founder of Skimlinks, an online advertising technology company. "It is competing with subjects such as media studies, PR and marketing, which seem much more exciting."[4]

Popular image is a problem. There are few role models for scientists in the media except for the popular televisions series, *Crime Scene Investigation*. "There are no shows about scientists," remarked Paul Otellini, chief executive of Intel. "Ask the average eighth grader to name a scientist and they can't name one, but they know who the NBA [National Basketball Association] scoring leader is."[5]

Today's greatest career culture irony is young people's eager consumption of all the latest digital technologies, but overwhelming disinterest in IT careers. Yet, social media networks, such as Twitter and Facebook, cannot alone give them the technical and life skills required to have a thriving career in the global economy. This is a rising social, cultural, and economic issue.

The popular *Star Trek* series is unfortunately no longer widely seen. It offered a provocative view of a 23rd-century future that was complete in every detail. Well-educated techies dominated life throughout the World Federation of Planets. Yet, Captain Jean-Luc Picard read books while drinking his Earl Grey tea. His crew members performed Shakespeare's plays and played classical music. The starship's world was an interesting blend of advanced technologies, liberal arts culture, and even had its own historian. Attorneys were few, and financiers and the stock market absent.

Parents also have helped to perpetuate the bias against scientific and technical careers. Many were influenced by the media or their own personal job experiences. Headlines repeatedly trumpeted "Engineers Losing Jobs!" Everyone was taught that the "U.S. is entering a post-industrial era" and that "U.S. manufacturing is dead." Parents nurtured career aspirations in areas popularly enjoying high prestige and remuneration, especially careers in law or on Wall Street. The prestige factor and "greed is good" mentality abandoned health care or scientific careers to embrace Wall Street and the finance industry's illusions of "wealth creation."[6]

Today's Career Realities

Hard economic facts are starting to alter career perspectives. In 2011, the number of law school applicants fell by 11.5 percent. Business school applications also declined. Businesses and law firms are cutting back on hiring. Many haven't raised salaries for new hires in recent years. For the first time in a decade, the value of obtaining a law degree or an MBA is being openly questioned.[7]

This is also true for many students pursuing college degrees in majors that are currently among the most popular, such as communications or graphic design, or ones in theoretical fields with little immediate connection to jobs outside of academe. Especially because of the high cost of obtaining a college education, students and parents are more carefully assessing the employment opportunities for graduates in specific fields. They are grilling career and college counselors and enrollment/admission officials on job placement rates for specific majors and certificates.

However, it would be better if career exploration and planning began much earlier. What parents really need is access to a flow of information regarding jobs and careers in their city/town/region for themselves and their children. This needs to start in elementary school.

Students need a diverse curriculum that can be adjusted to their learning aptitudes, rather than a typical lockstep literary approach to teaching and learning (see Chapter 2 on different learning aptitudes). Children can also enjoy and profit from job and career exploration in their classroom or by on-site visits to diverse local employers.

By middle school or junior high school, a personal career and aptitude assessment should be completed by every student. A school counselor needs to review this information with each family. Instead of waiting until high school to think about the future, this information gives a family time to more realistically discuss "What do you want to do when you grow up?"

Business-Skills Disconnect

From executive leadership to high-skill manufacturing, business leaders' cries are getting louder—"We can't find enough talent!"[8]

Corporate America failed to understand the big talent picture. Many believed in the fantasy that the United States could move from a technology-manufacturing-based export powerhouse into a postindustrial services consumption economy that would grow and prosper with even less business investment in worker education and training.

"That idea was flat wrong," says Jeffrey Immelt, CEO of General Electric. "Our economy tilted instead toward the quicker profits of financial services."[9] Immelt and many other leaders missed the gathering skills storm.

Now, GE is scrambling to transform itself from the big buildup of GE Capital back into a manufacturer of energy-thrifty washers and dryers, fluorescent light bulbs, jet engines, and other advanced manufacturing technologies.

For the remainder of this decade, the business competition for scarce talent will be unprecedented. Companies large or small will be hard-pressed to find good employees and retain them. Some studies already estimate that an additional 20–35 million workers with postsecondary education will be needed by 2025. Where are they?

For American businesses, the issue has clearly moved from talent management to talent creation. Jennifer Schramm at Society for Human Resource Management agrees that "Eventually, more organizations may conclude that providing education assistance is a cost-effective solution to the shortage."[10] What are they waiting for?

Although the United States has some of the most educated workers in the world, it has stopped educating/training enough people in the mid-level tech skills jobs that are most needed across every business sector.

Many companies pay lip service to their commitment to train and educate the next generation of skilled workers; but their funding is inadequate. Fifty percent of manufacturing executives surveyed by Advanced Technology Service, Inc. said that their training expenditures were only 1–5 percent of their total budgets.[11] Many small businesses resist the idea of providing any training at all.

A 2011 Accenture survey found that only 21 percent of U.S. workers responded that they acquired new skills through company-provided training over the past five years.[12] Robert Terry, editor of the *Learning Transfer Survey Report*, also points out that "According to successive empirical studies, only five to 20 percent of what is learned finds its way back into the workplace."[13] The concept of "just in time training," whether e-learning, classroom, or blended learning, is often compromised by the lack of time given employees to learn; low-quality curriculum; poorly trained instructors; or a lack of employee/line manager interest and support.

Training and education can help employees develop their talent for workplace innovation and raise individual performance. While advocating that businesses reinstate their in-house training programs or corporate universities, Nick Jones, chief executive of Ligentia, a global logistics company, remarked, "During the past three years [2008–2011], they've cut back hugely and are no longer supplying the industry with talent."[14]

A basic management fantasy seems to be at work over the skills-jobs disconnect. On the one hand, executives report a growing difficulty finding qualified people. Fifty-one percent even say they are increasing their training budgets (Deloitte, 2012).[15] Yet, on the other hand, most businesses prefer to invest only in more equipment and not their workers. "People don't seem to come in with the right skill sets to work in modern manufacturing," says Dan Mishek, managing director of Vista Technologies in Vadnais Heights, Minnesota. "It seems as if technology has evolved faster than people. . . . You don't have to train machines."[16]

U.S. companies since 2009 have increased their equipment and software expenditures at a faster pace than in the last three economic recoveries. The Economic Policy Institute concluded (2011) that this shows that regulatory costs or market uncertainty are not their biggest worries.

Others hoard their cash. Forty-one percent of corporate treasurers say this trend has grown over the past year (2012). These corporate security blankets are expected to grow further.[17]

Business Culture Fantasies

Short-term thinking supports a pervasive business culture career fantasy in U.S. boardrooms. The quick, the cheap, and the easy drive most business talent development strategies. The weakest link in this business culture fantasy is the continuing focus on outside hiring to get the skills the business needs. Recruiting both from outside America's domestic workforce or outside their own business means few employers are providing training and education opportunities for their own employees or for the next generation of workers. Too many businesses have given up on investing in the future of the U.S. workforce.

This is not a new American business strategy. The United States has been very dependent on foreign labor over the past 100 years. Think of the throngs of immigrants processed through Ellis Island until almost 1920. They provided a tidal wave of low-cost labor that helped establish America's first assembly lines and grew our industrial might throughout World War II. When that conflict ended, a large number of displaced Europeans, including German technicians, scientists, and engineers, helped America expand its technological leadership for the next 40 years.[18]

However, by the 1980s, U.S. businesses needed more high-skilled technical workers than they could obtain through America's domestic talent pipeline. As the pressure increased for more skilled people, they created two talent safety values: foreign direct investment and H-1B talent visas. In the main, they have gradually pulled back from the alternative of job training or career education programs.

First, U.S. multinationals exported millions of high-wage jobs that they couldn't fill in the United States. These jobs went to other high-wage countries. This also required significant expenditures for plants and equipment in these nations. Table 4.1 lists the 2009 high-wage employment of U.S. firms in sample countries: Second, U.S. business began the mass importation of skilled foreigners. They have used the United States H-1B visa program that annually granted 65,000 six-year job visas for foreign workers. This has proven to be an extremely popular program. In 2007, it took only two days for businesses to file applications for all the 65,000 allocated visas. In 2008, this fell to one day.[19]

In 2001, Jim O'Neill, a Goldman Sachs economist, invented the term BRIC for Brazil, Russia, India, and China, thereby creating a new grouping of significant emerging economies. Since then, South Africa has been added (2011) to make them the BRICS. However, U.S. business attention has primarily focused on China and India. Their perception is that these two nations act as a bottomless well of talent for their businesses.

Long-term forecasters tell us India and China may inherit the earth. Their arguments for touting these two rapidly growing markets are at first glance overwhelming.[20] Other pundits warn that China and India will become superpowers eclipsing the United States. In the following discussion,

TABLE 4.1   High-Wage Employment of U.S. firms in Sample Nations

Nations	# of Jobs
Canada	1.0M
The United Kingdom (Scotland & England)	1.1M
Germany	615,000
France	529,900
Total	3,244,000[1]

[1] David Wessel, "U.S. Firms Eager to Add Foreign Jobs," *Wall Street Journal*, November 22, 2011, B1; Gordon, *2010 Meltdown*, 29–30

we review the challenges they both are facing on the rocky road to becoming high-tech super economies. The growing talent shortage in both China and India is a key issue that is further complicated by a host of third world socioeconomic problems.

China and India start from a lower economic base. Their huge populations are waiting to consume. Their colleges and universities do not produce an inexhaustible supply of highly skilled scientists and technicians. Ongoing economic liberalization has given them significant economic power.

Some see the rise of India and China as a major economic game changer. "Future historians will surely call this epoch 'the great convergence,'" says economist Martin Wolf.[21] Are they on the way to achieving a new global power balance?

India wants the respect conferred by its rising IT power. But a rickety infrastructure and widespread corruption challenge its credibility as a great power. China's state-controlled capitalism is forging into uncharted territory, run by a fascist-type police state that fears political liberalization. Something must change.

These and other major limitations cloud the future of China and India. A major war for talent is now underway from Chinese tech manufacturers to Indian IT firms as they hunt for skilled workers. This has serious implications for a U.S. business community historically overdependent on importing skilled people from abroad.[22]

We will now consider the many talent challenges and a vast array of socioeconomic obstacles facing both these nations. They must overcome these significant impediments to create and sustain an effective education-to-employment system that meets the talent needs of their own domestic economies.

China—The Bandit Kingdom

State Capitalism over All

In 2011, the China colossus became the world's largest exporter and second largest importer. It has the world's largest workforce. China possesses 33 percent of world currency reserves and the largest trade surplus. It has the world's biggest cache of personal savings and is the largest importer of many raw materials.

To achieve this seeming economic miracle, China became one of the few communist regimes to successfully liberalize into a booming capitalist economy, though with Chinese characteristics. This seems an unprecedented combination.[23]

The answer, China's cheerleaders will tell you, is the Communist party's exerting a tight grip on every aspect of life. The model is called State Capitalism. It is not a new idea. Here is how it works. State-owned enterprises (SOES) and other so-called national champions aggressively acquire advanced technologies. The government manages China's exchange rate to benefit these exporters. The "Big 4 banks" control the financial system with $11 trillion in assets. They supply low-cost capital loans to China's domestic industries. SOES also get capital to buy foreign oil and minerals that fuel rapid economic expansion.[24]

In China's State Capitalism, political power is centralized. The Communist party's Central Organization Department makes all the appointments to both state-owned companies as well as governmental bodies. In reality, China's State Capitalism is a vast patronage system. Many of China's SOES are controlled by the army. Most are not very profitable, averaging about a 4 percent return.[25]

This system has other major economic limitations. The government-owned steel industry is a good example. It is ranked as the largest in the world. However, at least 50 percent is nonperforming, in the opinion of Robert DiCianni, manager, Marketing and Analysis at ArcelorMittal, USA. China's mills and equipment are often antiquated. Much of their steel production operates at a loss.

So many of these SOES in every business sector are run by political apparatchiks that they are commonly referred to as red entrepreneurs. The number of China's SOES is now on the rise.[26] Many of China's more lucrative sectors, such as the telecoms or green technology, are dominated by these SOES. Consequently, Chinese business leaders operate in the shadow of a secretive and repressive ruling Communist party.

China's State Capitalism is an unscrupulous competitive weapon used to advance the interests of these SOES by undermining their competitive rivals in the United States or the European Union, states Ian Bremmer in *The End of the Free Market* (2010). This is a colossally reckless strategy. "How do you fight against enormous subsidies, low-interest loans, cheap labor and scale, and a government strategy to make you No. 1 in solar?" complained Conrad Burke, president of Innovalight, a competing U.S. Silicon Valley company.[27]

Nor is the Chinese judicial system independent of the Communist Party. The chief justice was not trained as a lawyer. He was a career policeman in the security services.

China's media, religious groups, and civil society are severely restricted. In 2010, China's spending on internal security surpassed national defense for the first time. This happened after protests engulfed the Arab world reinforcing Beijing's growing concern about public unrest.

Over the last six years, China has tightened its grip on electronic communications, including shutting down over 130,000 Internet cafes. More recently, the government disrupted Google Inc.'s email services and other services used to circumvent Web censorship.

In China, political rivals are systematically eradicated. Liu Xiaobo, a longtime advocate of political freedom was sentenced (2010) to 11 years in prison. Social dissidents disappear into labor camps. The environmental campaigner Wu Lihong has also been jailed. Anyone who dares to challenge the system pays a stiff price.[28] Total control reigns supreme.

A New Brand of Fascism?

This raises important questions over China's increasingly repressive political culture. Has a country that has long called itself socialist really become brutally capitalist? China increasingly resembles earlier 20th-century dictatorships.

The Fascist Corporate State was first conceived by Italy's Benito Mussolini. Later, it was Adolf Hitler's Nazi Germany that perfected the system of state control over corporate interests, thus manipulating all aspects of industry, the economy, and employment. Hitler also used a huge repressive police state to eliminate opposition political groups. Today, Communist China has become the new fascist corporate state of the 21st century.[29]

Since 2003, China's miracle economy has rested on two pillars that are now shaky: exports and real estate. Real estate land grabs by local authorities have ignited thousands of protests. The crashing of a Chinese real estate bubble could lead to widespread national unrest.

"When we talk about China's economic power, we should be careful not to overestimate our strength. China's rapid gross domestic product (GDP) growth will be meaningless if these imbalances remain unsolved," says Yi Xianrong, director of the Financial Institute at the Chinese Academy of Social Science, a state-backed think tank.[30] Let's examine the potential global impact of both the talent crisis and real estate bubbles.

The "Ant Tribe" Needs Skills

Asia's awe-inspiring model of economic development started after World War II with Japan's ascent from the ashes of defeat. First, start on the most labor-intensive rung of industrial development by making the lowest value, simple products. Then, slowly move up the value chain as you build up a new infrastructure of skilled talent, logistics, and capital. Gradually begin exporting low skill/low wage jobs to poorer countries. This is the economic model the Asian Tigers—South Korea, Taiwan, Singapore, and Malaysia— copied from Japan, and now China is following the same path.

China has developed the world's largest manufacturing workforce, over 112 million people. But according to Yasheng Huang, a Sloan School of Management professor at MIT, despite all the hoopla that China is moving rapidly into "knowledge production, the economy remains driven by manual labor, low-cost and low-margin manufacturing" to absorb the huge mass of rural peasant labor.[31] In his journey across China from farm to factory, Peter Hessler in *Country Driving* (2010) says that the plant bosses he meets are proponents of "low investment, low-quality products, low profit margins, and low education by their marginally literate employees."[32] Up to now, China has rightly been viewed as the low-cost manufacturer to the world.

However, as China ascends to a higher phase of economic development, firms in its industrial heartland are beginning to reinvent their businesses. The TAL Group, a garment manufacturer, is moving beyond piecework. In a partnership with J.C. Penney, they are electronically managing their production of dress shirts from the factory floor in Don Guam to the retail shelves of Connecticut. Manufacturing costs have risen rapidly due to growing shortages of more skilled technical workers.

The Topnew factory is on the outskirts of Beijing. It is the largest plant in the Topnew Knitting Group. The recent labor crunch has motivated them to automate. A $500,000 computerized machine will replace many semi-skilled workers.[33]

There are two underlying drivers behind China's labor shortages. First, China's birth rate has been steadily decreasing since the introduction of the one-child policy in 1977. It has averted 400 million births in 30 years. The supply of people aged 15–24 entering the workforce peaked in 2005 at 227 million, and is predicted to fall to 150 million by 2024. Some manufacturers who can't find enough low-skilled workers are closing down production lines and idling factories. China already has drained its once vast reserves of unemployed rural workers.[34]

Second, as China gears up for high-tech manufacturing, it is facing a deficit of skilled talent. This includes skilled technicians for growing advanced manufacturing, chemical and pharmaceutical industries, financial services, research and development personnel, and qualified managers. Yin

Weimin, minister of human resources and social security, warns that the human resources structure does not match its need for talent and ". . . has become a bottleneck in China's goal to build an innovative country and for the shift of its economic development pattern."[35]

China is now the world's largest exporter of technology goods—laptop computers, mobile phones, and DVD players. Typically only assembled in China by foreign companies, their high-value components come from elsewhere. As China has moved up the value chain, this is creating talent problems.[36]

Ask senior Chinese executives what is their main problem. "The shortage of talent!" will be at the top of their list. Much of this talent bust is due to a Chinese education infrastructure that has not developed fast enough to keep up with the ever more rapid government-driven evolution of the economy. Talent may be the weakest link in China's economy over the next decade.

A Manpower global talent study (2006) based on a survey of 90 percent of the world's 500 largest multinational companies revealed a critical shortage of Chinese engineers, IT workers, and other professionals. Over the past five years, Chinese talent shortages have continued to worsen.[37]

China graduates over 600,000 engineers annually (2004) from its post-secondary institutions. Surely this will more than provide an adequate STEM-prepared workforce? But numbers do not tell the whole story. Great quantity does not equate to high quality. China is losing its talent war. The McKinsey Global Institute estimates that only 10 percent of Chinese engineering graduates meet the global professional standards of major U.S. and European firms. Their talent deficiencies include limited language proficiency, poor quality STEM education, personal cultural work issues, and job accessibility.[38]

Two separate Duke University studies (2006–2007) revealed that the quality of education in India and China is considerably lower than U.S. standards. These studies found that the focus is on quantity not quality and that ". . . there appears to be a factory-like approach to turning out some graduates."[39] The bottom line for China *The Economist* concludes is that "There are not enough engineers and scientists to produce high-tech goods across the board."[40]

China's reliance on rote learning and the Confucian tradition of unquestioning acceptance of what is taught undermines critical thinking skills for personal initiative and the practical, applied skills of graduates in engineering, finance, life sciences, and management. McKinsey also found that between 2010 and 2020 China will need to hunt down 75,000 additional managers with some form of global experience.[41] In summing up the overall talent picture, *Financial Times* economist Martin Wolf concludes that China is a "colossus with feet of clay."[42]

Millions of these college graduates are stacking up—at least 100,000 in Beijing alone, according to a 2010 estimate. They have a new name—"the ant tribe." Chinese sociologists came up with the term. It is a reference to their great numbers. Their undergraduate degrees usually come from a mushrooming crop of substandard provincial schools. The jobs most can get barely pay a living wage. "College essentially provided them with nothing," concludes Zhang Ming, a political scientist and outspoken critic of China's inferior education system.[43] When an economic crisis occurs, they will be a source of instability.

In the first six months of 2012, six million full-time jobs were created in China. Labor ministry surveys showed demand for talent outstripping skilled worker supply in 91 Chinese cities by a record amount.[44]

To help make up for these major skill shortages, the government has started a new talent hunt designed to attract some of the 35 million from the Chinese overseas diaspora back home. At least 200,000 Chinese have already returned. They call them *hai gui* or sea turtles. This Chinese word for turtle can be pronounced like the word for coming home.

To win this talent battle, the Chinese government has introduced mind-boggling incentives for expatriates: bigger apartments, chauffeur-driven cars, access to fellowships at the best universities, and important jobs in shiny new office buildings. Wei Liu returned in 2003, after working in Palo Alto and Colorado Springs for Hewlett-Packard. Dr. Shi Yigong, a Princeton University molecular biologist, returned in 2008 to become the dean of life science at Tsinghua University in Beijing. Rao Yi left Northwestern University in 2007 and became the dean of the School of Life Science at Peking University in Beijing.[45]

The fact that China has a major systemic structural problem in creating enough talent should really come as no surprise. During the Great Leap Forward, all universities were closed. They only reopened in 1978. The class of '82 was the first graduating class. Its members are coming into power now. In the early 1980s, China began inventing its own capitalist economy. It will take several more decades and a loosening of Communist Party control for the country's institutions to begin catching up to the demands of their own labor market for a bigger, freer, more high-quality education-to-employment system.

The number of students returning to China in 2011 was up 40 percent, compared to the previous year. In 2012, China introduced a new

"Exit-Entry" law. It includes a talent introduction visa for overseas Chinese who are citizens of other nations that facilitates opening businesses and trading in China.[46]

In the near term, it may prove very difficult for China to avoid major social unrest among its underskilled migrant rural workers as a major economic downturn begins. The bottom line for U.S. business—there is little surplus skilled talent left in China to recruit for overseas jobs no matter how high the United States raises its H-1B visa quota.

The degree of euphoria regarding China's economy on which the world economy has become so dependent has reached alarming heights. The huge government-ordained expansion of bank credit over the past two years will eventually lead to a spectacular burst of the real estate bubble, producing vast losses. The only question is—how soon?

Fraud and Corruption

How accurate are China's official government statistics? Leaked U.S. diplomatic cables bemoan "man-made" Chinese GDP numbers. In early 2011, China's National Bureau of Statistics stopped publishing the official index of national property prices. This only added to the already widespread frustration and skepticism about the quality of the country's official economic data.[47]

China now has a well-earned reputation for pervasive business, academic, and scientific corruption. Fraud remains rampant. There is misconduct across a wide range of activities, including intellectual property theft, blatant reverse engineering of technology, unbelievable levels of graft at every level of government, falsified data, bogus college/university degrees, cheating on tests, extensive plagiarism, and fabricating scientific data for professional journals.

There is growing evidence of Chinese government complicity in widespread cyber-espionage attacks. McAfee, the U.S.-based security company, issued a report in August 2011 stating that a single perpetrator mounted cyber attacks on the computer networks of 72 governments, companies (including 11 defense contractors), and organizations in the United States, Canada, Japan, South Korea, Taiwan, Switzerland, and the United Kingdom.[48] Such attacks could gain access to a variety of sensitive data ranging from military secrets to industrial designs and other intellectual property.

The Pentagon's 2011 annual report, "Military and Security Developments Involving the People's Republic of China," provides corroboration of extensive Chinese cyber espionage. Two Chinese military publications were named that identified "information warfare as integral to achieving information superiority and an effective means for countering a stronger foe."[49]

Mandiant, an American security firm, issued a 60-page study in 2013, with compelling evidence that China's People's Liberation Army conducted hacking attacks during the past seven years on 115 U.S. companies. China immediately denied the charge saying that their own country is a hacking victim.[50] However, what other country has devoted major governmental resources on this scale to help its companies to continue to grow at breakneck speed?

Beijing touts the triumph of its so-called socialism with Chinese characteristics. Unfortunately, as the *Wall Street Journal* states, "Its defining characteristic is theft."[51]

Postmodern Communist China has adopted a "rule by law," but has never embraced a "rule of law." Too many Chinese laws and regulations lack clarity. Enforcement is arbitrary. China's courts are subject to political influence. Property rights in China remain insecure.

Instead of law, *guanxi* (connections) with government officials rules. China has a largely decentralized government with an estimated 36 million officials mostly at the local level. Beijing's role is one of oversight, not detailed enforcement. This has allowed local officials to exploit their *guanxi* to enrich themselves through rampant kickbacks, bribes, commissions, and other schemes.

This freedom from bureaucratic oversight has allowed many businesses to be created or liquidated overnight. Instead of paying taxes, companies often just make minimal payments to the local government. To whatever extent businesses operate outside the law, they are subject to shakedowns from local to higher officials.

My interviews with both U.S. and Chinese business leaders consistently revealed that they divide the main costs of successfully doing business in today's China into three parts: a third for operations and labor, a third for fixed investment (plant, equipment, etc.), and a third for bribery of government officials at every level. A major modern global economy cannot indefinitely sustain this stratospheric level of corruption.

A Bulldozed Environment

At a China briefing in Chicago, the subject of Beijing's weather was mentioned by a returning U.S. government official. He commented that after four days in Chicago, he finally was able to stop coughing. Also, he said that Chicago's impressive skyline with its background of blue sky and white clouds was a sharp contract to the perpetual thick fog of Beijing.

The official government line is that this haze is not pollution. But the *China Daily* article, "Exposure to Smog Is Severe Hazard" (December 6, 2011) acknowledged that Beijing's lung cancer rate has increased by 60 percent over the past decade, even though there was no change in cigarette smoking habits.

The effects of unbridled corruption and arbitrary government regulation are evident in the massive development projects that are laying waste to the country's natural environment. "The Chinese miracle is built on a raw, bulldozed landscape of unrelenting horror," says the *Economist*. This has led to an "airpocalypse," a brown cloud thousands of kilometers across China that is fed by fires, diesel fumes, and many other forms of pollution.

Masses of floating garbage near the Three Gorges dam threaten to clog key floodgates on the Yangtze River. Water quality and scarcity are further problems. An acute water shortage across the Beijing region is beginning to limit future growth. But since the 1980s, 170 golf courses have opened. When it comes to water-hungry fairways, officials turn a blind eye for a price. The drought has hit eight of China's provinces reducing much of the wheat crop. Beijing shows little sign of reigning in golf or skiing (using artificial snow). Developers get away with this by simply calling golf by another name. Never mind the environment.[52]

A "Knock-Off" Culture

A further cloud on China's economic future is its blatant flouting of intellectual property rights. Chinese regulation of the private sector has often been characterized as "one eye open, one eye shut." The American Chamber of Commerce surveys of the business climate in China consistently show that the violation of intellectual property rights is one of the top concerns of U.S. companies in China.[53] The "shanghai" (knockoff) culture is so deeply rooted in corruption at many levels of society that it is hard to know where to start any effective crackdown. Ninety-eight percent of foreign-owned businesses have been the victims of at least one fraud, concluded a report (2011) by Kroll and the Economist Intelligence Unit.[54]

In China's latest wave of piracy, counterfeiters don't just copy goods. Now they replicate down to the smallest details entire successful Western retail stores. If imitation is the highest form of flattery, this cloning in China takes intellectual property theft to a stellar level. IKEA, Apple, Nike, Walt Disney, and Dairy Queen are all suffering major revenue losses from these fake stores. Some of these Chinese proprietors say that their stores' similarity to a recognized brand is just a coincidence.[55]

This is happening against a backdrop of continuing government efforts to force foreign companies to transfer their business and technological know-how to Chinese companies in exchange for market access. Starting in 1999, Beijing announced that all providers of encryption-related software would be required to disclose their source code. Industry experts say this would exclude foreign players from most of the Chinese market for fear of losing control over their proprietary software or force them to develop exclusive Chinese products.

Then, in 2006, China introduced their indigenous innovation program. This would require foreign companies to both design and produce their products in China. Beijing said this would encourage homegrown invention. Might its true purpose be to facilitate technology transfer by theft?

A host of companies, including Google, Goldman Sachs, General Electric, Siemens, and BASF, have blasted Chinese thievery. Over time, they anticipate that Chinese commercial theft will hollow out their capacity to compete. "I'm not sure that in the end they want any of us to win or any of us to be successful," Jeff Immelt chief executive of GE complained.[56]

Other experts go even further. The U.S. Chamber of Commerce has called China's indigenous innovation program "a blueprint for technology theft on a scale the world has not seen before."[57] This program is commonly viewed as a proposition that will be a win for China and a loss for foreign multinationals.

A report by the U.S. International Trade Commission, "China: Effects of Intellectual Property Infringement and Indigenous Innovation Policies on the U.S. Economy" (2011), estimated that U.S. firms operating in China with intensive investments in intellectual property lost at least $48.2 billion in 2009 alone. This rises to as much as $90.5 billion if foregone sales, royalties, and license fees are included.[58] "A China that leads the world in the theft of intellectual property, computer hacking, and resource nationalism will prove extremely destabilizing," stated Jamie E. Metzel, executive vice president of the Asia Society and a National Security Council official in the Clinton administration.[59] In short, China roundly deserves to be branded the "bandit kingdom".

Reading the Tea Leaves on the Future

In 2010, the Chinese government announced a policy of broad national support for developing seven new strategic industries: high-end equipment manufacturing (aircraft, high-speed rail, satellites); alternative fuel cars; biotechnology; environmental technologies (energy efficiency, pollution control); alternative energy; advanced materials; and next generation IT (cloud computing, advanced software). Furthermore, in June 2010, the government released "The National Medium- and Long-Term Talent Development Plan (2010–2020)," in which it announced plans to increase its pool of skilled talent from 114 million to 180 million by 2020.[60]

Currently, skilled talent shortages are causing wages in China to spike. Also, a global wave of consumer demand is feeding a surge in commodity prices. Inflation has begun to take hold, with a price rise of 5 percent or more each year. In June 2011, the yearly rise was 6.4 percent, the biggest jump in three years.

No bigger question hangs over the world economy than the future of China's economic growth. China's version of state capitalism may have reached its limits. Many warning signs are flashing red.

China's explosive growth has largely been driven by a low-wage export economy and massive investments in infrastructure and real estate. Over-aggressive local government spending on new roads, bridges, subways, and showpiece condo and retail projects have led to a wave of nonperforming loans. This has spawned a major real estate bubble. The central government has attempted to stop the breakneck lending of recent years. This has not proven very successful. The hope that China's economy will have a soft landing is disappearing as its real estate bubble continues to expand.[61]

This bubble has made it easier for the government to put off dealing with a host of socioeconomic problems. Yu Yongding, a former People's Bank of China official, warns that China will need to change its current system of state capitalism by reducing the underlying gap between the rich and the poor, since "a serious backlash is brewing."[62]

China must pay heed to the ever-changing currents of globalization. Over the past decade, manufacturers in high-cost nations, such as the United States, have raised worker productivity to become more competitive. They have reorganized operations and invested in new labor-saving technologies.

Hal Sirkin, manufacturing expert at BCG, a Chicago-based consulting group, believes that soon it will no longer pay for U.S. companies to outsource production to China. "They will find their costs are no higher if they do the manufacturing at home."[63] Other logistics experts also agree with this reshoring forecast. China needs to find a new economic model.

Starting with Deng Xiaoping's observation in 1992 that "There is good social order in Singapore," the Chinese have been fascinated with this prosperous city-state. They value its authoritarianism and state industrial policy. But the Chinese ignore the core of Singapore's success—a laissez-faire economic system. Foreign multinationals flock to Singapore for its excellent infrastructure, well-educated workforce, open trade routes, the rule of law, little corruption, and low taxes.

Sooner rather than later, Beijing will have to adopt some of these same government reforms with the same gusto as their economic reform. Chinese communist ideology is in decline. The legitimacy of the party's ruling class rests on continuing economic growth. But with rising income, demands for greater political participation will inevitably follow. How will China solve this problem?[64]

There are many in the Communist Party today who have never supported this Red Capitalism. They see a potential return to the social excesses and turmoil of China's prerevolutionary era of the 1930s and 1940s. One of the former rising stars in the Communist Party, Bo Xilai, was touting the virtues of the isolationist policies of Chairman Mao. However, what he and others do not understand is that without China's dramatic opening to global markets and Western finance, its remarkable physical transformation since 1978 would have never happened.[65]

The lack of transparency of China's State Capitalism also contributes to even more skepticism regarding the country's long-term financial viability. The U.S. Securities and Exchange Commission is investigating accounting practices and disclosure procedures at a number of Chinese companies listed on U.S. exchanges. In April 2011, James Doty, chairman of the Public Company Accounting Oversight Board (PCAOB), the U.S. government accounting regulator, complained in testimony before Congress that his group's inability to inspect the accounting work of these Chinese firms was "a gaping hole in investor protection."[66] This poor access to financial information led to a major sell-off of China's overseas-listed companies (6/11). If China is to become a reliable business player in international financial markets, it can start by repairing its reputation with investors by giving the PCAOB access to work done by auditors in China.

China's $4 trillion massive foreign exchange reserves have given the world a largely false appearance of vast national wealth. Yet, Beijing's ability to use them in a crisis is very limited.

Many wealthy Chinese are transferring their assets to other countries. According to the China Merchants Bank and Bain & Company publication, "2011 China Private Wealth Report," 60 percent of Chinese people with a net worth of over $15 million have already left or are planning to leave. The United States, Australia, and Canada are the most popular destinations for these wealthy Chinese. Some say retirement or education motivates their change in citizenship, but making their wealth safe seems the most prominent concern. The fears about the future means that their wealth will not be placed back in China.[67]

China is drowning in nonperforming investments financed with credit. These bad bank loans are soaring while local governments face insolvency. The country is littered with ghost cities and crumbling infrastructure projects. The coming cyclical bust will discredit this state-led capitalism growth model that allocates credit based on politics rather than market opportunity.

Protests against the Chinese government appear to be gaining strength. In the past, children have died in earthquakes due to shoddily built schools or were poisoned with impure milk. Peasants were thrown off their land to build high-rises. Because members of the middle class were victims of the high-speed train tragedy of July 2011, the government did not succeed in covering up its consequences as in the past. Its hubris, incompetence, and corruption were exposed. If China's sleek high-speed rail system is not safe, how sound is the banking system or the party management of the economy, including its development of more skilled talent? There is no consensus within the Communist Party on how to ensure its survival in a time of increasing economic uncertainty and social upheaval. Whether there will be a gradual shift to a more open pluralistic system or a wrenching period of political disorder in the near future remains to be seen. However, the era of China providing a seemingly unlimited pool of talent for the United States and other industrial nations appears to be at an end.[68]

India–"The License Raj"

Losing Momentum?

In both India and China, the hunt for skilled talent has become a major business issue. But they are very different nations. India is the world's largest democracy. In 1991, India abandoned its Soviet-style centrally planned socialist economic model and its famous "Hindu rate of growth"—3 percent a year. Manmohan Singh, then India's finance minister, initiated capitalist reforms that jump-started economic growth.

Suddenly, India leaped ahead to become a land of opportunity. It created 40,000 new millionaires by 2009 and much better times for hundreds of millions of its citizens. Yet India is a land of paradox. The benefits of its economic growth are spread very unevenly among India's 1.2 billion population. UNICEF's 2010 data shows that 42 percent still live below the international poverty line of $1.25 per day. Forty-six percent of all children remain malnourished (2011). Rural unemployment is at nearly 30 percent (2011).

India often resembles a failing state. India's stifling bureaucracy makes doing business extremely difficult; the so-called License Raj nurtures widespread corruption. The public school system is in shambles. Talent growth is constricted because academic quality is so poor in many of India's higher educational institutions. India's infrastructure for roads, power, water, and railways is shockingly inadequate. This has accentuated the massive growth of urban slums.

Corruption is increasing. Rapid economic expansion has created more opportunities for graft. India's boom has enriched a minority, while leaving most mired in poverty. This flawed trickle-down economy has only helped to further fuel a decades-old Maoist insurgency that now is the nation's biggest internal security threat.

After 20 years of economic reforms, this wasn't supposed to be the picture of how agrarian India would be transformed into an industrial powerhouse. India ". . . is in danger of losing its momentum," says Rajiv Kumar, director general of the Federation of India Chambers of Commerce and Industry.[69]

What Talent Dividend?

One of the pillars supporting India's continuing economic boom is the demographic fact that about half the people are under the age of 25. India's demographic dividend promises both a gigantic future workforce and potentially a huge consumer middle class.

Before 2030, India will overtake China as the most populous nation on earth when its population attains 1.45 billion people. However, India's population will be far younger. It will have the world's largest workforce—986 million people. But without access to better education and quality skills training, this talent dividend may turn out to be a fantasy. Illiteracy now stands at 26 percent. India's weak educational system still dooms millions of ill-educated youth to little hope of gainful employment.[70]

Talent: Myth versus Reality

Because of its huge population, India potentially offers a vast supply of workers. It churns out 600,000 engineers every year (compared to 84,000 in the United States). More than 200 multinationals have R&D centers in India tapping these phalanxes of engineers. Also, an enormous pool of expatriate PhDs, who have worked in the West, are now being lured to return home by good job opportunities.[71]

Yet multiple studies have raised warning flags on the employability of the graduates of Indian technical colleges and universities. Aspiring Minds has developed the AMCAT standardized employability test, comparable to the Graduate Record Examination in the United States. The test results help companies evaluate thousands of Indian engineering and computer science students. AMCAT gauges students' analytical, verbal, and quantitative skills, and assesses business problem solving, teamwork, and other critical thinking competencies. Aspiring Minds reported in 2010 that only 4.2 percent of the engineers evaluated were fit to work in a software product firm. An additional 17.8 percent were found to be suitable for an IT services company. But they would all require up to six months of additional special training. These were even worse findings than the 25 percent employability figure from an earlier McKinsey Global Institute survey (2005).

While India's best universities, such as the India Institutes of Technology, are on par with U.S. Ivy League schools, there are only 16 of them. Yes, there has been a four-fold increase in the number of students in India's engineering colleges: from 390,000 in 2000 to 1.5 million in 2011. But this vast expansion has come at the expense of quality. A study by India's National Association of Software and Services Companies (NASSOM), found that 75 percent of these technical graduates and 85 percent of general college graduates were unemployable.[72]

Much of the reason for this is that India's higher education system is built on a foundation of sand. Free compulsory education for every child in the age group 6–14 was only legislated in 2009. For the majority of students education in today's India is just plain lousy.

Teachers are absent in droves and masses of unidentified pupils crowd decrepit schoolhouses that are often devoid of basic instructional materials or even drinkable water. India's workforce is 35 percent illiterate. Just 15 percent of students reach high school and only 7 percent graduate. About half of India's girls remain illiterate. This is startling to most people who have been told by such books as *The World Is Flat* (2005) or the documentary film *Two Million Minutes* (2007) that India is a model of educational excellence supporting a vast pool of talent.

The *2010 Annual Status of Educators Report* by Pratham, a nongovernmental organization that aims to improve education for India's poor, surveyed the performance of children in 13,000 grade schools. While it found that over 96 percent of eligible children were enrolled, almost 50 percent of fifth graders can't read at a second grade level. Only 36 percent can do simple division, a decline from 2009. Also, 9–15 million children still remain out of school. This is an educational disaster.[73]

One of the Pratham report's authors, Amit Kaushik, thinks that India must make an urgent turnaround "if the next generation is not to be lost." Azim H. Premji's aim is to do just that. He is the chairman of the Indian IT giant, Wipro. His education foundation is working at 1,500 elementary schools helping to train new teachers in better teaching methods. The aim is to substantially raise student reading skills, math literacy, and reasoning skills. Like Microsoft founder, Bill Gates, Mr. Premji is a billionaire. He hopes his foundation working in both public and private schools will eventually make a difference for tens of millions of India's children.[74] Another 11,500 grade schools are still in desperate need of a similar transformation.

At the other end of the talent prep spectrum stand the top business schools, the India Institutes of Management (IIM). Over 242,000 students took the annual entrance exam for just 2,200 seats (2009). Expansion of these top higher education institutes has been slowed by tight government regulations.

There are now 13 IIMs in India, as 6 more campuses were added since 2010 due to increasing student demand. They differ from other nations' elite MBA programs because upon graduation most students are placed in secure, well-paid jobs. India's businesses are literally starving for these top business school graduates. They are needed to manage fast-expanding operations in many business sectors.

India's talent gap also has spurred the development of a wide array of private schools. They annually produce a bumper crop of 100,000 graduates. Unfortunately, India has no independent accreditation agency to assure quality for its business schools. The result is that Indian business graduates' knowledge and qualifications range from world-class to very poor. In the opinion of Shobha Mishra Ghosh, director of the higher education department at the Federation of Indian Chambers of Commerce and Industry, only 5–10 percent of these private business schools are delivering a quality education.

To help close this talent gap, the government in 2010 sent parliament a bill that would allow foreign universities to set up branches in India. It was defeated. Over 100 foreign educational institutions already offer vocational, technical, or management courses to experienced executives. America's Fuqua School of Business at Duke University is affiliated with the Indian Institute of Management and already offers corporate executive programs. However, Duke cannot operate its own business school in India.

An important talent source for India's businesses is the 160,000 students who annually study abroad. Taking a page from Communist China in the war for talent, the India government established a Ministry of Overseas

Indian Affairs and a Return and Resettlement Fund to help hunt down and lure expatriates to return home. About 100,000 returnees are expected to move from the United States to India between 2009 and 2014, projects Vivek Wadhwa, a researcher at Harvard University. Many will join multinational companies, start new businesses, or even join the government bureaucracy.[75]

Public-private partnerships are another type of initiative being employed to tackle India's shortages of skilled workers. In 1952, the Indian government began opening vocational centers to supply India with skilled technicians. Since then, while technology has leaped forward, the nearly 2,000 state-run technical training schools have barely changed. However, since 2007, hundreds of businesses across India, including Ispat Steel, Hero Honda, Tata Motors, and Mafatlal Denim, have entered into new partnerships that have collaboratively upgraded many of these institutes' curricula and technologies. Unfortunately, not every training center director has enthusiastically embraced these partnerships. "It's a slow process," says Subhash Chawra, founder of Chawra Plastics, a specialty plastic packaging company. "But we feel we are moving in the right direction, even if it's not as fast as we want it to be." His business has a permanent employment sign up—"Help and Supervisors Wanted." But no one has turned up.[76]

As we have seen, the crux of India talent problem is the poor employability of large numbers of young people. This is the origin of the nation's talent paradox—high unemployment linked to labor shortages across the economy. Wages rose about 13 percent in 2011, according to Hewitt & Co., because of widespread talent shortages. Business executives and policymakers alike worry that the country is failing to provide skill training to the huge cohort of poor, rural workers. India must create a viable education-to-employment system. "In the next four or five years, there is a higher probability that India's growth machine will stop—because it can't create the skills—rather than because it can't create jobs," stated Jahangir Aziz of J.P. Morgan Chase.[77]

India needs more talented workers and fast. The World Bank (2009) predicted that less than half of the skilled people needed will be found to build and modernize its roads, water delivery, power systems, and housing over the next decade. India's already heavily overburdened physical infrastructure has been starved of investment for decades, and consequently the skills of maintenance workers have drained away.[78]

But will India pick up this slack? Until India's human capital talent base is deepened and physical infrastructure overhauled, the nation's inexorable rise in the 21st century is far from assured. What is certain is that for the immediate future a declining number of India's most talented will be attracted to jobs in the United States, Canada, or the European Union.

Graft, Bribes, and Talent

Corruption has been identified by many inside and outside the country as the biggest issue confronting India. Corrupt state bureaucracies are undermining multinational expansion in India. "Under normal notions of competition in the market economy, the most efficient firms (would) get to the top. (But) in parts of the economy afflicted with corruption, the most rotten firms get to the top," says Ajay Shah, a professor at the National Institute for Public Finance and Policy.[79]

In 2010 and 2011, a number of corruption scandals rocked India. One of the most flagrant examples was the government payment of $80 per roll of toilet paper for the 2010 Commonwealth Game in Delhi. Activists and some lawmakers have supported establishing a "Lokpal," an independent national ethics agency with wide-ranging power to investigate and prosecute graft and bribery on the part of senior elected officials, members of the judiciary, or government bureaucrats at all levels.[80]

Ratan Tata is one of India's most successful executives. He has been chairman of the Tata Group since 1991. Since then, he has transformed the organization into India's best known conglomerate, including companies within and outside India, with holdings in automobile manufacturing (both the Tata Nano and Jaguar), consulting, steelmaking, software, luxury hotels, and the tea and coffee industries.

Mr. Tata is a booster of India. "Economically it is a much more open environment," he says. The free enterprise system works well, ". . . until you need approvals . . . Then you still have problems and maybe more acute than you did before." Paying bribes isn't his style. They do not fit into his ethics. "Maybe I'm stupid or old fashioned, but I really want to go to bed at night saying I haven't succumbed to this."[81]

Manmohan Singh, India's prime minister, has pledged to tackle the corruption issue. This is perhaps the biggest test of his premiership. But will he do it? It is time for India to fundamentally restructure its business climate with such serious reforms as an open, competitive bidding system, viable public procurement policy/standards, and an end to public servant corruption.[82]

Insurrection or Skills?

The extreme poverty and high illiteracy prevailing in rural India pose significant challenges to the Indian government. These inequities have helped to fuel a Maoist insurgency that has continued for 40 years in remote areas of eastern and central India. Prime Minister Singh has termed this guerilla movement India's biggest security challenge. Recently, this insurgency has grown in severity and extent. Maoist Naxalite rebels have attacked trains, mines, pipelines, and seized control of villages. In late 2009, the government launched Operation Green Hunt deploying over 50,000 paramilitary police in five Indian states. However, this effort proved ineffectual during 2010, as 1,169 people were killed in Naxalite attacks, the highest number of yearly casualties ever.[83]

More than policing is the need to end this insurgency, as enormous disparities in income and educational attainment are feeding it. One program to remedy this is the Mahatma Gandhi National Rural Employment Scheme, a $9 billion effort to employ the poor by rebuilding the antiquated infrastructure in India's most backward rural areas. But, according to senior government officials, the program is riddled with corruption. Less than half of the new road and irrigation projects begun in 2006 were completed by 2011. Workers complain about being forced to pay bribes to get these jobs. They frequently were not paid in full. Most importantly, they aren't learning new skills for future long-term employment that will enable them to break out of their cycle of poverty.[84]

As we have seen, India is running out of skilled talent to build a modern economy. Most of its current workers remain in the agricultural sector. As this sector mechanizes, these farmers are ill-suited to work in either 21st-century agriculture or to move into other growing business sectors.

To boost the size of its middle class, India must successfully address the employment and talent challenges of its rural poor. India's long-term attractiveness to foreign investors as a major consumer market will certainly be enhanced by moving more of its citizens into the economic mainstream through equipping them with the education and skills needed in a modern economy.

"Anything Is Possible"

In 1951, Jawaharlal Nehru, India's first prime minister, prepared the nation's initial economic plan. He predicted a 2.1 percent annual growth rate. His forecast was mildly ambitious. Even if sustainable, Nehru calculated that a 600 percent increase in national wealth was required before India's masses would reach a "really progressive standard of living." Under British rule, India's economy had crawled along with a 0.1 percent growth each year.

For decades, the Indian state of Bihar bumped along at Nehru's low growth rate. Then, in 2010, Nitish Kumar, the current chief minister, announced the state had reached an 11 percent average growth rate for the last five years. This made rural Bihar the second fastest growing economy in the country. How did this miracle happen?

Elected as a reform candidate, Mr. Kumar first tackled crime and corruption at all levels, even targeting local members of Parliament and the state assembly. Then, he opened schools for 2.5 million non-attending children. In one year, medical clinics raised patient visits from 30 to 300 per month. Bureaucratic rules were loosened, and local graft punished, thus freeing billions of dollars for such infrastructure projects as new roads, street lights on narrow lanes, more police stations, schools, and water pumps.

"If even Bihar can change, then anywhere in India can change," says Shaibal Gupta at the Asian Development Research Institute. "With good governance, good policy, and law and order anything is possible."[85]

On July 24, 1991, Manmohan Singh, then serving as the finance minister of India, presented a budget to the parliament that changed his country and the world. Singh began opening industries to foreign capital and reformed custom regulations. He abolished production quotas and many businesses licenses. Singh began opening India's economy to the world.

India in one generation has seen its GDP per person rise by 230 percent. So, what now needs to be done for more people to experience a middle-class lifestyle? Singh's reform process is only half finished.

The miserable state of India's physical infrastructure is a major constraint on the economy. The government of Manmohan Singh has given unprecedented attention to this infrastructure deficit. They plan $1,000 billion worth of spending over the next six years. However, bureaucratic, unresponsive local governments have crippled infrastructure development across much of the country. Political corruption often siphons off money from the cities to state governments, perpetually delaying improvements. As a result, the better-run and better-educated states in western India attract more overseas investors than the poorer, more corrupt states in the east. This has caused great regional economic disparities and feeds social unrest.

First, there needs to be a dramatic reduction in graft and crony capitalism at all levels. Second, the war for talent and education must be radically expanded so that quality education matches quantity education, in order to supply the human capital that will allow India's economy to move up the value chain in the services and goods it produces. Third, pervasive infrastructure bottlenecks that are choking economic expansion need to be eliminated, while also improving the physical environment of rural areas and India's megacities.

There can be no doubt that India as an increasingly unfettered democracy will continue to rise. Its speed of development will be largely determined by how fast old ways of thinking adjust to the realities of the global economy.[86]

Who Will Win the Battle over Skills and Jobs?

In 2011, I attended an impressive performance by the China Philharmonic Orchestra (CPO). Since their December 2000 Beijing inaugural concert, they have toured the world and were selected in 2009 by Gramaphone as one of "the world's ten most inspiring orchestras." The program for this California performance stated that they were chosen "for almost single-handedly bringing Western classical music to the ears and hearts of a vast nation, for whom it had been forbidden for decades. They have taken it upon themselves to educate the country, and (alongside others) are making a pretty good job of it."[87] The CPO is an outstanding example of how far China and India have evolved culturally, economically, and socially over the past 30 years.

Yet, where are they now heading? Will China and India continue supplying the United States and other industrial economies with the talent they need for stable economic growth? Or will China and India through expansion of their own talent pool eclipse the U.S. economy and attain global economic dominance?

A serious inflationary threat has been spawned by growing talent shortages. In China, coastal wages are up 17 percent (2011). Indian inflation is averaging 9 percent, with wages increased by an average 13 percent (2011).[88]

How does the United States compare in a comparative talent run-up against these nations? For all its troubles, America remains the world's only economic superpower, but its talent pool is out of sync with the technological growth of the global economy. The American talent pool has become increasingly underpowered and overreliant on importing foreign talent. Additional investment by American business in U.S. human capital creation is urgently needed.

China

In contrast, China is an adolescent, as its young economy arose in 1978 from the ashes of the disastrous Great Leap Forward of the Mao era. It has benefitted from the advantage of its huge population and cheap labor. Now comes the hard part. As the economy matures, institutional changes in social/political structures are required along with massive investments in human capital development.

China now faces a major employment crisis. The 30-year low-cost/ low-wage manufacturing era that fueled its economic miracle is now over. China's 53-million migrant worker army is growing increasingly restless over low wages and a lack of employment benefits.[89]

Other cracks also are appearing in China's boom. Credit Suisse citing alarming levels of credit expansion warned of slower growth for the overall economy (6/11). Local government and state-owned or backed enterprise debt totals amount to well over 150 percent of China's 2010 GDP, according to Victor Shih, a political economist at Northwestern University. (By comparison, the U.S. debt-to-GDP ratio is 93 percent.)[90]

It is clear that China's greatest challenge is institutional change. After 90 years of existence, the Chinese Communist Party finds itself in crisis, as especially China's rising middle class views it as an entrenched elite. "The fact is that many people today foster hatred for government officials and hatred for the rich," says Yang Jisheng, a former government journalist and author.[91]

More Chinese economists are now predicting sharply lower annual GDP growth. This could undermine middle class support of the Communist Party that has been based on the so called Beijing consensus, the contention that people don't think a lot about freedom of action, free markets, and democracy as long as capable bureaucrats deliver major economic growth.[92]

The Soviet Union's Communist system collapsed amazingly quickly. It was a degenerate government based on hypocrisy and corruption. Its major scientific successes in nuclear weaponry and the space race were based on information theft or unsustainable spending levels. Is China now on the same path?

China needs to establish neutral legal institutions across the entire country that abolish corruption and contain crony capitalism, if it hopes to achieve high-income status, global leadership, and a high-skilled workforce.[93] Without this flexibility, its future success is uncertain. China once erected its Great Wall to protect itself from outsiders. Its future economic development and that of its talent system may be constrained by reluctance to move beyond the cultural constraints of the past.

India

The old Hindu Economy is now past history. But India's spectacular growth of recent years is beset by many political and social issues. Economists and business leaders now believe that India's high inflation rate (9.1%, May 2011) is the by-product of broad economic structural failure driven by severe skilled talent shortages, a dysfunctional transportation and power infrastructure, and the unrealistic expectations of many of its citizens.

Unless serious efforts are made to redress a growing human capital deficit, India's economy may stall, as it attempts to move up the value chain into more sophisticated IT services and manufacturing. Someday, India may challenge the supremacy of the United States in path-breaking scientific research, but not in the foreseeable future. It lacks the large-scale, high-quality university graduate programs needed for an abundance of such breakthroughs.

India has many advantages that China lacks. India has a democratic political system and an Anglo Saxon legal code. Also, India's younger age cohort is slated to continue growing, with the nation's population passing China's by 2030. There is much talk about the India's demographic dividend, but this will only be an illusion unless the quality of India's entire national talent development system is significantly upgraded.[94]

Safety Valve Failure

How does the United States fare in the talent race against China and India? Our review has shown there is a growing mismatch in India and China between their available talent pool and domestic economic demands for more skilled human capital. Other serious socioeconomic issues complicate their efforts to increase the number of highly skilled workers. There are strong indications of late that much of the euphoria about China, or in the longer run India, overtaking the United States as economic superpowers has been fading.

U.S. business leaders still believe that America remains the best location for the world's top scientists and engineers. But a World Economic Forum study reported that the majority of U.S. patent filings by many American companies are now being made by foreign nationals living in the United States (General Electric 64%, Merck 65%, Cisco 60%).[95] This motivates many in the U.S. business community to continually lobby the Congress to open wide a talent safety valve, the annual H-1B foreign visa quota, from 65,000 to over 100,000.

The talent tide has been turning as talent hunters in India and China woo their nationals to return home and become active participants in their burgeoning economies. At the same time, the United States has tightened immigration policies and raised visa application fees to screen out potential terrorists from entering America. It can now take up to a decade to obtain permanent U.S. residency. Finally, many other nations are tapping the same STEM talent pool by offering attractive employment opportunities and permanent citizenship to foreign nationals. Canada, Germany, England, Singapore, Brazil, Australia, and others have significant shortfalls in their workforces. They are all on this same talent hunt and are offering attractive employment opportunities and permanent citizenship to foreign nationals.

In 2011, the World Economic Forum found that more Indian immigrants were moving back to India than were moving to the United States. A separate Kauffman Foundation study, *Losing the World's Best and Brightest* (2009) that surveyed over 1,200 foreign nationals attending U.S. colleges and universities, found that 32 percent of Indian students and 52 percent of Chinese students believed that stronger job opportunities awaited them in their home countries rather than in the United States.[96]

The Chinese Ministry of Education estimated 108,000 Chinese citizens who had studied abroad returned to China in 2009. This was over a 56 percent increase over the previous year. In 2010, nearly 135,000 Chinese students returned home, a 25 percent increase from 2009.[97] Bin Wolfe, people leader for Ernest and Young's Asia-Pacific region, concurs that Chinese students in the United States are increasingly moving back home. Her July 2011 assessment is quoted in the *Wall Street Journal*: "There is a lot of competition out there. People with strong experiences and bilingual skills are in high demand."[98]

A 2010–2011 survey sponsored by the Kauffman Foundation found that 72 percent of Indian immigrants who returned home said that opportunities to start their own businesses were better or much better than in the United States. For Chinese returnees, the figure was more than 80 percent.[99]

For these and other reasons there recently have been wild fluctuations in U.S. H-1B visa applications (see Table 4.2). Some have argued that the new $2,000 fee on the H-1B visa application, substantial legal fees, or extra security scrutiny can be disincentives for companies and potential applicants. The most recent surge may be the result of the current downturns in the economies of China and India. This may be motivating more of their nationals to seek U.S. employment rather than returning home. However, once these nations' current economic problems are resolved, we can reasonably expect their skilled talent demands to increase, thus providing incentives to more of their nationals to again seek opportunities at home.

H-1B visas cannot solve the present or future skilled talent requirements of U.S. business. The continued effort of the chief executives of major U.S.

TABLE 4.2   Time Fluctuations in Reaching
H-1B Visa Quotas

Year	Time to Fill Quota
2008	1 day
2009	8 months
2010	9 months
2011	33 weeks
2012	10 weeks
2013	5 days[1]

[1] Neil G. Ruiz and Jill H. Wilson, "The End of the Race for H-1B Visas," Brookings Institution, June 13, 2012, http://www.brookings.edu/blogs/the-avenue/posts/2012/06/13-immigration-ruiz-wilson; Hiawatha Bray, "High-Tech Visa Quota Filled in 5 Days," *Boston Globe*, April 6, 2013, http://www.bostonglobe.com/business/2013/04/05.

technology companies to increase the number of H-1B visas is a business culture fantasy whose days are largely over.

As Georgetown University's Center on Education and the Workforce STEM report warns, "Whether we can continue to employ this strategy as wages become more competitive in other countries remains an open question. It is unlikely that we will continue to be able to successfully compete for the top international talent."[100]

Peter Cappelli, an economist at the Wharton School of Business, points out that current large U.S. companies are pursuing a talent strategy of filling 66 percent of job vacancies from outside their organizations. This is a radical policy departure from a generation ago when 90 percent of U.S. jobs were filled from within organizations.[101]

As we have demonstrated, a job and skills disconnect is triggering a rising tide of vacant jobs across the U.S. labor market. This is sure to increase as more skilled people retire and job-skills requirements continue to rise. H-1B visas will only produce a tiny fraction of the number of skilled people needed. Instead, American business needs to invest time, treasure, and talent into rebuilding an effective 21st-century U.S. education-to-employment system.

For decades, U.S. business has gorged itself on foreign talent as one of the cheapest, fastest, most leveraged ways to meet its talent demands. Compelling evidence shows that those days are largely over. The falsehood of this business culture fantasy is now being exposed for what it is.

American business needs to get back in this skills and jobs game. Parents, students, and the business community need to discard their outdated career and business culture fantasies and fully grasp that the U.S. economy has entered a new Cyber-Mental Era, which has fundamentally changed the global demand structure for jobs and careers. The hunt to provide for America's future talent needs to begin at home or it won't happen.

"A blind and ignorant resistance to every effort for the reform of abuses and for the readjustment of society to modern industrial conditions represents not true conservatism, but an incitement to the wildest radicalism," said President Theodore Roosevelt in 1908.[102] He understood what a responsible society needed to do in that era of change. Does America's culture today share his insights?

Business needs to invest again in the current and future U.S. workforce. Parents everywhere need to heed, consider, and act on what was told to school children in Philadelphia: "When students around the world in Beijing, China, or Bangalore, India, are working harder than ever, and doing better than ever, your success in school is not just going to determine your success, it is going to determine America's success in the 21st century."[103] President Obama's words foretell either America's future or her epitaph.

Chapter 5

The "Big Lie"

The United States' failure to educate its students leaves them unprepared to compete and threatens the country's ability to thrive in a global economy.[1]
—Harvard Kennedy School

Americans often have strong opinions about school reform. Most parents believe that their own child's school is doing just fine. The problem is in another school district, town, or inner city. This is the "big lie" that feeds into the status quo culture of American schooling.

A mounting number of U.S. and international reports are raising red flags regarding the current condition of American education and on how little has been achieved in nearly 40 years of school reform efforts. A key problem is the great disparity in the quality of American education. As Microsoft's Chairman Bill Gates has remarked, "Our public schools range from outstanding to outrageous, and where a child's school is located on that spectrum is a matter of luck."[2]

In most parts of the world, the quality, content, and funding of public education is primarily determined by the national government, often as an extension of economic development policy. In the United States, on the other hand, the 50 state governments and local communities have considerable influence over the content, quality, and funding of public education.

There are islands of excellence in U.S. education at all levels. The United States has many of the world's finest institutions of higher learning that attract large numbers of the best and brightest students from many other nations. But, although the United States invests more in its schools than any other nation, the results of the general education system largely range from mediocre to downright dismal.

The reports that follow identify choke points in American education that are eroding our international standings and impeding efforts to equip today's students with the knowledge needed for success in life and at work.

U.S. Slips in International Rankings

In 2008–2009, the United States ranked first in the World Economic Forum's Global Competitive Index. In 2012, America had fallen to number seven. A key factor is how successful a country can raise income levels and opportunities for its people. A more competitive economy grows faster.[3]

As Don Peck points out in *Pinched* (2011), "Most important, of course, an innovation economy depends on an excellent education system and a highly educated workforce."[4] In 1990, the Organization for Economic Cooperation and Development (OECD) ranked the United States first in the world in the percentage of 25–34 year-olds with college degrees. By 2010, the United States had slipped to 14 among OECD nations.[5] For most of the 20th century, our educational critical mass exceeded all nations, based on America's human capital "exceptionalism." Today, that "exceptionalism" is gone.

The percentage of Americans who are well educated is below average, relative to other rich nations. The National Academy of Science now warns us that "In a world where advanced knowledge is widespread and low-cost labor is readily available, U.S. advantages in the marketplace and in science and technology have begun to erode."[6]

The United States participates in three major international exams: Program for International Student Assessment (PISA) tests the 15-year-old students of 57 nations and regions in math, science, and reading. This test is sponsored by the OECD. The Trends in International Math and Science study (TIMSS) tests fourth and eighth grade students in math and science. Thirty-six to forty-eight nations/regions participate. The Progress in International Reading Literacy Study evaluates fourth grade reading comprehension. Forty nations/regions participate.

A Harvard Kennedy School study found that from 1995 to 2011 the test scores of U.S. students on these international exams improved by approximately one grade level. Three states improved the most: Maryland, Florida, and Delaware, with Massachusetts, Louisiana, South Carolina, New Jersey, Kentucky, Arkansas, and Virginia completing the top 10. Overall, 24 nations trailed the United States and 24 nations appear to be improving faster.[7]

For example, in the 2009 PISA results, only 32 percent of American 15-year-old students were proficient in mathematics. The United States came in 32nd among the nations. Twenty-two other countries significantly outperformed American students, including 58 percent of Korean and 56 percent of Finnish students. While 42 percent of U.S. white students were math proficient, this proficiency rate was surpassed by *all students* in 16 other countries, such as Japan, Germany, Belgium, and Canada.[8]

The 2011 TIMSS test results were somewhat better. The math and science scores of U.S. eighth graders were not significantly lower than the top performing nations. Students in seven states, Massachusetts, Minnesota, North Carolina, Indiana, Colorado, Connecticut, and Florida, scored higher than the international average in both subjects. However, only 7 percent of U.S. students scored at the advanced level in math, in contrast to 48 percent of eighth graders in Singapore and 47 percent in South Korea, the two best performing nations. This huge lag is a cause for serious concern.[9]

It is very important to have a balanced perspective on the major political and cultural differences between the United States and other high-performing countries, when weighing American students' test performance. However, we shouldn't use these differences as excuses.

There is some good news. In total numbers, the U.S. produces more high-achieving students than any other country studied. In both reading and math, America has more high achievers than Germany, France, and the United Kingdom combined. The United States has a very large population of high-achieving readers. This group is larger than all the combined high-achieving readers of Japan and Korea.

But there was a lot of bad news as well. The United States is the largest world economy ($15.6 trillion GDP, 2012) and has the third-largest national population (314 million, 2012). Our huge sophisticated economy requires a larger proportion of high-achieving students in reading, math, and science than we are currently producing. In mathematics, fewer than 10 percent of American students scored at highest PISA achievement levels. This was below the OECD average of 12.7 percent. Five nations, South Korea, Switzerland, Finland, Japan, and Belgium, had 20 percent of their students attaining the top performance levels.

This dearth of high-performing American students was termed "one of the most disturbing findings," by Mark S. Schneider, vice president, American Institutes of Research, former commissioner, National Center for Education Statistics. "In the modern economy, you need a lot of well-trained smart people to drive innovation, to drive creativity."[10]

In total numbers, the United States produces many more low-achieving students than any other OECD industrial country, including developing nations like Mexico and Turkey. In reading and math, the number of low-achieving American children exceeds the total combined number of similar students in Germany, France, the United Kingdom, Italy, and Japan.

Fifty percent of African American students are low achievers in math. This is a higher proportion than in any other OECD nation except Chile and Mexico. In reading, only Mexico scores lower than these U.S. students. A final disturbing note for many parents—in both reading and math test results—is that the American educational system now produces about an equal number of low-achieving white as well as black students.[11]

A 2009 McKinsey study, "The Economic Impact of the Achievement Gap in America's Schools," based on an analysis of OECD data stated: "By underutilizing such a large proportion of the country's human potential, the U.S. economy is less rich in skills than it could be. The result is that American workers are, on average, less able to develop, master, and adapt to new productivity enhancing technologies and methods than they could otherwise have been."[12]

The report summarizes its economic findings: "The persistence of these educational gaps imposed on the United States the economic equivalent of a permanent national recession."[13]

The Nation's Report Card: Mediocrity Enshrined

In the past two decades, national initiatives to improve U.S. K–12 education have been in the spotlight. The U.S. Department of Education launched the National Assessment of Educational Progress (NAEP), also known as the Nation's Report Card, to measure the performance of students across the nation at the 4th, 8th, and 12th grade levels. NAEP tests in reading and math for fourth and eighth graders have been administered largely at two-year intervals since 1992, with results reported on a 500-point scale and at four skill levels: Below Basic, Basic, Proficient, and Advanced.

While there have been some gains in mathematics scores, overall results have been mediocre to almost flat over the past 20 years. The greatest advances were in fourth-grade math, where students scoring at proficient or above rose about 21 percentage points from 18 percent to 39 percent. At the eighth-grade level, there was about 14 percent increase. Reading scores, however, increased only 4 percentage points or less. Still, the 2011 NAEP results reveal a significant cohort of low achievers, as 18 percent of fourth graders and 28 percent of eighth graders scored below basic in mathematics. In reading, 34 percent of fourth graders and nearly 25 percent of eighth graders had below basic scores.[14] U.S. Secretary of Education Arne Duncan offered this assessment on the 2011 NAEP results: "While student achievement is up since 2009 in both [4th and 8th] grades in mathematics and in eighth-grade reading, it's clear that achievement is not accelerating fast enough for our nation's children to compete in the knowledge economy of the twenty-first century."[15]

In the 2009 NAEP science testing, only about a third of fourth graders, 30 percent of eighth graders, and a fifth of high school seniors scored at or above the proficiency level. At the advanced level, only one or two students in 100 make the cut. A smaller number of 12th graders were proficient in science than in any other subject the NAEP has tested since 2005 except history. In 2011, when only eighth graders were tested in science, 32 percent scored at proficient, a mere 2 percent increase. In the newly computerized 2011writing assessment, only 27 percent of students in the fourth and eighth grades scored at or above the proficient level.[16]

These results show why it is very important for students to catch up academically before eighth grade. As an ACT analysis states, "Waiting until high school to address preparation gaps is too late for the majority of students who have fallen behind, particularly for those who are Far Off Track. Catching up those students is a daunting challenge even for the most effective high school."[17]

High School Dropouts: A National Disaster

Eight hundred and fifty-seven student desks were arrayed near the Washington Monument on the National Mall (June 2012). Eight hundred and fifty-seven students drop out of high school, every single hour, every single day, according to the College Board. This adds up to one million students each year. Although there has been some improvement in U.S. dropout rates, a 2012 OECD report ranked the United States 22nd among 27 developed countries in its rate of high school completion.[18]

Billions of dollars have been spent on stemming the U.S. high school dropout disaster. Though by some measures that tide has been reduced, Russell W. Rumberger, University of California, Santa Barbara, and director of the California Dropout Research Project, concluded that the national graduation rate is worse now than it was 40 years ago (83.1%, 1972).[19]

Measuring high school graduation rates has long been a muddled mess. First, no uniform method has been used by all 50 states. Second, there is no uniform age for compulsory high school attendance: Eighteen states set the dropout age at 16, 11 at age 17, and 21 at age 18 (2012).

A 2012 analysis, conducted by *Education Week*'s Educational Research Center, concludes that the national high school graduation rate was 73.4 percent for the class of 2009. Graduation rates improved over the past year by 1.7 percent for African Americans and by 5.5 percent for Latino students.

But rates among Asian Americans and Native Americans, dropped from 1 to over 2 percent; the graduation rate for white students remained the same.[20]

Although some states and individual school districts are improving, 10 states have lower graduation rates than a decade ago. In California, 43 percent of Hispanic students dropped out between 2005 and 2009. Only 10 percent earned a college degree. The high school dropout crisis still claims over one million students annually; 4 in 10 minority students will not graduate.[21]

Another significant distortion in official high school graduation statistics comes from including General Educational Development (GED) recipients with four-year high school graduates. These are high school dropouts who by passing an exam are certified as equivalent to those who receive a high school diploma.

By 2008, 20 percent of all annually issued high school credentials were GED certificates. "A substantial body of scholarship," warned James J. Heckman, an economist at the University of Chicago, and Paul A. LaFontaine, at the American Bar Foundation, "shows that the GED program does not benefit most participants, and that GEDs perform at the level of dropouts in the U.S. labor market. The GED program conceals major problems in American society."[22]

The states are now being forced by a federal requirement to use one uniform method to calculate high school graduation. However, the states are resisting dropping their dropout shell game.

Who is to blame for America's dropout factories: weak parenting, weak principals, weak teaching, and unenforceable truancy laws? We still seem to be years away from American society accepting its shared responsibility for the high school dropout crisis.

Another nasty secret at many underperforming high schools is that they graduate students who are at the fifth grade level in academics, organization, and behavior. Caleb Rossiter, a former high school teacher now at Washington University and the Institute for Policy Studies, recounted his experience as a math instructor at a high-poverty public high school in Washington, D.C. Only 10 percent of his math class was present more than three days a week and 50 percent attended two days or fewer each week. Hardly any of the chronically absent did any classwork or homework. Yet, only 68 percent failed the class! They attended a Credit Recovery program after school for a few weeks. These students magically earned the credit without taking a mastery exam.

What can be done with the millions of students performing well below grade level who attend such high schools? As Rossiter states, "Clearly, if students enter high school with elementary-school skills, graduation is a long shot and college is a mirage."[23]

The public conversation needs to focus on joint efforts uniting parents, schools, and community agencies in finding solutions to this crisis. We will see how some U.S. regions are doing just that in Chapters 6 and 7.

Armed Forces Qualification Test Finds Basic Skill Deficits

Nearly 25 percent of recent high school graduates who try to join the U.S. army now fail the Armed Forces Qualification test, which includes aptitude tests in math, reading, science, and problem solving that measure the skills necessary for enlistment. The Education Trust report, "Shut Out of the Military," found that failure rates were even higher among Hispanics (29%) and African Americans (39%). These results are very worrisome because prescreening filters out those who are ineligible to take the test. Pentagon data (2004–2009) showed that 75 percent of those aged 17–24 don't even qualify to take the test because they are physically unfit, have a criminal record, or didn't graduate from high school. In the final analysis, for every 100 potential recruits only 19 qualify to join the army. Marine, Air Force, Navy, and Coast Guard recruits need even higher test scores.[24]

Tom Loveless, an education researcher at the Brookings Institution, stated, "A lot of people make the charge that in this era of accountability and testing, that we've put too much emphasis on basic skills. This [Education Trust] study really refutes that. We have a lot of kids that graduate from high school who have not mastered basic skills."[25]

ACT and SAT Exams—College Readiness Low

The SAT and ACT are the two national examinations taken by high school students seeking college admission or meeting state or school mandates. In 2012, over 1.6 million high school seniors took each exam.

The ACT average composite score in 2012 of English, math, science, and reading abilities was 21.1. This score has remained flat over the past four years. The maximum ACT score is 36. Only 25 percent of high school students taking the ACT in 2012 met its benchmark for being college ready in all four subjects; 28 percent did not meet any of the benchmarks. Two-thirds met the criteria in English and 50 percent in reading. But these numbers have been falling or stalling rather than rising.[26]

During the 1970s, verbal SAT scores began to decline. This drop became so significant it forced the College Board to renorm the verbal SAT scores in the mid-1990s. Yet the downward trend still continues. The SAT average reading score was 529 in 1972. In 2011, it had fallen to 497. The maximum SAT critical reading score is 800. For the high school class of 2011, the average reading and writing scores were the lowest ever recorded and the 2012 scores in both areas were one point lower.[27]

In 2012, only 43 percent of SAT takers graduated from high school, with a level of academic preparedness associated with a high likelihood of college success. "This report should serve as a call to action to expand access to rigor for more students," warned College Board president Gaston Caperton. "When less than half of kids who want to go to college are prepared to do so, that system is failing."[28]

Not surprisingly, these academic deficiencies have resulted in a rise in remedial education for first year college students. About 40 percent of entering students must take remedial coursework before they can enroll in courses carrying college credit. This raises costs to public two- and four-year schools, and means higher costs in time and money for these students as well.[29]

Hope for the Future

The last two chapters reviewed the issues behind the growing structural unemployment crisis in the United States. Left unchecked, the United States faces serious potential economic and social consequences. Yet, in the past, America overcame a similar crisis.

Over 100 years ago, the United States developed its current education system. From 1890 to 1920, the nation's economy shifted from being primarily agricultural to one based on industrial production. Urban areas swelled as factories and offices grew and large numbers of immigrants came to America for better economic opportunities. Public schooling in the cities took on the task of assimilating the newcomers and providing them with the ethos and education needed for jobs in offices and factories.

Community, business, and political leaders came to see the links between supporting an education-to-employment system and social progress. Samuel Gompers of the AFL, newspaper publisher Henry George, industrialists Henry Ford and Andrew Carnegie, inventor and scientist Thomas Edison, and politicians, such as Theodore Roosevelt and Woodrow Wilson, all joined together in supporting and building mandatory, tax-supported public education.

This system fostered education and skills for this new age plus a work ethic that included punctuality, respect for authority, quality workmanship, and self-discipline. The United States was the first nation in history to attempt to create and support such an education-to-employment system. It has served the nation well.

For most of the 20th century, through two world wars, the rise of the American middle class, and the collapse of the Soviet Union ending the Cold War, this educational arrangement worked very well. It transformed America from a rural, agricultural nation into the world's number one economic superpower.

Here's how it worked: since 1970, about 25 percent of the population graduated from college; 40 percent graduated from high school, some going on to additional technical or postsecondary education; the bottom 35–40 percent had a hard time in school, and more dropped out with each passing decade of the century. (These are approximate ranges.)

Because this U.S. educational game plan worked for so long, for so many, most Americans came to believe that only a fraction of the population (particularly future managers and professionals) were capable of really benefiting from quality education programs. So, why spend more money on the rest?

It was a closed system that compartmentalized life into three separate segments: education, career preparation, and work. The smarter kids went on to college from high school to prepare for white-collar careers. The others were funneled into vocational education, apprenticeships for blue-collar jobs, or went straight into the workplace.

The system then erected a high brick wall separating the real world of work from the theoretical world of education and career preparation. People openly talked about the year you got out, as if high school or college were a prison. Apprenticeship education existed in its own limbo between these two worlds. Most people never crossed over the wall again. Yes, professionals, executives, salespeople, and advanced technicians did receive some training and development. But most workers were lucky even to receive on-the-job training. Historically, college tuition reimbursement has been the most underused U.S. employment benefit. This was basically a closed education-to-employment system for most workers.

Now, times have changed. As the world moves into the Cyber-Mental Age, it is the human brains behind the technology that make innovation happen. Without this talent, businesses are left with a pile of useless hardware and software.

Unlike the last 50 or even 70 years, during which U.S. business had an almost unquenchable thirst for men and women with minimal education, 21st-century technology has less and less use for them. In every type of business, there is a demand for knowledge workers (i.e., persons with specialized career training and a sound liberal arts education). With job content changing so fast in every field, continuing education updates and greater mental dexterity is a necessity for almost every worker.

Today and into the foreseeable future, because of the historic rate of human technological progress, business is becoming more and more dependent on jobs that call for the majority of all employees to exercise their brains rather than just their brawn.[30]

In the world's tech economy, the skill differences between white-collar and middle-skill jobs are blurring, and many workers are being left behind. "Both the quality and quantity of the labor force are not keeping pace with the demands of a skill-based economy. . . . Labor force quality, as proxied by education, has stagnated," contend two University of Chicago economists, James Heckman and Dimitriy Masterov, in a report that has cited Federal Reserve Chair Ben Bernanke.[31]

Diane Swonk, chief economist and senior managing director at Mesirow Financial, concurs with this analysis. "We delayed the pain and papered-over the problem," but "the recession washed that away." She predicts that a lasting outcome of the recession will be a "skills shortage driven by educational inequality."[32]

The picture of the U.S. economy that has emerged is one of abundance and poverty: abundance of labor, poverty of talent. Christopher Thornberg of Beacon Economics calls it a barbell economy. Urban centers, such as Los Angeles, Chicago, New York, have not only a greater than average share of college graduates, but also of those who have dropped out of high school.[33] On Labor Day 2012 a *Chicago Tribune* editorial, "The Pernicious Jobs Gap," acknowledged the Chicago area had ". . . thousands of jobs that many residents can't fill because they lack the needed education and training." The *Tribune* demanded the Chicago community ". . . close the gap between the skills that employers want in their new hires and the education of those available to fill the jobs.[34]

Advance Illinois, an education advocacy group, in its 2012 report clearly shows that education deficits begin early in Illinois and persist. Only one-third of fourth grade students read at grade level. Less than one-third of Illinois ninth graders go on to complete a college degree. Its verdict on the current condition of education in Illinois, "The world is passing us by . . . our schools are not getting the majority of students where they need to go."[35]

Economic history discloses that the spread of new technologies does not destroy job growth, but that over time new jobs requiring new skills eclipse jobs that become obsolete. This only occurs, however, after policy makers provide the resources to make it happen. The current problem is that too little is being done to help those students and adults who are being left behind.

What is the impact on hiring today? In an interview included in a 2012 *Insight on Manufacturing* article, Jim Golembeski, executive director of the Bay Area Workforce Development Board, recounted the experience of a large Green Bay, Wisconsin, manufacturer. In September 2008, this company had 134 job openings and received 850 applications for these positions. Only 17 people were hired. Why? Because they lacked a high school diploma or a GED and work experience, 450 applicants were eliminated; 208 failed an eighth grade level reading and math test or a manual dexterity test. That left 192 people. They were all individually interviewed and assessed for character, interpersonal skills, teamwork, and reliability. In the end, this employer only found 17 people with the desired qualifications.[36]

However, at least 66 percent of all Americans possess average intelligence. Some have higher abilities. The great American employment challenge is to double the number of smart people—the kind of people the Green Bay manufacturer was looking for. We have the knowledge to do this. We still have the economic means.

The future of the United States hangs on putting an end to the big lie. We can continue to deny a school culture of enshrined mediocrity and the dumbing down of American society, or we can face up to reality. As Wendy Kopp, the founder of Teach for America, warned, "In the face of a crisis that threatens our economic and civic strength and our ideals as a nation, we have to overcome our differences and pull together, or we will all fail together."[37]

A new U.S. talent era has arrived. The availability of better-educated people with up-to-date career skills now determines where businesses will locate in the United States and elsewhere in the world. Those communities that learn to better collaborate for 21st-century renewal of their workforces will retain their economic base and attract new businesses. Those that cling to the status quo will wither and die.

In the next two chapters, we explore the dynamics behind regional job and economic renewal in the United States and other nations. RETAINs are acting as change agents to update and expand local businesses, jobs, and economies.

Part III

The Breakthroughs

Chapter 6

Regional Talent Innovation Networks (RETAINs)

Organizations failing to be proactive to help create a skilled labor pool may very well face their own demise in the long term.[1]
—Richard Melson, Cambridge Forecast Group

U.S. Employment Revival

It may surprise most Americans to learn that one of our least populated states (672,000) has become the shining star in today's job market. In fact, North Dakota has reversed a long demographic decline, as people are moving there from nearby Minnesota and Iowa, and even from far sunnier and warmer California, Texas, and Florida. The state has grown about 5 percent since 2000. Another indicator of its popularity is that over 44 percent of its college students come from another state! Why this stampede to the northern plains? It can't be for its mild winter weather!

In 2012, North Dakota's unemployment was about 3.0 percent, the lowest among all the 50 states. With its economy booming, 16,500 jobs remain vacant. In contrast, the U.S. unemployment rate stood at over 8 percent with 30 million Americans jobless or underemployed, even though about five million jobs were vacant. What is the untold story of this state's job machine?

Since the early 1990s, North Dakota has made growing progress in diversifying its economy and its talent pool of skilled workers. State Senator Karen Krebsbach traces this movement back to the 1980s when farm consolidation and the increasing mechanization of agriculture was causing the state to lose population and jobs. This encouraged some conservationists to actually propose turning much of the high plains states into a new national park!

At this crucial point, North Dakota leaders crafted Vision 2000 to begin diversifying the economy and reversing population flight. Later, business leaders, community and educational institutions, and political leaders on both sides of the aisle formed the Committee of 100 to develop a strategic economic change plan. Over the last 20 years, they have continued this collaboration for the transformation of North Dakota's economy and workforce.

A concerted statewide effort has diversified and expanded the state's well-educated, high-skill workforce from its agricultural base into a talent pool supporting a wide range of business sectors, including information technology, green industries, biotechnology, unmanned aerial systems, and energy. These initiatives have attracted Microsoft, Aldevron, Northup Grumman, and over 2,400 IT-related businesses across the state. In agriculture, North Dakota still leads the United States in 11 cash crops, but this sector only employs about 7 percent of its workforce.

Adding further icing to the economic cake is the recently developed Bakken Belt of shale oil, natural gas, and coal. Also, North Dakota is ranked ninth among the states in wind-generated energy. These energy initiatives have created 13,000 new jobs.

Overall, between 2001 and 2012, North Dakota added over 50,000 new jobs to its economy. Its gross domestic product per capita in 2009 was the highest in the United States, and its personal median income is among the nation's highest.

The key component of North Dakota's success has been broad community collaboration in every part of the state to generate a modern talent creation system. A broad network of partnerships among businesses, community organizations, educational institutions, and governments have established and funded Regional Talent Innovation Networks (RETAINs) to rebuild the local and state education-to-employment systems. At present, career education and information programs are provided in elementary and secondary schools, job/career information is disseminated to students, parents, and adult workers, and current workers and the unemployed are offered continuing education and training. There are career academies, career and technical education and training centers, and college-level career programs in each of the state's major cities—Fargo, Bismarck, Grand Forks, and Minot. In rural areas of the state, regional career academy centers have been established to supplement electronic instruction beamed to smaller schools. Across the state, 20 Centers of Excellence supported by 190 private sector partners are headquartered at postsecondary institutions.

North Dakota's RETAINs have also played a role in strengthening the overall quality of the state's elementary and secondary schools. Eighty-six percent of its students graduate from high school (versus 73% in the United States as a whole). In a combined study of PISA-NAEP test scores, 41 percent of North Dakota students reached the proficient level in math versus 32 percent for the entire United States.

However, North Dakota recognizes that much more needs to be done to have the workforce it needs for the next decade. The state projects that between 2008 and 2019 over 131,000 jobs will have to be filled; 69 percent (93,000 jobs) are replacements for retiring baby boomers, and 38,000 are new jobs. The health care, IT, education, engineering, and energy areas are projected to be strong growth areas.

The governor and other leaders I met in North Dakota underlined their determination to face this talent challenge and expand the efforts of their RETAINs. One prominent state official said to me, "Eighty percent high school graduation isn't good enough! Why not 100 percent?" After meeting businesses executives, politicians, educators there, I have come away with the strong impression that civic engagement is alive and well in North Dakota. North Dakota may have a small population, but it stands as a working laboratory model of how to build long-term collaboration at the community and state levels. How much lower does the U.S. labor market have to sink before there is a public consensus on its structural collapse? Magic bullet answers from the political left or right cannot defuse this crisis.

Systemic change supported by civic engagement is a challenging and long-term process. If the people of North Dakota are doing this, why can't the people in the other 49 states? How much more economic pain will they need to feel before getting started?[2]

We Are Not Helpless!

Most Americans know that something bad is going on in their communities. There is a growing sense of cultural disintegration. Robert Putnam in his book, *Bowling Alone: The Collapse and Revival of American Community* (2000), documents the decline in many forms of social and civic involvement in America.

The sheer volume of bad news in the media may leave many average Americans feeling helpless to deal with seemingly overwhelming social and economic problems. Luckily, there are many Americans who see the need for promoting systemic change, not wallowing in despair.[3]

Throughout our history, the United States has faced difficult economic times and overcome them. Our culture has encouraged individual flexibility and innovation that has led to new products and services, enhanced productivity, and job growth.

Between 1890 and 1920, industrialization and the consequent growth of U.S. cities led to the disintegration of social structures and institutions and the need to find new ways to preserve traditional American values. Eventually, conditions eroded to the point that people took a risk on new leadership.

The Progressive movement arose to combat such abuses as urban slums, exploitative working conditions, and corrupt political organizations. Yes, there were both Democratic and Republican Progressives during that era. President Theodore Roosevelt energetically promoted the Progressive agenda at the national level.

One of the singular achievements of the Progressive Era was the extension of public schooling throughout the nation. By 1918, all of the then 48 states mandated K–12 tax-supported compulsory education enforced by truancy laws with teeth. This was revolutionary for its time. It encountered opposition in every state. The United States was well ahead of the rest of the world in adopting the first modern education-to-employment system! For example, the United Kingdom did not set up similar mandates until 1946 and Ireland in the 1980s.

Most historians agree that these decades also saw an unprecedented boom in association building. Americans of all classes and conditions created and joined a broad spectrum of voluntary organizations, most of which have endured to the present. These associations promoted a wide variety of causes—civic, religious, fraternal, ethnic, labor, business, professional, and veterans were among the most prominent. While some began at the national level, most were formed at the community level, and then spread laterally to other communities. Ordinary people—amateurs—formed clubs and organizations that promoted self-help and civic engagement as popular debate about local issues became part of the U.S. culture.[4]

That was our economic and social revolution 100 years ago. We need to do it again!

Lessons from the Grassroots

Technology is the easy part. Today, the hard part is to coordinate across-the-board cultural change in communities to successfully face the new economic and employment realities.

What is the concept behind these RETAINs? Why are they being formed? First, to stop population and business flight from a region or state. Second, to reverse tax base decline. Third, to end falling enrollment in community schools, stop declining governmental services, and turn around local economic stagnation. Community members are uniting to find solutions in a time of regional crisis. They want to retain their life, viability, and spirit to build a better, hopeful future for their community. To do this, they must retain their local talent and develop its capacity to innovate.

From their beginnings in the 1990s, the RETAINs movement has been about much more than just economic development, or school reform, or tax reform. RETAINs are regional, cross-sector, public-private partnership hubs. They act as intermediaries, rebuilding the pipeline that connects people to the job market. RETAINs are reinventing a 21st-century education-to-employment talent creation system for our tech-driven, knowledge-based economy. RETAINs see themselves as a joint undertaking in community building and reviving the U.S. free enterprise system (or the esteemed cultural and economic values of any nation). The key words here are "bottom-up collaboration" defined as joint authority, joint responsibility, and joint accountability among all the partners.

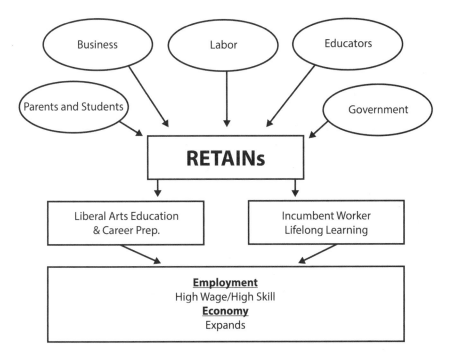

FIGURE 6.1   Regional Talent Innovation Networks' Shared Vision

RETAINs succeed because individual groups form a new shared vision of a larger community arising from a variety of isolated silos (see Figure 6.1). Each group has its own agenda and needs. But each also has an influence on the whole community and each depends on the success of the whole community.

United We Progress, Divided We Fall Behind

No individual business or organization can rebuild a regional workforce by acting alone. The U.S. business culture has traditionally treated its involvement in schooling as a part-time charitable activity. Now, more and more local/national business leaders are beginning to see that workforce development is not charity, but that the very sustainability of their business and community are dependent upon it. RETAINs help refocus this dialog so that all of a region's partners consider becoming more interdependent. Even the largest corporations now are beginning to realize they cannot solve their talent shortages by themselves, without participating in regional workforce systemic change.

Critics of business-education partnerships often charge that corporations want total control and that their intent is to set up factory schools to train people for dead-end jobs, rather than higher skilled middle-class occupations. This could not be further from today's reality.

RETAINs help businesses large or small give up some of their independent decision making and control by sharing in shaping a region's new talent creation system. "Interdependent strategic alliances are beginning to be implemented," says Randall A. Yagiela, founder of Michigan's Transformation Connection, "where the pain of not changing exceeds the pain of collaborating."[5]

RETAINS promote joint business, governmental, educational, and societal efforts to overturn the status quo. In the current talent debate, RETAINs are where private economic/career pursuits merge with public affairs.[6]

Successful businesses are beginning to integrate talent development with their broader strategies. Combining business expertise and stature, with the overall public and commercial power of a RETAIN, helps address today's fundamental business sustainability challenge—rebuilding the talent pipeline.[7]

Another factor that may deter individual companies from investing in training is that they fear newly trained workers will be poached by another company. RETAINs link regional employers together as a collaborative network that integrates training organizations, educational institutions, and other community-based organizations. This reduces the individual companies' investment in employer-provided education and training. RETAINs help minimize the poaching risks and promote a more positive overall regional business culture of sharing rather than stealing workers from each other.

The talent needs of companies are changing at an increased pace. Regions need to be more creative in their workforce development systems. RETAINs help produce innovative responses to meet unique community needs and industry talent requirements. RETAINs promote vision, vitality, and commercial ingenuity.[8]

RETAINs are regional in their makeup, often stretching over multiple cities and countries. In large metropolitan areas, multiple RETAINs based on a neighborhood or local community focus may also be workable. Regional collaboration has a powerful funding appeal.

RETAINs are focused on talent creation in the broadest sense, with an important economic development subtext. They focus on the process of building an innovation network by aligning many small communities into a new education-to-employment talent creation system that eliminates redundant services and fills in the gaps with new initiatives (see Figure 6.2).

"Talent is the #1 economic development advantage for any region," states Randy Yagiela, president of Michigan's Transformation Connection.[9] By studying a region's talent pool, companies can find out what they could become through short- and long-term training and education opportunities. Yagiela also believes RETAINs give local businesses more opportunities to share real-time data about required job skills with school systems.

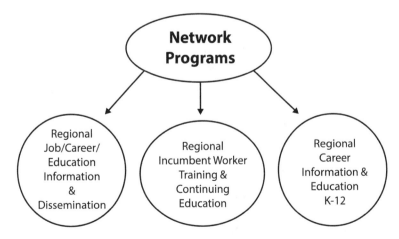

FIGURE 6.2   What RETAINs Do

RETAINs are growing, as the lines have blurred between the need for community economic development and workforce development. The systemic means to these ends is creating a larger talent pool of smart people. The occupational mix of that pool of talent will evolve over time, as well as the new talent system that RETAIN builds and supports.

RETAINs challenge community leaders to reexamine long-held beliefs. "RETAINs must have an energized, focused, and determined leadership that understands today's challenges and gives more than lip service to advanced solution thinking, rather than what has always been done, or they will not succeed," stated Robert Zettler, workforce consultant, Richland County OneStop, in Mansfield, Ohio.[10]

For much of the U.S. history, there has been a tradition of unusually widespread citizen participation in civic causes during times of crisis. "Americans do not abide very quietly the evils of life," Columbia University historian Richard Hofstadter reminds us. "We are forever . . . demanding changes, improvements and remedies . . ."[11]

RETAINs are all about inventing things. Today, every community still contains dozens of people who do want to create something—people with ideas and ambitions for a better future. This includes entrepreneurs who have built successful businesses. They represent a knowledge resource to tap about people management, IT, HR, outsourcing, cost control, media, fundraising, and so on. "Such creative individuals are bold and unconventional—possibly able to propose original answers that taxpayers and politicians desperately need in these straightened times."[12] But they need information and contacts, as well as having obstacles cleared out of their way. Americans have always prized a national culture that encourages ingenuity, exploration, and invention.

RETAINs apply civic activism to the talent crisis. They provide individuals, businesses, and community leaders with a clearer pathway for taking direct responsibility in nurturing the talent needed for each new generation's success.

RETAINs can trigger this regional conversation. After speaking to a group of local community leaders about these issues, I received this response: "Like many communities, the Rockford (Illinois) area is also facing a shortage of skilled workers at a time when local unemployment is extremely high," said Darcy Bucholz, executive director, Boone and Winnebago Counties Workforce Investment Board. "Your plan to change the way future workers are educated and your illustrations of how other cities are heading in that direction was thought-provoking. . . . Our goal in scheduling your presentation was to be a leader in starting the conversation about the realities facing the Rockford community."[13]

Since then, Laurie Preece, executive director of the local nonprofit Alignment Rockford, has worked with community leaders to begin establishing college prep/career academies. A career pathways program supported by local industry partners will open the first high school career academies in 2013, with the opening of three other high schools planned in 2014.[14]

Joel Kotkin, author of *The Next Hundred Million: America in 2050* (2011), observed, "It is here—at the grass roots level—that you can best glimpse the essential sources of American resiliency. American society draws most of its adaptive power not from its elite precincts but through the efforts of communities, churches, entrepreneurs and families."[15]

This is what happened in Fargo and across North Dakota where high tech has joined agriculture, manufacturing, and energy to build one of America's strongest local economies. This was not easy. It took time to build, and still continues to evolve. But the concept of a RETAIN is at its heart. There are now many more RETAINs with their own stories in progress across the United States and in other parts of the world.

Chapter 7

Future Jobs at the Grassroots

RETAINs must find new, better, and much faster methods for changing community attitudes and engaging community participation. Those who can't grasp this challenge and resolve it will wither and die.[1]
—Robert Zettler, Workforce Consultant for the Richland County OH Commissioners

Bridges to the Future

Transformation is never easy. Changing a region's employment and cultural outlook takes both time and perseverance. In many of the case studies that follow, a local crisis pushed a community to take action on the talent front. The individual leadership shown in each instance depicts how civic activism can take many different creative paths to achieve meaningful change. All of these Regional Talent Innovation Networks (RETAINs) and other talent initiatives are still works in progress. But they have sustained support through their initial stages and are making advances in transforming their education-to-employment system for the talent requirements of a 21st-century workforce.

High School Inc.

Orange County, California, is one of America's wealthiest regions. It is the home of the original Disneyland. Nearby is Santa Ana, a working-class community of over 300,000 people and home to the second largest concentration of small manufacturers in the United States. Among them are high-tech companies, such as Textron Aerospace Fasteners, Power Wave Technologies, and Aluminum Precision Products, Inc.

By the late 1990s, these companies began to run out of local talent. Two-thirds of local eligible workers lacked the skills for entry-level jobs. More than 150,000 Santa Ana residents came from Latin American countries making English fluency a major employer issue. While Orange County prospered, Santa Ana businesses began leaving and 20,000 jobs were lost.

In 1998, the Santa Ana Chamber of Commerce formed a taskforce of business-community leaders to craft a solution. They documented a growing job-skills disconnect between the talent requirements of area businesses and the education and training local institutions were providing to students and adult workers. This gap was particularly large for companies with IT and other science, technology, engineering, and mathematics (STEM) job vacancies.

Santa Ana first organized Bridge to Careers. Over the next six years, it provided local residents with job readiness programs supported by several hundred local businesses.

In 2007, High School Inc. (HSI) was established to act as a catalyst for the formation of liberal arts, college prep, and career academies. It encompasses six career academies within Santa Ana's Valley High School: the Global Business Academy, Culinary and Hospitality Academy, the Healthcare Academy, the Transportation and Logistics Academy, the Engineering and Manufacturing Academy, and the New Media Academy. Each of these academies has either received or is in the process of obtaining entry-level job certification for graduating students.

The Santa Ana high school district's collaboration with the HSI Foundation has resulted in improved graduation rates for students attending these academies. Because of their overall success, the school district has committed to working with the foundation and the local business community to replicate these academies at other Santa Ana high schools. "Unless the public and private sectors can get together," states Cathie Olsky, Santa Ana deputy school superintendent, "we will all be out of business."[2]

HSI has combined the efforts of businesses, educators, parents, and community organizations to build a new talent creation system and become a first-of-its-kind true community high school. Dale Ward, CEO of the HSI Foundation believes that "The academies provide rigorous and comprehensive educational pathways to sustainable personal careers. Our student graduates will be better prepared to support a family, their community, and also sustain local businesses in Santa Ana and beyond."[3]

Windy City Solutions

The Chicagoland area has the largest concentration of small manufacturers in the United States. The region is a major and growing transportation hub, IT nexus, an important commodities financial center, and is home to major academic and research institutions.

A 14-county tristate metropolitan region has a population of about 9.5 million. The city of Chicago contains 2.7 million people. The metro area's population is relatively young and is the 10th largest labor market in the OECD. Its working-age population (4.2 million, 2012) is aging.

Within the city and Cook County, a skills-jobs mismatch is very evident with 240,000 unemployed residents and a pool of over 200,000 vacant jobs (September 2012).

With a high school graduation rate of 56 percent in the City of Chicago, the large number of dropouts far outstrips available low-skills jobs. "Even in the currently depressed labor market," an OECD/Chicagoland Chamber of Commerce review concluded, "there are not enough individuals qualifying for the jobs that demand some higher educational attainments beyond a high school diploma."[4] Only about 670,000 people (20%) of the City/Cook County population fit into this category of "some college."[5] This places the Chicago economy at a dangerous economic tipping point.

According to a 2012 Brookings Institution report, there were 3.5 job openings in Chicago for every unemployed worker with a bachelor's degree or higher. On the other hand, there was less than one job available for every person with no more than a high school diploma.[6]

When having a bad day on the job, Mayor Rahm Emanuel said he finds himself "staring right into the whites of the eyes of the skills shortage." He related, "I had two young CEOs in the health care software business in the other day, sitting at this table. I asked them: 'What can I do to help you?' They said, 'We have 50 job openings today, and we can't find people'"[7] (see Table 7.1).

Chicago's serious efforts at systemic workforce change began 10 years ago. In 2004, Mayor Richard M. Daley announced plans for sweeping education/school change through the Renaissance 2010 Initiative, starting with 60 new elementary and high schools that were to be reopened as charter schools, contract schools, or career academies. These new schools offered a wide range of specialized and traditional college prep curriculums. The Chicago Community Trust and the Gates Foundation raised $50 million to cover start-up costs. Area businesses adopted a school providing further financing and volunteers.

TABLE 7.1   Chicago Area Occupations with Most Vacant Jobs January/
February 2012

January/February 2012	
Title of Occupation	Openings
Computer Occupations	38,315
Health Diagnosing and Treating Practitioners	16,799
Advertising, Marketing, Promotions, Public Relations, and Sales Managers	10,468
Financial Specialists	9,687
Business Operations Specialists	9,060
Operations Specialties Managers	8,715
Other Management Occupations	8,030
Sales Representatives, Services	7,766
Supervisors of Sales Workers	6,886
Engineers	6,678
TOTAL	122,404

Source: Jonathan Rothwell, "Education, Job Openings, and Unemployment in Metropolitan
America," Brookings Metropolitan Policy Program, August, 2012. http://www.brookings.edu/
research/papers/2012/08/29-education-gap-rothwell. Used by permission.

In 2012, about 53,000 out of 400,000 Chicago public school students
were enrolled in more than 100 charter schools. The city has plans to increase the number of charter schools to 600 over the next five years.[8]

Austin Polytechnical Academy

On Chicago's West Side Austin Polytechnical Academy is a pre-engineering
career academy high school organized by the Chicago Renaissance Manufacturing Council. The seven square mile Austin neighborhood was once
home to 20,000 manufacturing jobs. In 2012, only 2,000 remained. Unemployment stands at 19.3 percent, with 41 percent of children and about 30
percent of adults living in poverty.

Austin Polytech is operated jointly by their parent nonprofit, Manufacturing Renaissance, and the Chicago Public Schools. Sixty Chicago area
manufacturers have partnered with Austin to provide financial assistance
and expertise to prepare students for college and careers in advanced manufacturing, including Johnson Controls (energy efficiency products), Hud-
son Precision Products (machine parts), WaterSaver Faucets, and Winzeler
Gear (plastic precision gears).

In June 2012, 58 Austin Polytech seniors from its second graduation class had completed three-to-four years of pre-engineering classes combined with an enriched liberal arts program, and also had learned about manufacturing opportunities through job shadowing and paid internships. Almost every one of these graduates will attend college. About 90 percent earned at least one nationally recognized credential from the National Institute for Metalworking Skills (NIMS). (Twenty percent of Austin's graduates are pursing career tracks in manufacturing and engineering either through full-time employment and part-time school or through their college majors.)

Adult workers are also being reskilled at the Austin Manufacturing Training Center (AMTC). In-demand career skills, such as computer numerically controlled (CNC) machinery training and industry-recognized certifications, are being offered for adult workers on Chicago's West Side. Adults can earn up to 5 NIMS credentials.

Both Austin Polytech and the AMTC directly address the local job-skills mismatch by equipping Austin area city students and adults with the education required to begin an advanced manufacturing career. The strength of this polytechnical model of education developed by the Manufacturing Renaissance has encouraged other regions in the United States and in the Chicago region to also consider adopting these programs. McClymonds High School in Oakland, California, is currently in the early stage of developing the Austin model.[9] Dan Swinney, executive director of Manufacturing Renaissance, believes, "We are seeing the beginning of a public/private movement that seeks innovation and development in manufacturing as the means to promote a sustainable and restored society."[10]

Instituto Health Science Career Academy

Another charter school, the Instituto Health Science Career Academy, was begun to address the shortage of Latinos in the health care field within the Chicago metro area. Part of the Chicago Public Schools, this career academy will fully integrate studies in the health sciences with a rigorous liberal arts curriculum. Instituto will provide not only a quality college prep program, but also offer students professional certifications in entry-level health care careers (i.e., physician assistants, pharmacy technicians).

Instituto will ultimately serve 600 students. Its new $22 million Chicago West Side facility features 32 high-tech classrooms, 10 science labs, and a nursing simulation lab. The facility is owned by Instituto del Progreso Latino, a leading nonprofit community-based organization.

The Metropolitan Chicago Healthcare Council played a major role in forming this career academy. Chicago health care sector partners, such as Baxter International, Inc., Rush University Medical Center, and Children's Memorial Hospital, contributed both financial and human capital expertise to develop a successful academic model.[11]

Early College STEM Schools

Five technology companies—IBM, CISCO, Microsoft Corporation, Motorola Solutions, and Verizon Wireless—are partnering with the Chicago Public Schools and Chicago City Colleges to prepare students for careers in science and technology. The five Early College STEM Schools are located in diverse Chicago neighborhoods. Each company has developed a curriculum and is providing mentors and internships for a specific career academy. Each is also supplying technology equipment and professional development for the teaching staff. Instruction will be offered in such subjects as website development, software programming, database management, network engineering, and security.

Each student will be able to graduate in four years with a high school diploma and college credits toward an Associates of Science in Computer Sciences or Information Technology. Cheryl Hyman, chancellor of the City Colleges of Chicago, states, "We believe that the new model will help greater numbers of young people obtain post-secondary degrees that will lead to meaningful careers."[12]

These STEM high schools are being organized around best practices developed by IBMs P-TECH career academy, opened in Brooklyn, New York (2011). The IBM International Foundation helped develop the curriculum.[13]

Skills for Chicagoland's Future

On the adult worker unemployment front, the nonprofit Skills for Chicagoland's Future was established to fill immediate opportunities and to tailor job training programs to fill the specific vacant jobs of Chicago area employers. This grew out of an earlier Chicago Career Tech Program initiative (2009) that helped test the feasibility of this concept.

Launched in late 2012, Skills for Chicagoland's Future is employer demand driven with an initial goal of filling 650 jobs in its first year of operation contingent upon funding. With the collaboration of the Chicago-Cook Workforce Partnership (local Workforce Investment Act board), it will match likely trainees to specific job vacancies. "We are an advocate for business hiring needs to the workforce system, and an advocate for hiring the unemployed to business," stated Marie Trzupek Lynch, president and chief executive officer of the organization.[14]

This initiative coordinates a full spectrum of training from in-house at employers to local public/private postsecondary education institutions. Customized job training will generally be funded by 50 percent from the employer and 50 percent from government job training funds. All business sectors and the full spectrum of jobs will be eligible throughout Chicago and Cook County.[15]

Chicagoland Workforce Funder Alliance

The formation of the Chicagoland Workforce Funder Alliance is another positive move to better develop a new unified workforce development system. This initiative is to help provide financial support to intermediaries organizing workforce partnerships across business sectors. The Chicago Community Trust, Joyce, McCormick, Polk, Fry, and other foundations will fund the Alliance's grants.[16]

Coordination Challenge

The above Chicagoland workforce/education programs are representative of the many initiatives now underway. However, they do not constitute a coherent RETAIN for structured change.

The 2012 OECD report finds the talent creation and education-to-employment system remains fragmented into "uncoordinated and incoherent education and training programming . . . de-linked from businesses across the region." It concludes that this failed system arises from the weak cooperation between businesses, education, and government.[17]

Chicago, New York, Los Angeles, Dallas, Atlanta, and other major U.S. urban areas all face some of the same infighting among entrenched forces that are hard to overcome because of the sheer size of the populations involved. However, these challenges are not insurmountable nor will they simply vanish. As we have seen, Chicago's leaders have already launched some significant initiatives.

Several regional RETAINs might help focus the will to change large urban areas business-institutional arrangements. Bringing to scale a new education-to-employment system in large urban areas seems most likely to succeed, if RETAINs are formed by the different local communities that make up a region. Major metropolitan areas need to align their policies and investments through partnership hubs to meet the talent demands of their advanced manufacturing, health care, financial, service, and other appropriate local businesses sectors. Private business investment needs to be matched with an increased flexibility of new or existing federal workforce programs to help rebuild metropolitan education-to-employment systems. This will happen only after each community clearly accepts the necessity for fundamental changes.

The Community Education Coalition

In 1997, a group of community leaders in Columbus, Indiana, home of Cummins, Inc., began to build a seamless talent creation system from preschool to career education and lifelong learning. The Community Education Coalition (CEC) is the area-wide RETAIN that has established Columbus as a regional center, fostering strong linkages between education and workforce-economic development. Over 100 companies located in 10 Indiana counties help fund and participate in middle and high school career education pathways linked to careers in the advanced manufacturing, health care, and hospitality/tourism sectors.

An Advanced Manufacturing Center of Excellence supports services for students and workers in advanced manufacturing, technology, and metrology. The Health Education Network supports two technical education centers, and includes 7 hospitals, 5 postsecondary institutions, and 14 partners.

CEC collaborates closely with Ivy Tech Community College, Indiana University, Purdue College of Technology, and WorkOne, to offer more specialized programs and workforce training. CEC also manages the Columbus Learning Center that offers classroom space to all of the above organizations.

CEC's success has been built on mobilizing the region's civic engagement. This RETAIN has attracted new business to the region and reduced unemployment—all by investing in the current and future human capital needs of the region's economy.[18]

"M-Powered"

HIRED is located in the St. Paul-Minneapolis area. It is a nonprofit organization founded in 1968 that acts as an intermediary to better connect employers to job seekers.

In 2005, HIRED became part of M-Powered, a partnership that includes Hennepin Technical College, local employers, and industry associations. This partnership prepares people for employment in high-demand manufacturing specialties. Unemployed workers, with some but not all the required job skills, are placed in intensive paid job training. Trainees receive a combination of classroom instruction at the technical college and company-provided training. At the end of the program, successful candidates are hired by local companies.

M-Powered successfully blends public and private funding to fill vacant business jobs. A wide variety of companies participate in planning and implementing programs. They include specialty metal and plastic manufacturers, makers of biomedical devices, and other medical technology firms.[19]

The "Pre-Hire" Redemption

Mansfield, Ohio, is situated in the midst of an area that experienced an extensive shutdown of manufacturing operations beginning in the 1980s. In 2001, the Center for Housing Policy determined that Mansfield had the cheapest real estate in the nation, largely due to its massive idle GM plants and six mostly vacant industrial parks.

Also closed was Mansfield's huge federal prison. This is where Tim Robbins and Morgan Freeman filmed the movie *The Shawshank Redemption*. Perhaps, this movie's message of self-help and hope prefigured Mansfield's own future of economic redemption?

The Mansfield manufacturers who have survived the waves of economic shutdowns did so because they were innovative and developed the use of very efficient new technologies and operating systems. This has meant that they need workers with more advanced manufacturing skills, plus a willingness to learn and adapt to a more flexible, team-driven production environment.

Since 2001, Mansfield has pioneered worker retraining programs built around a growing collaboration between business and government. Their new Pre-Hire Training program is a great new step in that direction.

Pre-Hire acts as an intermediary between local employers and adult training programs. It helps them develop short-term concentrated training courses to reskill unemployed workers for vacant jobs. The Pre-Hire network of employers is assisted in selecting those workers most likely to complete this advanced training. Pre-Hire uses the best trainers available from the three local workforce training providers.

Each trainee receives 80 hours of classroom and hands-on tech-lab training over a four-week schedule. This includes additional just-in-time training, team participation classes, and work ethic discussions. To date, the Training Workers in the Advanced Pre-Hire Method has graduated 21 classes in Crawford, and Richland counties using this new business and worker friendly training program.

Eighty-eight percent of the workers who completed the Pre-Hire program received full-time employment. In addition to providing preparation for the advanced manufacturing sector, Pre-Hire can be used to train workers for employment in health care, information technology, and alternative energy occupations.

"All the money we've spent on job skill training, we absolutely can prove that people get jobs as a direct result of training," said Ed Olsen, a Commissioner in Mansfield's Richland County.[20] In 2010, the local unemployment rate was more than 12 percent. By September 2012, it was below 8 percent.

This Pre-Hire partnership between business and government has worked so well that the State of Ohio is sharing details of Pre-Hire so that other counties can establish similar job training networks.

"The Pre-Hire results are really good news for our regions," says Bob Zettler, a workforce consultant. "With other community leaders we have rekindled a hopeful future for our businesses, workers and communities as we take more positive steps forward to rebuild the Mansfield regional economy."[21]

Winds of Change from the New North

The New North geographic region covers the 18 northeast counties of Wisconsin. Since it started in 2005, New North, Inc. has grown to become a RETAIN that now has the support of over 100 private investors. It fosters collaboration among a long list of private and public sector leaders and governmental entities.

New North acts as an intermediary in workforce and career development that enables key industry sectors to build stronger employment pipelines. It is a regional hub for such groups as Northeast Wisconsin (NEW) Manufacturing Alliance, Northeast Wisconsin Educational Resource Alliance, North Coast Marine Manufacturing Alliance of NEW, and several health care alliances for the region's 49 hospitals and surgical centers.

With 24 percent of New North's workforce in manufacturing, it is not surprising this sector's labor needs have been in the regional employment spotlight. Paul Rauscher, president of Economy Machine and Tool (EMT), began noticing in the mid-2000s that too many employees were nearing retirement. There was not enough local talent in the pipeline to replace them.

"We have a skilled labor shortage in manufacturing," Rauscher insisted. "This isn't just an EMT thing or a New North thing. It's happening across Wisconsin and the country."

In January 2006, Rauscher met with Ann Franz, strategic partnerships manager at Northeast Wisconsin Technical College, to discuss this talent challenge. "Today's factories aren't dark and dingy. They are bright and full of technology. These are exciting jobs with endless possibilities," asserted Rauscher. "We had to get out there and share our story . . . If we didn't, no one would know."[22]

Six months later, the NEW Manufacturing Alliance was born. Starting with 12 manufacturers it grew to 101 members (2012). Their growth coincides with the expanding skilled labor shortages. A Manufacturing Vitality Study of the region showed that in 2011 only 29 percent of 173 companies had difficulty finding skilled workers. However, by 2012, the talent shortages had grown to 45 percent.[23] In September 2012, there were over 33,000 vacant jobs across Wisconsin with over 10,000 in the New North Region.

The NEW Manufacturing Alliance has made a proactive collaborative effort to tell their story about careers in advanced manufacturing to local students in middle schools, high schools, and local community/technical colleges. The alliance actively recruits students using plant tours, career speakers, and job shadowing. The Alliance's message states Franz is "that manufacturing is a vibrant, well-paying career is resonating with people."[24]

The alliance also posts its member companies' employment opportunities on its website (www.newmfalliance.org), showing training, education, and skills required for each job. Many member companies offer tuition reimbursement for their employees and actively engage with apprenticeship programs to train new workers.[25]

The alliance's career education and information efforts helped support the introduction of a Computer Integrated Manufacturing Module Laboratory. This 44-foot trailer houses 12 CAD/CAM computer stations, two CNC machines, and other equipment to give rural high school students a hands-on exposure to modern manufacturing. The lab will serve 10 schools and up to 240 students a semester.[26]

The North Coast Marine Manufacturing Alliance is another important area partnership initiative that includes seven manufacturers and three institutions of higher learning. Marinette Marine, one of northern Wisconsin's largest employers, has a major contract to build 10 littoral combat ships for the U.S. Navy. This company has been particularly active in contacting local high schools to recruit students for its training program that it operates in conjunction with Northeast Wisconsin Technical College.[27]

What has brought about all of these successful collaborative partnerships? "A lot of this is in the water," says Jerry Murphy, executive director of the New North. "People have recalibrated themselves over the last five years (2007–2012)."[28]

The New North's winds of change are getting stronger. This RETAIN has motivated more people to put their collective toes in the water to rebuild the career pipeline across multiple sectors thereby creating more good jobs for the people and economy of NEW.

Prairie Advantage

Outside Chicago, there is a state called Illinois. Many people think of this vast prairie as only fit for growing corn and soybeans. Then there is Danville.

Like Mansfield, Ohio, Danville, Illinois, was particularly hard-hit in the late 1980s with the closing of its General Motors auto plant and, soon afterward, nearby parts subcontractors. Overcoming this shock, Danville organized a RETAIN to rebuild its regional economy and workforce.

In 1998–1999, the Chamber of Commerce, Economic Development Commission, and Workforce Development Board formed a joint regional collaboration, the Vermilion Advantage. This RETAIN has gradually developed a variety of programs and services, including K–12 STEM programs and activities, career information and education, high school career academies, scholarships, and job postings. Vermilion Advantage programs are financially supported by companies, local public and private educational institutions, and governmental entities.

The Vermilion Advantage groups its over 54 member companies and agencies into four clusters: manufacturing, logistics, technology and services, and health care. Its 442jobs.com website provides information on the range of occupations within each cluster, career profiles, and current job openings.

The Vermilion Advantage also works with 39 elementary and secondary schools, public and private, as well as 5 youth organizations to rebuild the pipeline connecting students to potential careers. These educational and informational programs feature a career exploration laboratory, character and ethics development, applied math/science experiential learning, exposure to the physical sciences and engineering professions, project-based learning, and a cutting-edge gateway to technology educational program.

The Vermilion Advantage has helped facilitate the house system within the Danville High School. There is a Freshman House and three upper houses—New Tech High, Global House, and ACE House (Academy of Creative Expression). Also, the "Finish First!" program was instituted to raise awareness about the importance of completing high school, and thus boosting the region's high school graduation rate.

The future looks bright for the Vermilion Advantage in its role as a regional intermediary in education-to-employment and workforce development. Apprenticeship, worker training, and career education are growing across the area. Other adjacent counties are discussing possible links to build a broader network of businesses and service agencies.

"Vermilion Advantage will continue to help the regional economy expand," says Vicki Haugen, Vermilion's president and CEO, "so long as the community leadership remains committed to a brighter future built on job growth and business innovation."[29]

Other Significant U.S. Talent Initiatives

There are numerous RETAINs and other important talent initiatives across the United States. Here is a brief sampling for your further exploration.

Partners for a Competitive Workforce—Cincinnati, Ohio

This is a collaboration that includes over 150 organizations in health care, manufacturing and construction, the United Way, Greater Cincinnati Foundation, Chamber of Commerce, and the National Fund for Workforce Solutions. For over 10 years, Partners has addressed skill shortages in the tristate region (Ohio, Indiana, Kentucky) through worker retraining. This public-private partnership also supports career pathways programs.[30]

New Century Careers, Pittsburg, Pennsylvania

Since 1997, over 1,300 machinists have been trained through New Century Careers (NCC), a collaboration that links over 150 manufacturers in a nine-county region around Pittsburgh with local technical schools and community colleges. This RETAIN's programs range from sponsoring high school student technology contests to worker retraining for entry- or mid-level jobs. NCC also supports apprenticeship training for local companies at three sites through the National Tooling and Manufacturing Association.[31]

"NCC has a proven track record of finding talented and motivated individuals who are interested in a manufacturing career path and equipping them with the skills necessary to get started," attests Dan Fogarty, Human Resources Manager at Schroeder Industries. "We are lucky to have NCC and don't know what we would do without them."[32]

Talent 2025—West Michigan

Talent 2025 is a coalition of over 60 organizations encompassing 13 western Michigan counties. Its mission is to act as a catalyst to ensure an ongoing supply of skilled talent for the region. It acts as an intermediary to facilitate collaboration among employers, educators, and community leaders to improve the talent creation system. Talent 2025 working groups range from initiatives on early childhood development and K–12 education all the way to postsecondary career-education programs. Their goal is to advance proven strategies that will align the talent creation system with the economic needs of the region, thus improving business sustainability, competitiveness, and enhancing the quality of life throughout west Michigan.[33]

National Fund for Workforce Solutions

This nonprofit national partnership was established in 2007 to help close the workforce skills gap. The fund has raised over $30 million from the Rockefeller, Ford, J. P. Morgan, and Microsoft foundations, as well as many local organizations, to rebuild regional talent creation systems. To date, it has helped to fund over 30 RETAIN partners that provide training to job seekers and entry-level employees. (For a list of regional collaborations, visit www.nfwsolutions.org/regional-collaboratives.)[34]

100Kin10

The innovation fund, 100Kin10, is a broad-based national network of foundations, businesses, educational institutions, and others committed to expanding STEM teaching and learning. In 2012, a number of foundations pledged $24 million to initiatives seeking to recruit and prepare 100,000 new STEM teachers over a decade. To become a partner and be eligible for funding, an organization must be nominated by an existing partner. An application is then submitted to 100Kin10.[35] (For more information visit the website http://www.100kin10.org/.)

Purdue Center for Regional Development

Located at Purdue University, the Purdue Center for Regional Development (PCRD) develops new ideas and strategies that contribute to regional collaboration, innovation, and prosperity.

PCRD, in cooperation with a number of other organizations, has compiled the iRegions database with information on 1,400 regional organizations nationwide, including a brief description of each collaboration, the area served, and contact information.

This searchable Excel database can help you become familiar with RE-TAINs in your region or aid in the formation of broader public-private collaborative RETAINs. To access this information, go to www.pcrd.purdue. edu and link to iRegions Innovative Regions.[36]

International Talent Development

Cooperative programs for building talent are thriving in many parts of the world. Many particularly center on education-to-employment. Here are a few examples.

Singapore

Singapore is one of the world's fastest developing economies. The close links between education and economic development has helped to develop leading-edge industries and a highly talented workforce. There are three educational tracks for secondary school graduates: junior colleges, polytechnical institutes, and the Institute for Technical Education (ITE). The latter two focus mainly on career preparation. The five polytechnical institutes offer three-year diploma courses in various fields, such as engineering, business, accountancy, and nursing. In 1992, Singapore's vocational education was revitalized with the creation of the ITE, which has upgraded the content, quality, and public perception of this educational option. On three high-tech campuses, ITE offers one- and two-year certificates developed in close coordination with the business community.[37] Singapore's postsecondary education is built upon a strong foundation of educational excellence. In all the 2011 TIMSS and PIRLS international test results, Singapore was in the top four in country comparisons. These tests included reading at the fourth-grade level, mathematics at the fourth- and eighth-grade levels, and science at the fourth and eighth grade levels.[38]

Penang Skills Development Centre—Malaysia

Since 1989, this privately-run nonprofit training center has educated over 128,000 workers. The Penang Skills Development Centre (PSDC) has a base membership of over 130 companies. It has proven essential in maintaining Penang as the electrical and electronics hub of Malaysia, earning it the title of the "Silicon Valley of the East."

The PSDC collaborative model brings together the best of industry, education, and government in four industrial estates, with 775 plants employing over 170,000 workers. All the other states in Malaysia have followed the PSDC model establishing 11 additional regional skills development centers throughout the nation.[39]

The Dual Systems of Germany, Switzerland, and Austria

Though differing in some details, Germany, Switzerland, and Austria have long maintained very successful career/technical education systems in which career preparation combines paid training at a business site and school attendance. An apprentice spends from three to four days a week at a business and the remaining one to two days at an educational institution.

Germany's Dual System has the longest track record. There are apprenticeship programs for about 350 separate occupations. About 60 percent of German youth choose to enter apprenticeship programs that average three years in length. Currently, 1.5 million Germans annually participate in apprenticeship programs. About 70 percent of German companies with over 50 employees participate in this dual system. Although the extent varied among the 16 separate German states, in 2011 about 2 percent of apprenticeship openings went unfilled.

In Austria, about 40 percent of secondary school graduates opt to enter apprenticeship programs in about 250 occupational areas. Both large and small firms participate, with 40,000 companies training 120,000 apprentices in 2009.

In a country of only eight million people, 58,000 Swiss companies provide Vocational Education and Training (VET) to about 80,000 apprentices. After nine years of schooling, almost 66 percent of Swiss teens choose the VET program. Apprenticeship training is available in nearly 250 occupational areas. Apprenticeships are from three to four years in duration and the average starting salary for a VET in a commercial program is $50,000 a year.

The predominant feature of all three of these national apprenticeship systems is the extensive cooperation among businesses, trade organizations, and educational institutions. Businesses are directly involved in preparing curriculum content with educators and trainees. In all three of these nations, the youth unemployment rate is below that of other OECD nations. In October 2012, less than 3 percent of Swiss youth were unemployed, when the comparable rate for the United States was 12 percent and the European Union (EU) 22 percent.[40]

Ursula von der Leyden, Germany's minister for labor and social affairs, terms the German dual system "the classic public-private partnership," which she believes would aid other European nations with high rates of youth unemployment. Her message to other EU nations is: "Whether it is painful or not, because we have a globalized world, we have to undertake reforms to improve our competitiveness."[41]

Denmark—"Flexicurity" Aid

Historically, about 20 percent of Danes change jobs each year. This is very high for EU economies. Yet Denmark has maintained, even during the current worldwide slowdown, a relatively low unemployment rate for Europe (7.9%, 7/12).

An important reason for the fluidity of Denmark's labor market is its Flexicurity System. Denmark's laws make it relatively easy to dismiss an employee. But if a Dane loses a job and needs additional skills for a new position, the government subsidizes courses at local technical colleges. These talent updates are often partially funded by a new employer and even sometimes by the previous employer. This process has kept the Danish labor economy very flexible and highly responsive to business talent needs, and provides increased job and career security for individual workers.[42]

Denmark, however, has a growing skills deficit which is prompting a debate on its tough immigration policy. Henning Gade, chief consultant at the Confederation of Danish Employers, has estimated that Denmark will need 150,000 new skilled workers by 2020 in various areas, such as IT, engineering, and biotech.[43]

Moving Niagara Forward

The Niagara Region in the Ontario Province of Canada is home to 460,000 people living in 12 municipalities. It includes Niagara Falls, a famed tourist destination. Family-owned light industries dot the area. The population is aging and the younger people often move to Toronto. In October 2011, this author was invited to speak at a conference that was held in the city of St. Catharines where the local unemployment rate was 9.2 percent at a time when Canada's overall unemployment figure was 7.2 percent.

This conference came about because the community leaders there are determined to boost the economic development of their region. George Darte is the community leader, who got the ball rolling. He is a past president of the International Order of the Golden Rule, an association of independent funeral home directors encompassing the United States and Canada. I first met George when I addressed a national convention of this group in 2009. Members of this association across Canada and the United States are faced with a shortage of morticians over the next decade. Because of one of my earlier books, they looked to me for solutions to take back to their home communities.

George Darte immediately started the conversation about my coming to the Niagara Region to discuss the wider picture of global talent shortages. He wanted other community leaders to hear and read about how RETAINs are addressing local and regional talent development to retrain workers, expand career information and information programs, and attract new businesses to an area. Darte commented, "I'm sick and tired of having jobs leave. I want to see us grow business back into the Niagara region."

Sometimes, it only takes one person to spark community action. Darte is an active member of the local Greater Niagara Chamber of Commerce. He worked with Walter Sendzik, the chamber's CEO and his staff, to organize a half-day conference "Moving Niagara Forward." As Sendzik stated, "We need to expand our business collaboration throughout the area and overcome parochialism to address this talent crisis."

They convened 50 women and men from the business, education, government, union, and health care sectors to learn how the global talent revolution will affect Ontario and their region. Like most of us, they want to see local towns and businesses prosper and grow and prevent the flight of families and businesses from their area. Kithio Mwanzia, the chamber's director of public policy and government relations, thinks that there is a need for workforce development action across the Niagara region. "There's certainly a skills gap. It's such a critical time with so many discussions about economic development. We need to act now," he said.

This was just the beginning of the public conversation energized by the networking at the conference. George and his colleagues represent the growing civic activism that I have witnessed many times in the United States, Canada, and around the world. These people are far from helpless or hopeless. They have embarked on the road to renew the education-to-employment talent system through a Niagara Region RETAIN. This will not be easy, and it will take time. But their personal resolve to meet this community challenge of rebuilding their jobs pipeline is intense. It's their contribution to the future prosperity of Canada.[44]

Final Thoughts

Global talent creation is not a zero sum game. It is not true that if some nations expand their talent pool, others must lose. In fact, every nation can grow their talented people into a stronger economic force, as shown by the analyses in the last two chapters. RETAINS are helping people and businesses better adjust to the lightning speed of current labor market changes.

We are in a watershed era of historical transformation driven by major technological advances. The key challenge is rethinking how we create stronger learning skills for more people. During this transition, it is slowly and often painfully becoming apparent that tomorrow's job, career, and life successes will only be earned by those who more fully develop their personal talents.

RETAINs act as catalysts that bring together different segments of individual local communities to create new talent systems for a 21st-century workforce. To achieve that goal in the near future, we must bring RETAINs to scale across our society. What new business and governmental policies will be needed? The next chapters will consider the work ahead.

Part IV

The Future

Chapter 8

A New
Business Agenda

But just as important as revitalizing policy is reshaping attitudes . . . let's
summon the can-do spirit that has made America the land of innovation.[1]
—Robert J. Stevens, Chairman, President,
CEO, Lockheed Martin

Walk the Talk

Many executives ranging from major corporations to medium-sized and
small businesses complain that they are having increasing trouble finding
skilled talent for 21st-century jobs. At both the *Wall Street Journal*'s CEO
Council meeting of 100 chief executives in November 2011 and the *Wall
Street Journal*'s second annual meeting in June 2012 of approximately 40
chief financial officers (CFOs) of major corporations, one of the top priorities was improving human capital. "[T]he U.S. must improve the skills of
workers to aid in export growth," said the CEOs from Kaiser Permanente,
Oracle, Dow Chemicals, Caterpillar, Intel, Fed Ex, Navistar, and a host of
other Fortune 500 companies.[2]

The CFOs agreed on the top priority of creating an innovative workplace by "getting the culture and talent right." Joseph Zubretsky, CFO of
Aetna Inc., stated that "Innovation is where our financial capital meets intellectual capital."[3]

The CFOs also concurred on the need for a "functional, robust and
modern educational system," said Joe Kaeser, CFO of Siemens AG.[4] Private
industry should do its part by building more technical education programs,
the group advised. However, most companies only rely passively on their
local education-to-employment system of schools, colleges, and internal

training to continuously renew a pool of skilled talent of adequate size and quality. But this once successful approach isn't producing the talent business needs today.

Corporations, such as AT&T, Microsoft, IBM, Intel, Hewlett-Packard, United Technologies, Boeing, Caterpillar, and many others, support a broad array of programs designed to improve talent creation. These include community high school dropout prevention, high school career academies, college scholarships, employee tuition assistance, student math, science, or robotic competitions, math/science professional development for teachers, and STEM/pre-engineering curriculum development assistance.

Businesses and foundations are also providing financial assistance to nonprofit organizations, such as Jobs for the Future, SkillsUSA, IC Stars, and Year Up, which focus on specific areas of talent development. These programs are providing guidance on educational practices to improve skill development.

What impacts have these programs had over the past 20–30 years? How sustainable are they? Where have they been scaled up to improve a region's talent system? The answers point to the need for RETAINs to act as intermediaries. They can plug these individual programs into overall systemic change efforts and make them locally sustainable through a broader public/private cross-sector partnership policy.

Serious reform requires changing business policy, and that means political debate inside and outside a company. This is where RETAINs can help businesses focus on training and systemic educational change. In the case studies we have reviewed, business leaders dialogued with educators, unions, politicians, and other community leaders to build new sustainable talent creation structures.

Top company executives participated in local RETAINs and tackled tough questions. They acknowledged that some of their steps would be seen as political and unpopular at first. But they took the heat when there was push back. This is the process that made transformational talent change possible.[5]

Without more talent, how can business help the U.S. economy grow? As Robert J. Gordon, Northwestern University economist notes, a major obstacle is the leveling-off of America's educational excellence. U.S. business needs to adopt policies that make adult education far more available and far more compelling.[6]

U.S. business must look beyond the short-term economic and profit fixes of the immediate past. For this decade, pro-growth business policies must focus on increased productivity. This will come from enlarging the pool of talented workers who can make better use of advanced technologies to produce more competitive products or services.[7]

Many successful companies now integrate their strategic talent development strategies into their broader business sustainability model. But most don't even try. Perhaps, half of all U.S. businesses have prepared an employee talent development plan. Of these, most are not implementing the program. This trend can be seen from the 2013 Conference Board's CEO Challenge survey. Executives in Europe and Asia ranked human capital as the number one challenge they faced. However, U.S. CEOs listed human capital fifth, behind operational excellence, government regulation, customer relationships, and innovation.[8]

A 2011 survey by the Society for Human Resource Management found that 28 percent of organizations are not even pursuing broader sustainability issues, let alone training and development. The obstacle is perceived cost.[9] About 80 percent of employer-sponsored training expenditures are made by 20 percent of the largest U.S. companies. Most of these expenditures are for those in the top ranks of these organizations. Leading-edge STEM companies, however, do invest in advanced technical and scientific training for a broader range of their employees. But most workers are lucky to even get on-the-job training.

Building employee skills is now a more critical task than ever for U.S. business. Though the United States invests nearly $1 trillion, or about 7 percent of its output in education and training each year, many workers are still left behind.

The Manpower Group reported (2012) that 28 percent of U.S. employers were providing additional training to overcome talent shortages However, this was well below the average of 37 percent for employers surveyed in other western hemisphere nations.[10] Why is U.S. business so reluctant to train its workforce?

The majority of executives and small business owners rarely think about the potential impact of talent shortages. This will only begin to change when they personally experience how the skills and jobs mismatch threatens the sustainability of their business.

Training Magazine's Annual Training Industry Survey reveals a highly erratic pattern of business training expenditures (see Table 8.1). At a time when talent development is more crucial than ever, 2012 training expenditures fell below the 2001 level! Yet, U.S. corporations in the past few years have been sitting on a big cash cushion that has reached over $3 trillion (2012).[11] So, why don't more businesses train?

TABLE 8.1   U.S. Business Training and Education Expenditures

Year	$ (Billion)	+/– % Rounded
2001	56.8	+5
2002 & 2003	52.8	–5
2004 & 2005	51.4	–
2006	55.8	+7
2007	58.5	+4.8
2008	56.2	–4
2009	52.2	–7
2010	52.8	–
2011	59.7	+13
2012	55.8	–6.5

Source: Compiled from Training Magazine Annual Training Industry Surveys, 2001–2012.

Answering the "Big Three" Objections to Training

Most business people firmly voice their belief that "Training doesn't work!" The argument goes like this: "It's a waste of time and money. I pulled myself up by my own bootstraps, so why should I spend money on my employees? Anyway what are we paying taxes for? My responsibility as a CEO is to maximize shareholder value, period." (Or in the case of a small business owner, "My responsibility is for the continued well-being of my family, period.")

Business opposition to employee training/education is often based on the "Big Three" objections:

#1—"Most training produces little or no worker performance improvement."
#2—"If you successfully train workers, they will be poached by your competitor."
#3—"Training doesn't have an accurate financial metric. You can't monetize return-on-investment (ROI) for training programs."

Here are some answers to help change your perspective about training's role in your business.

#1—"Training doesn't work" versus Sustaining Your Talent

Several years ago, a CEO challenged this author to reduce to one page an understandable proof of how training and education could produce innovation in his business. What I produced is seen in Figure 8.1.

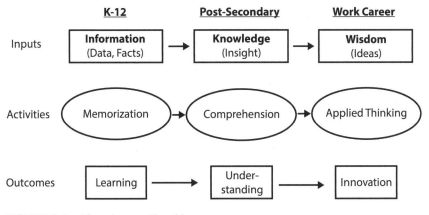

FIGURE 8.1   How Innovation Happens

How does innovation happen? Luck? Genius? Personality? Evidence shows that most people's ability to innovate develops gradually over time.

As students move through elementary and secondary school, they need to both amass information through memorization and also develop their capacities for learning. By adolescence, they should be fully proficient in learning how to pursue and assimilate new knowledge.

More of today's students attend postsecondary programs centered on career development. The young adult begins to experience some of the "ah-ha" moments in life, including a growing comprehension of the basic nature and demands of specific occupations. Previously acquired data and facts are utilized to form new mental maps that provide greater understanding of how the world functions.

When young adults enter the workplace, many face the challenge of putting theory into practice for the first time. They need to employ all the information they have gained, plus their problem-solving and critical thinking skills to generate new ideas that in turn produce innovative products or services.

Apple's Steve Jobs was once asked what made his company special. He replied, "It's in Apple's DNA that technology alone is not enough—it's technology married with the liberal arts, married with the humanities, that yields us the result that makes our heart sing."[12]

Let's translate. This is the century of technology. Innovators will win the game. You need workers who have married the sciences to the liberal arts. People who have developed new ways of thinking, new ideas, and can creatively employ their imagination to tell a story about a new product, service, or way of doing business. These are the people who have bridged the "science friction" gap (see Chapter 4). They have the capacity to recognize and exploit the potential of new technologies. They are the competitive edge your business needs to develop.[13]

The late Peter Drucker also described management as a liberal art. He argued that management was essential for all human endeavors, and thus had a social function in addition to a business role. Instead, for the past 20 years, Wall Street and MBA programs have focused businesses on short-term profit. This culture threatens the essential core talent sustainability of businesses and organizations.

U.S. business executives often allege that today's university graduates are poorly prepared for the complex jobs that companies need to fill. Ironically, many institutions of higher learning have weakened their liberal arts requirements that increase the depth of students' knowledge and better develop their critical thinking skills. In the past, businesses recruited liberal arts majors because of their broader education and inquiring minds. Their business knowledge was developed through training programs that rotated them through the major departments or sectors of the company. They often emerged suggesting a fresh approach to chronic organizational problems. The most promising were mentored as future leaders.[14]

Many of the best CEOs and managers I have worked with had this background. Now, an entire new generation needs to be given the same opportunities. Turning all colleges and universities solely into career or technical academies will do little to solve the current shortages of creative younger managers.

In this Cyber-Mental Age, U.S. businesses are continuing to move further toward complex higher cost products and services based upon advanced technology in order to remain globally competitive. These operations are based upon the levers of highly adaptive management systems and advanced technology. This strategy also requires specialized talent at many levels to support higher performance, innovation, and quality levels. This new workplace structure blurs the line between workers and management. To produce increased productivity and profit, businesses need to actively engage the eyes, ears, minds, and emotions of all their people. Training can be one of those important levers.

A company's training and education programs need to be specifically targeted to employee performance and business productivity issues. On the one hand, poorly designed, sporadic, flavor-of-the-month, scatter-shot training, or training solutions applied to paper over bad management decisions usually are a waste of time and resources. How many of yesterday's bright management ideas were rushed through your organization before they were given the time to be properly implemented? Change fatigue and disillusionment with training are the results.

On the other hand, high quality training is properly designed for the targeted audience. Enough time is allocated for people to learn and think about how to utilize the new applications on the job, and maybe even practice them. Management must clearly support such changes and facilitate their implementation within the organization.[15]

E-learning is now all the rage. On the plus side, this training method is good for self-paced, well-educated workers. It can be delivered anywhere, at any time. Management has great control over its content. Pure e-learning is cheaper, as it eliminates employee class time, travel, classroom space, and trainers.

On the negative side, research shows that most employees need to physically interact with other people in a classroom setting. Classroom courses bring together students and trainers/teachers in real time, where the instructors can quickly gauge what is not being understood and adjust their instruction to remedy the situation. Learning succeeds best when it encourages a dialogue. It is least effective when it becomes a monologue.

Blended learning combines the best of both worlds. Computer instruction is used to provide learning modules for which it is best suited, such as imparting new factual information or procedures. Trainers/teachers become facilitators using a team teaching approach. Blended learning matches the best instructional mode to the course content and performance objectives of the learners.[16]

Many businesses are already working nonstop to remain relevant. Their leaders realize that the need to constantly adapt is the new reality of the Cyber-Mental Age. Computer technology is transforming the nature of jobs in almost every business sector. In many cases, what workers learned in school is miniscule compared to what they need to know today. Constant training updates help them stay relevant and sustain their companies in a future of rapid change.[17]

Training works boils down to this: is your company willing to allocate the time and financial resources needed to implement effective training programs throughout your organization? If yes, training and education will enhance your organization's performance, productivity, and profit. If no, your company may not remain sustainable, and innovation will decline as your pool of talent will begin disappearing.

#2—"If you train people, they will be poached" versus Training Promotes Loyalty

Larger businesses can more easily afford in-house training. Some operate corporate universities. RETAINs are now helping smaller companies engage in employee development. RETAIN networks are establishing regional skill training centers or developing partnerships with local postsecondary institutions. This enables smaller employers to develop the skills of new hires and provide current employees with training updates. Such combined efforts greatly reduce an individual business' training costs.

The stronger the RETAIN network, the less likely workers will be poached. Current anecdotal evidence from RETAINs suggests that widespread business participation in these networks can reduce worker poaching by as much as 75 percent among its members.

This is also the case for small business engaged in RETAIN internship/apprenticeship programs through local high school career academies, community colleges, or union programs. Encouraging widespread small business participation in such regional programs helps all the partners, as program costs are shared and all can benefit from a larger local pool of trained talent.

Much to their regret, companies are finding out that if you don't train employees, you are likely to lose them. This is particularly true among the young and skilled. Higher achieving 30-year-old workers are switching employers on average after 28 months. Exit interview research finds that lack of training and workplace mentoring drives them away. Training can improve younger worker's loyalty, if it is also clearly linked to a future career path. If not, they will take their skills and education to another company that better maps out their potential for the future.[18]

Training is also important for updating the skills and retaining employees who are in their 50s and 60s. Andrew Hill, *Financial Times* management analyst asserts that "Companies that wish to attract and retain skilled staff must now apply the same flexible thinking and close attention they focus on recent graduates to employees entering the last quarter-century of their careers."[19]

General Electric spends $1 billion a year on its elite management college in Crotonville. Novartis sends top managers to regular off-site training. Andy Grove, head of Intel, spends at least a week a year teaching up-and-coming executives. So did G.E.'s Jack Welch and A.G. Lafley at Procter & Gamble.[20]

Small as well as large businesses need to understand that talented people will be in even greater shortage as this decade advances. They will consider careers at a company that best trains, mentors, and maps out a joint future with them.

#3—"Training results can't be measured financially" versus ROI Models Provide Contrary Evidence

Human capital is the sum total of individual intelligence built on the acquisition of skills, training, and educational experience over a lifetime.[21] There is widespread skepticism that a quantifiable ROI can be calculated for training/education programs. Executives want this training ROI calculated in various terms, such as a business contribution, business alignment, business value, and a direct connection to the business.[22]

"Picking the right metrics is the key to creating real value from training," says McKinsey and Company.[23] Today, companies around the world, both large and small, are doing just that.

The key to accurate ROI calculations is obtaining access to essential business operational data and using spreadsheet analytics to measure results. This data includes profit margins, gross revenue, and operational results data. This process requires cooperation among different business units inside an organization in gathering and analyzing this information.

Our research has shown that training needs to be targeted to specific employee performance issues. Higher quality training produces a higher ROI, since it produces stronger changes in employee behavior and thinking.[24]

There are many ROI methods now available to employers for such in-depth quantitative evaluation of training/education programs. Many of these ROI measures use evaluation software.

One example is the "Human Capital ROI Nine-Step Worksheet." It estimates the business monetary returns both before and after most skill, training, or education programs. This method can also be used to make comparisons between in-house training versus potential outside training vendors.

It also addresses three serious issues that until now have compromised accurate financial training measurement:

1. Training effectiveness versus other business variables: Did the results come from the training program or some other business factor?
2. Training transfer: Unless you have a way to calculate the "average" training transfer back on-the-job, you will inflate the training's ROI.
3. Depreciation of training: Even the best training programs do not permanently improve a business. You need to depreciate a training program's benefit over time.[25]

The Human Capital ROI Nine-Step Worksheet is a file to be used in an Excel spreadsheet. It can be downloaded free of charge in two forms at http://www.imperialcorp.com/humanCapital.html. (See Appendix 2 for more details.)

Today, many of the world's leading businesses outside the United States are beating America at the innovation game by paying more attention to training ROI. Rather than ignoring this relationship, they are building their future competitiveness through coordinating the use of advanced technologies with the development of appropriately skilled talent. America's chief competitors are investing more in their companies' human capital through employee job training, executive development, and student career education.

Overturning Yesterday's Logic

The talent system's current structural collapse has accelerated over the past two decades. Rebuilding this system will not be easy. It will take time. As a McKinsey Global Institute study states, "To create the jobs that America needs to continue growing and remain competitive, leaders in government, business, and education will have to be creative—and willing to consider solutions business has not tried before."[26] The good news is RETAINs are providing a cross-sector cooperative framework for such innovation.

Talent creation will not be robust unless business people, educators, and government come to fully understand the enormous untapped potential of the U.S. workforce. As Peter Drucker warned, "The greatest danger in times of turbulence is not the turbulence; it is to act with yesterday's logic."[27]

To change that logic, we are seeing an increased business focus on workforce analytics, workforce planning, regional career education, and employee performance management. These human capital issues are often the hardest for a business to manage well.

Talent creation can be wasted if a company doesn't know what skills its workers will need for today and tomorrow. Businesses need to establish an inventory of their employee's current skills. They then must chart a path for future innovation and employee creativity within their organization. Finally, companies must decide how far their own culture and the community will push for a new talent creation system.

Since private sector businesses account for the lion's share of U.S. jobs, they need to spearhead the creation of a 21st-century talent system. Businesses need to develop their talent internally, and also work with educators and communities to redevelop the education-to-employment system.

More outreach programs are vital. Students and parents need to be informed about how technology has transformed workplaces and talent requirements. Ties between schooling and work should be fostered through internships and apprenticeships.

RETAINs are helping more and more companies to cooperatively address the talent challenge at the regional level. Now is the time for a new business agenda to scale up the RETAIN model, rather than looking for answers from Washington. America has done this before. We can do it again. It's in our genes!

Chapter 9

Government Realignment

Without adequate investment in skills, people languish on the margins of society, technological progress does not translate into economic growth, and countries can no longer compete. . . . In short, skills have become the global currency of 21st-century economies.

—(OECD, 2012)[1]

Local, state, and federal government agencies and professional regulatory groups have major roles to play in the success of partnerships for talent creation. Government policies that encourage and assist business investment in training prospective or incumbent employees need expansion. Government regulation touches all levels of the education from preschool to graduate programs. The education-to-employment system requires major structural reforms. Student learning is an incremental process. Failure at one level can lead to failure at the next. Government involvement is vital in raising standards, fostering educational equality, and offering more education options at all levels.

Investing in Human Capital

In 2010, Intel President and CEO Paul Otellini announced a $3.5 billion initiative, "Invest in American Alliance," to target innovation at multiple clean tech, information tech, and biotech companies. Intel and 16 other tech companies also pledged to hire more college graduates to create the new products and services of tomorrow.[2] But Otellini was silent about human capital investment.

Human capital is the sum total of individual intelligence built on the acquisition of skills, training, and education over a lifetime. It is the applications of this talent in a knowledge-based economy that creates real value and innovation for every business.[3]

"Little constructive dialogue about elevating human capital as a source of competitive advantage takes place among key stakeholder groups: the business community, government, labor and others," asserted Thomas A. Kochan, management professor at MIT's Sloan School.[4] That is about to change.

Tom Peters, America's senior management guru, asks why in a random 30-minute interview with a typical CEO he is unlikely to hear a word about employee training and education. "I would hazard a guess that most CEOs see an IT investment as a 'strategic necessity', but training expenses as a 'necessary evil.'" Peters argues that new business rules need to be written to solve the current talent crisis. He calls for "A human capital development manifesto at the enterprise and national government level."[5]

Robert I. Lerman, an economist at the American University, the Urban Institute and Germany's Institute for the Study of Labor, suggests that a low-cost intervention to encourage more employer training and education is to acknowledge the asset value of human capital. "The change would recognize in income statements and balance sheets that training investments generate assets that yield future benefits," Lerman states. In addition, Lerman believes that "Since employer-sponsored training yields a high return, additional employer-sponsored training is likely to prove productive and improve the skills qualifications and earnings of American workers."[6]

The U.S. accounting system classifies employee training and education as a business expense, whereas building a factory or purchasing equipment or software is treated as an investment. We foresee this would continue to be the preferred treatment for closely held family and smaller nonpublicly held corporations.[7] But, particularly for publicly traded companies, this means that training expenses are deducted from quarterly earnings while investments in equipment or buildings can be depreciated over time (under Internal Revenue Service [IRS] regulations). This situation makes it harder for business executives who invest in worker training and education to make their numbers to meet Wall Street's quarterly financial expectations. If developing employee talent continues to be treated as an expense and not as an investment, it will perpetuate a negative mind-set about training and education throughout the business community.

Management expert Stephen Covey compared the current talent development situation to doing bloodletting as a cure for an illness, when you already understand germ theory. You can try to do bloodletting better, but the underlying business mind-set is that developing people is an expense to be avoided. Yet Covey asserted that "80 percent of all value added comes from people."[8]

How significant has training and education become as an intangible instrument in the U.S. economy? A study (2006) from researchers at the Federal Reserve Bank and the University of Maryland explored this issue. They found that businesses invest in many types of intangibles, such as research and development (R&D); training and education; databases and software; advertising and trademarks, to name a few. The rate of this type of business investment was fairly flat from the 1950s until the mid-1990s. It then began rising to around $1 trillion a year by 2000. This was the same level of expenditure that businesses were making on traditional fixed capital assets.

When the IT bubble burst after 2000, intangible investments never recovered. For example, by 2010, U.S. business was spending 10 times more on IT hardware than on training and education. However, by 2012 intangible investment in training and development had fallen below 2001 expenditures.

Yet, according to this study, by the late 1990s $1 trillion in annual economic growth being driven by business investments was being excluded from the gross domestic product (GDP) by out-of-date U.S. accounting practices. This study found that U.S. intangible investments were equal by 1995 to traditional "bricks-and-mortar" forms of capital investment in driving overall national economic growth.[9] But important change is now coming.

In 2013, the United States became one of the first adapters of a new international GDP accounting standard that will treat R&D as a capital investment rather than a cost. Brent Moulton, a manager of national accounts at the Bureau of Economic Analysis (BEA), stated, "The world economy is changing and there is greater and greater recognition that things like intangible assets are very important in the modern economy and play a role similar to tangible capital that was captured in the past."[10]

This change will enhance corporate profits since companies will no longer be counting R&D after depreciation as a cost. Also, the savings rate for private citizens and government will rise reflecting this increase in the nation's capital investment.

Steve Landefeld, director of the BEA, believes this is only the beginning in getting a more accurate picture of growth in the U.S. economy. "You need to go further in this exploration of intangibles. R&D is just a piece of the puzzle."[11] We strongly agree.

The Financial Accounting Standards Board (FASB) needs to update its accounting standards to allow businesses the option of capitalizing their expenditures on training, education, apprenticeships or internships. This is already allowed by the IRS under certain circumstances, if the training/education program expenditure is unique to the business.

For example, a bank buys a new computer system for $20 million. The cost of that equipment can be depreciated over its useful life, according to the IRS. In this case, it can be spread over 10 years. The computer manufacturer tells the bank that the technical training of current and future employees will require an expenditure of $400,000 in order to use the system over that time period. Purchasing managers tell us that adding the technical training costs to the purchase price of new technology is a commonly followed accounting procedure. Thus, the amount that the bank may depreciate is the actual purchase price of the computer system, set-up costs, and the employee training program to operate it over its useful lifetime or $20,400,000.

However, it is not the end of this story. Contemporary computer systems are very complex. They will only yield the promised productivity gains and enhanced employee performance advantages if the employees possess both the technical skills and required soft skills (i.e., systemic thinking, problem analysis, teamwork, statistical literacy, etc.).

In this case, bank employees will need additional training and education in math ($100,000), team building ($250,000), and interpersonal/customer service skills ($150,000). Under IRS rules, these costs also may be capitalized.

IRS Rule 96–62 states that "Training costs must be capitalized only in the unusual circumstances where training is intended primarily to obtain future benefits significantly beyond those traditionally associated with training provided in the ordinary course of the taxpayer's trade or business." We believe that the additional $500,000 in training required to operate this new computer system is an unusual deduction, in the sense it had never before been offered to the bank employees. It is now being offered for the use of new technology that will give this bank future benefits far beyond that associated with any training provided in the past. Using this rationale, the total depreciation of the bank's new computer system will be $20,900,000 instead of $20,400,000.[12]

In today's fast-paced knowledge economy, expensing training in publicly traded companies is an anachronism. Current U.S. accounting standards were written for a 20th-century mass production economy that changed more slowly and in which semiskilled and unskilled jobs predominated. During that time period, continuing professional education was largely reserved for executives and professionals. Today, it needs to include many more mid-level workers. The new economy requires a new talent-creating financial metric that appears as an investment on a balance sheet, so that businesses can track the impact of training and education investments on both short- and long-term profits.

Making more appropriate investments in any business' human capital raises the organization's potential ability to enhance worker performance, increase productivity, and make better use of technological enhancements that will raise profit margins. Large publically traded U.S. corporations are holding record amounts of cash on their balance sheets. Many of these companies are also reporting difficulties in finding skilled talent. New accounting standards from FASB and IRS regulations that allow businesses the flexibility to capitalize training, development, education, and internship expenditures will make human capital investment more attractive to business executives.

Specifically, capitalizing training will give U.S. businesses incentives to:

- Use training program to fill persistent vacant positions.
- Retrain current workers as new technologies become available or management structures change.
- Support apprenticeship and internship program pipelines for long-term sustainability.

All of the above will increase America's abilities to create more talented people. It will have an immediate and long-term impact on reducing U.S. unemployment. In addition to creating more jobs, capitalizing business training and education will help the U.S. economy rebalance away from consumption to increased high-tech investment, domestic production, and exports.[13]

For a future knowledge economy, it is "inappropriate to ignore the association between innovation, human capital, and knowledge acquisition on the one hand, and investment in intangibles, IT capital, labor-quality change, and multifactor productivity, on the other," concluded economists Carol Corrado, Dan Sichel, and Charles Hulton. "What is surprising is that intangibles have been ignored for so long and . . . the potential [financial] magnitude of this bias arising when they are excluded from economic growth accounting."[14]

The United States today urgently needs this new talent investment metric to help guarantee U.S. business technological leadership into the first decades of the 21st century. U.S. organizations with multinational operations are in an advantageous position to help stem global talent shortages. However, just as we have stated here, the McKinsey Global Institute warned in 2010 that many of our business leaders have doubts that American culture and society will back more rigorous educational standards in to order to produce the talented people with the knowledge and skills needed for high-tech jobs and careers.[15] If business does not make its vital contribution to talent and skill development, this warning will become a self-fulfilling prophecy.

Tom Peters forcefully advocates having "training in its broadest sense placed atop the enterprise agenda on a par with capital expenditures." Peters admits this human capital manifesto may seem "a long way from where we are now." But, as creativity becomes ever more important for business growth, "human capital investment . . . falls into a category of 'not optional.'"[16] We need everyone to get that message!

Improving Federal Job Training Initiatives

Business-government collaboration is not a new concept. NASA's Apollo Moon Landing Program illustrates how well it can work. Yet, most of today's government workforce development partnerships are limited to working with nonprofit organizations, rather than also including the for-profit business community in such partnerships.

Federal job training programs have a long history. Most were established to assist disadvantaged workers, especially dislocated workers and the long-term unemployed. They have gone through a series of metamorphoses over the past 40 years. The following are among the most prominent:

1. Comprehensive Employment and Training Act (CETA) 1973
2. Job Training Partnership Act (JTPA) 1982
3. Carl D. Perkins Vocational and Applied Technology Education Act 1960
4. The School-to-Work Opportunities Act 1994
5. Personal Responsibility and Work Opportunity Reconciliation Act (1996)
6. Workforce Investment Act of 1998 (WIA)

WIA established local Workforce Investment Boards to contract with local organizations for the provision of training programs and other services. These programs largely offered generic training for low-skill/low-wage jobs. They have largely failed. Forty-six point two million Americans (15%) today live below the poverty line (2012). Many more with incomes above the poverty line now have been pushed out of work by the long-term structural unemployment crisis. Weak formal education and little or no career skills limit their future employment prospects.

There has been growing criticism over the multitude of federal training programs that in addition to WIA do not appear to be coordinated or focused on employment opportunities in local communities. As we have seen, this recently has begun to change. Programs, such as Skills for Chicagoland's Future, HIRED (St. Paul-Minneapolis), and others, have begun to partner with local WIA boards to match unemployed persons with specific vacant jobs in businesses. These people receive job training at the businesses, supplemented by classroom instruction at local postsecondary institutions. These programs are funded through a combination of public and private company investment.

RETAINs offer a compelling model for expanding these public-private training collaborations. We also need to think more broadly about who needs to be trained. About 89 million eligible adult workers are not currently in the labor market. This encompasses large groups of Americans, including:

- Sequencing mothers, or women who have dropped out of the workforce to have children and then desire to return (27–30 million)[17]
- Boomers who have retired or will retire between 2013 and 2030 who might be employed at least part-time (70 million)[18]
- People who are physically or mentally challenged (20–22 million)[19]
- People in the criminal justice system (3–5 million)[20]
- Military veterans seeking civilian employment (10–15 million)[21]

In some regions and states, there are programs that retrain and reintroduce these workers into the labor market. Over the next 10 years, they will represent a pool of 76–100 million workers. Improved government-business collaboration could help mobilize this potential talent pool and transform a depressing neglect of human capital into a real asset for people, businesses, and the broader economy.

Deconstructing the Education Blob

"We have settled on a path of global mediocrity for students attending our most affluent schools and national marginality for those attending failing inner-city schools," commented Arthur Levine, a former president of Columbia Teachers College and the president of the Woodrow Wilson National Fellowship Foundation.[22]

First, a few words to all educators. If you are among the many dedicated professionals at every level who makes a maximum effort to help all students advance academically and grow into mature and responsible adults, we sincerely thank you for persevering in a difficult career. At times, you are disdained by many others who don't share your enthusiasm for teaching students and the love of learning.

The United States needs you. We wish to acknowledge your high value because the future of America is truly in your hands. We promise to better motivate and reward your daily efforts to maximize every student's potential.

To those that can't identify with this message, I offer a few questions for your consideration from the writer and author, Peggy Noonan. "Do you remember the mission? Do you remember why you went to work there, what you meant to do, what the institution meant to you when you viewed it from the outside, years ago, and hoped to become part of it?"[23]

The great disparities in the quality of American education and their serious social and economic consequences are sparking a wide variety of efforts to fundamentally alter the U.S. education system. Their aim is to assure that every student is better prepared for being a responsible citizen and is provided with a clearer pathway for securing a skilled career. Isn't that what the American dream in the 21st century is all about?

The high-speed education change train is about to arrive in your local community. You can get on board as part of the process or be left behind. The choice is yours.

Thirty years of government education reforms have been amazingly neutralized by most of the education establishment. Since the passage of the Civil Rights Act of the 1960s, there have been some minor improvements in minority achievement. But overall, there has been virtually no increase in the percentage of students graduating with the skills and education needed for 21st-century careers (see Chapter 5).

Entrenched vested interests regularly welcome the latest wave of reform in theory. They then destroy them day-by-day in generally unaltered schooling practices. Ronald Reagan's Secretary of Education William Bennett aptly tagged this reactionary bunch "the blob." In 2013, almost three decades later, he cited a President's Council of Advisors on Science and Technology report that by 2020 about one million more college graduates in STEM are needed than are currently expected. His response, "We are nowhere near meeting that goal. Our middling performance today stunts our nation's economic growth and drastically undermines the ability of the next generation to support itself and its country with well-paying, growth-producing and satisfying jobs."[24]

They have offered "three great excuses" for so many failing schools: inadequate government spending, economic inequality, and cultural indifference. These all are important factors, but other important components have now emerged.

Spending is important. But it seems to depend on how and on what the money is spent. While the United States is first in education spending, it lags behind many other developed countries on overall student achievement (see Chapter 5). Andrew Schleicher, head of analysis at PISA (an international achievement testing and ranking program), thinks that only 10 percent of the differences between nations in student learning has anything to do with money.[25]

Dan Goldhaber at the University of Washington believes that a family's income influences up to 60 percent of a student's school achievement. Australia has even wider income differences than the United States, but Australian students ranked 9th in reading, ahead of U.S. students who came in 15th (PISA, 2009). Shanghai, China, one of the world's least equal societies, placed first.

Popular culture is an important factor. In top-ranked Singapore, Hong Kong, South Korea, and Finland, parents universally push their children and schools to succeed, as do perhaps 25 percent of U.S. parents.[26]

Contemporary culture can also offer us conflicting education images. On the one hand, we read about the high school dropout crisis, but at the same time we read about students who complain that they are drowning in schoolwork. A federal survey of elementary and high school students produced the following provocative findings:

- Many schools are not challenging students and a large percentage of students report that their school work is "too easy." Thirty-seven percent of fourth graders say that their math work is too easy.
- Many students are not engaged in rigorous learning activities. A significant percent of both elementary and high school students report that they seldom or never receive reading or writing assignments that come up to standards for their grade level.
- Students don't have access to key science and technology learning opportunities. Seventy-two percent of eighth grade science students say they aren't being taught introductory engineering and technology concepts.
- Many students don't understand their teacher's questions. They report a failure to learn during class. Thirty-six percent of high school seniors report they seldom clearly understand what their math teacher presents or asks.
- Disadvantaged students often are less likely to experience quality learning in the classroom. Among middle school students only 56 percent usually understand what their science teacher is saying.[27]

While there is no magic bullet for exploding the U.S. education blob, in my view the road to progress includes expanding educational diversity by offering different types of schools within communities and school districts and enacting higher standards for the teaching and school management/administrative profession. Three ways of increasing educational options will be considered here: charter schools, comprehensive college prep career academies that include liberal arts studies, and apprenticeship education.

Charter Schools

In 1992, Minnesota became the first U.S. state to pass charter school laws. By 2012, there were over 5,600 charter schools in 41 of America's 50 states, enrolling more than two million students (4% of all students). Charters are publicly funded but independently managed. They are given the freedom to set working conditions outside the restraints of local education rules and union contracts. Many charter schools have been founded to address the achievement gap in the school performance of poor and minority children.[28]

Charter schools are highly diverse and have a mixed record of success. Charter school results vary by state and city. The Stanford University CREDO study found that where there is strong oversight (Arkansas, Denver, Chicago, Louisiana, and Missouri) charter reading and math gains were significantly better than traditional schools. Charters in Arizona, Florida, Minnesota, New Mexico, Ohio, and Texas scored poorly because of lax screening of charter startups, and almost no serious oversight thereafter.[29]

There are national networks of charter schools as well as individual local ones. The largest U.S. charter school organization is the Knowledge is Power Program (KIPP). Currently, there are 125 KIPP schools in 20 states and the District of Columbia that enroll more than 41,000 students. Over 87 percent of KIPP students are from low-income families. KIPP charter schools extend student class time, the length of school days, and require twice monthly Saturday classes and summer school. The goal of the KIPP program is to prepare students for success in college and in life through a rigorous learning program.

Students, parents, and teachers sign learning pledges that emphasize their partnership in the learning process. The sample parent's pledge includes ensuring their child fully follows the KIPP schedule of instruction and dress code, agreeing to check their child's homework every night, and trying to read with the child every night.[30]

Under Mayor Michael Bloomberg, New York City has opened over 100 charter schools, most in low-income communities. In 2012, about 67,000 students applied through a lottery for less than 15,000 slots at charters. Almost all came from high-poverty African American and Latino families.

Remarkably, these charter students slightly outperformed the entire state of New York by 7.2 points in math and only lagged 3.6 points in reading. New York State has far fewer poor children and minorities. This helps belie the contention that poverty undermines the possibility of significantly better student outcomes than those generally being achieved in public education.[31]

Charter schools, with proper oversight, are successful because they offer a local community the freedom to shape the school to the pupils' needs rather than to the interests of a central bureaucracy. They can fire weak teachers, spend funds as they wish, add time to the school day and year, use diverse curriculum content teaching/tutoring methods, offer teacher performance pay, better motivate their students, and pursue other promising strategies.

In "Learning from the Success and Failure of Charter Schools," published by the Hamilton Project at the Brookings Institution, Roland Fryer, a Harvard University economics professor, contends that school systems can benefit by adopting five practices:

1. Focusing strongly on teachers' professional development,
2. Using student data to individualize learning,
3. Providing "high-dosage" tutoring,
4. Extending the school day and the school year,
5. Promoting a culture of high expectations for all students.[32]

After two decades, there is huge public demand for the expansion of successful charter schools. Why? Chicago's Mayor Rahm Emanuel best summarized the possible reasons, "The success of a student depends on a dedicated teacher, a strong principal, and an involved parent."[33]

Comprehensive Career Academies

The development of a student's academic knowledge and career skills are no longer mutually exclusive silos. Both the informational content of 21st-century jobs and the speed of continuing labor market changes have now ended this division.

So, the choice is no longer college prep or voc-ed. But changing educators' mind-sets about the transformed nature of future jobs and careers and effective education for them remains an uphill battle. I met with a high school superintendent recently and we were discussing this transitional issue. The administrator became very agitated and finally yelled at me, "I've devoted my whole professional life so that my students wouldn't end up in the dead-end jobs of voc-ed."

Other educators also remain skeptical about career academies. During a workshop, a high school teacher told me, "Career academics are an effort to deny minority and other students a college education and entering the middle class. They are a political and business conspiracy to take over education and turn it into factory schools serving their own agenda not the students." This teacher's opinion is a denial of reality regarding career academies that I have observed across the United States. It does reflect the teacher's own educational development and a generational bias against a technologically driven economy with its changing career realities.

Some parents have complained to me that their children don't need all that math, science, history, English, or writing skills, let alone career training. Their message: "Just give them what we got in school, we need more good paying, low-skill jobs in America." My answer: "Our world has moved on. Jobs and careers have changed since your youth. Technology will make life in the 21st century better, but no one promised that it would be easier or require fewer skills."

Today's reality is that all students must be prepared for some form of postsecondary education—two- or four-year college degrees, technical certificates, or apprenticeships. Integrating the required 21st-century skills and career and technical education into the entire education system (elementary, secondary, postsecondary, workplace learning) will make this a reality. The required direction for all K–12 education is to prepare every student for this transition without remediation to a postsecondary education.[34]

This is the primary reason why liberal arts, college prep, career academies, or to adopt a simpler term for this discussion, comprehensive career academies (CCAs) are a growing phenomenon in high schools across the United States. Over 2,500 CCAs are already operating. Many are smaller learning communities within larger high schools. Some are stand-alone career high schools in health care, IT, and various STEM areas. They blend a stronger liberal arts curriculum with specific practical career education courses and internship experiences. Here are a few examples:

Philadelphia Academies, Inc.   They say that necessity is the mother of invention. Just 45 years ago, the first career academy program, the Philadelphia Academies, Inc., did not begin as a grand experiment or a project funded by a foundation grant. In 1968, the City of Philadelphia was in the grip of crisis. Race riots, economic stagnation, and widespread unemployment precipitated a new education alternative to resuscitate the future workforce.

A coalition of business and civic leaders focused on the astronomical high school dropout rate. They established the Electrical Academy under the sponsorship of the Philadelphia Electric Company within Edison Public High School. It began with 30 students who were promised employment upon their graduation.

Today, the Philadelphia Academies, Inc. as a RETAIN offers career academy programs in process technology; urban education; applied electrical science; biotechnology; business and technology; communications; hotel and restaurant management; auto technology; health care; and IT. Approximately, 6,500 students are enrolled in 13 high schools at 24 academy program sites. The 2012 graduation rate for career academy students was 84 percent, compared to 61 percent for non-academy students.

Over 300 businesses participate in supporting these diverse career programs. They provide about 33 percent of the programs' funding. Foundation grants supply about 30 percent, and 35 percent is publically funded. About 90 percent of career academy graduates continue into postsecondary education or begin a career.

As the first career academy in the United States, the Philadelphia Career Academies, Inc. pioneered and has continued to develop the academies model. This concept has attracted widespread business and community participation across America.[35]

Center for Advanced Research and Technology—San Joaquin, California   Founded in 2000, Center for Advanced Research and Technology (CART) is a CCA offering specialized programs in the professional sciences, advanced communications, global economics, and engineering. Over 1,300 eleventh and twelfth grade students from the Clovis and Fresno Unified School Districts are bused to CART where they attend half-day classes taught by educators and business people in state-of-the-art labs. Grundfos Pumps, DeVry University, Community Medical Centers, and Universal Biopharma Research are among the businesses currently supporting CART. About 95 percent of CART graduates attend postsecondary institutions.[36]

Alignment Nashville   Organized in 2004, Alignment Nashville is an intermediary organization addressing a broad spectrum of community strategic goals. One major focus has been establishing academies throughout all of Nashville's public high schools. Over 220 companies are now committed as stakeholders in these programs that are designed to offer students both career awareness and a stronger liberal arts education.[37]

Workforce Excellence, Coachella Valley, California   Fifteen career academies that serve approximately 2,500 high school students in Palm Springs, Palm Desert, La Quinta, and other Riverside County desert communities have been initiated by the Coachella Valley Economic Partnership (CVEP), a RETAIN created to enhance the region's economy and workforce. To develop the resources needed for Workforce Excellence, the CVEP is working with 75 community stakeholders, including K–12 and postsecondary educational institutions, the local workforce investment board, and area businesses. Within five years, the Coachella Valley Regional Plan for College and Career Readiness has a target of enrolling a minimum of 30 percent of the region's 20,000 high school students in career or interest-themed academies, pathways, or similar programs.

Current Workforce Excellence programs include health care; hospitality, recreation and tourism; arts, media, and entertainment; and advanced technology. To help rebuild the health care occupational pipeline, career exploration in health care is offered at the elementary school level. A coordinated postsecondary health care career education plan is now supported by the College of the Desert (the local community college), California State University San Bernardino, and the University of California Riverside, School of Medicine. In an additional physician education program, the Eisenhower Medical Center is supporting 55 family practice and internal medicine residencies with the goal of encouraging these doctors to remain and practice within this region.[38]

Overall CCA Advantages   CCAs give more young people tangible information about career possibilities and where they might go in life. CCAs blend abstract and experiential learning. The practical courses and internships expose them to opportunities in growing fields that they might ordinarily shun or know nothing about. Entering the world of work with a degree of protection and supervision combats the adolescent woe of motivation, as they learn about the skills required for specific jobs in real workplaces. CCAs help close high school dropout factories.[39]

CCAs offer students a powerful combination of liberal arts studies and career preparation programs that will help more young people enter postsecondary institutions and prepare them to continue a lifetime of learning updates throughout their adult careers. (For more information about leading CCAs across America, see Appendix 3.)

Apprenticeship Education

Apprenticeships are skill training programs that combine paid, supervised, on-the-job learning experiences with related classroom academic instruction. Apprenticeships provide students with an advanced set of skills leading to certification in a specific career area. These programs can be sponsored by trade unions or businesses. In 2011, over 398,000 people were enrolled in registered U.S. apprenticeship education programs.[40]

Union-based employers sponsor more than half of all registered apprenticeships. Though the skilled trades in the construction sector have accounted for the bulk of U.S. apprenticeships, growth is now occurring in the transportation, communication, and health care sectors. Overseas, many nations have expanded apprenticeship education into white-collar technical fields as well.

Trade unions help develop curricula and provide workplace-based training. Their special knowledge of the workplace and recruiting network of employers offer many advantages. Though trade unions have incentives to protect the interests of existing workers, particularly in times of economic downturns, the fact that many union members in the skilled trades are reaching retirement age should expand union apprenticeship programs in the near future.

U.S. business sponsors the other half of apprenticeship education. As we have seen, German, Swiss, and Austrian companies invest heavily in the dual system of apprenticeships in their own country. In the United States, they are modifying their models to the local market. Siemens began such an apprenticeship program at its gas and steam turbine plant in Charlotte, North Carolina.

To change the student's mind-set, these programs offer local high school students a facilities tour. "Everything in the factory is run by a computer, a robot, a laser—people don't think manufacturing is like that," explains Pamela Howze, plant training manager.[41] She informs students, their parents, and local guidance counselors, "They get paid to go to school, and they get paid when they're working here in the (work) shop [hands-on training], and they get paid when they are at the community college [classroom education]. That's a pretty lucrative deal for a young person." Upon their graduation, they will earn wages well above the regional average.[42]

Volkswagen operates a similar apprenticeship education effort at its new Chattanooga, Tennessee, car plant, but there the typical trainee age is 25–30 years old. German, Japanese, and Swiss companies in many parts of the United States also seek to involve local partners.[43]

The Apprentice School in Newport News, Virginia, was founded in 1919. Now largely supported by Northrop Grumman Shipbuilding, it offers 19 registered apprenticeship programs. Some are offered in conjunction with local community colleges and result in an associate's degree. During the entire course of the four- or five-year programs, Northrup pays apprentices hourly wage and provides them with full benefits. The base salary upon completion of the apprenticeship program is $50,000.[44] Northrup also has an apprenticeship program for high school graduates at its Avondale, Louisiana, shipyards.[45]

Apprenticeship programs are an important component of postsecondary career education. Completing a typical two- to three-year program is certainly just as complex as attaining a two-year associate degree from a community/technical college. For this reason, we need to consider this program an Apprenticeship College. This more clearly represents their advanced educational value and the complexity of their technical skill training.

Apprenticeship has been underutilized in the U.S. labor economy. We need each state to consider new legislation and regulation reform that will encourage additional apprenticeship programs at the college and adult education level. This means giving businesses, unions, and educational institutions incentives to collaborate and removing artificial regulatory walls that have in the past frustrated efforts to form or expand such important talent creation programs. (For more information on current registered apprenticeship programs across the 50 United States access: http://www.doleta.gov/OA/sainformation.cfm.)

Strengthen Teaching and School Leadership Education

The shining new academies we need will not come into existence without many better prepared master teachers who provide superior classroom instruction and principals who are effective leaders. Teachers need to be well-versed in their subject area of expertise and adept at using different instructional methods. Principals need to know how to lead a team of people in an educational setting, reach out to students and parents, and cope with organizational change. They themselves should be master teachers.[46]

McKinsey and Company studied the top 10 PISA-scoring school systems around the world to find out how to accomplish these goals. South Korea, Finland, and Singapore attract more of their society's best minds into teaching through a stringent selection and elongated education and training process. These nations recruit teachers from the top 5–30 percent of college undergraduates for rigorous, high quality, graduate teacher education programs. In contrast, the bulk of U.S. teachers come from the bottom third of their college class.

Better teachers take much longer to form. New teachers in South Korea, Finland, and Singapore start after obtaining graduate degrees and completing long teaching internships. In Finland, every school has a large number of special intervention teachers who act as tutors. These special tutors undertake an extra year of university study on individual tutoring methods to prepare them for this specialized instructional role. In contrast, most U.S. students begin teaching with undergraduate degrees that include short student teaching programs.[47]

South Korea, Finland, and Singapore also pay beginning teachers well by front-loading salaries so that they are comparable to those received by business school graduates. All these factors have, in turn, elevated the status of the teaching profession in the cultures of these nations.[48]

Outstanding school leadership is second only to quality classroom instruction as a key to improving student achievement. Yet, too much of principal development in the United States rests on studying the rules, regulations, and bureaucracy of education, not on mastering people management or team leadership. Too many principals are unable or unwilling to become good people managers, master learning-culture landmines, or strive for continuous improvement in an often hostile local culture. This is a big challenge.

In Singapore, a Leadership Assessment Center evaluates the core competencies and personality of each potential candidate for school principal. If passed, the candidate begins a rigorous six-month university program. Assessment continues throughout the process, washing out many trainees. At the end of the program, only a candidate who has fully mastered the principal leadership program is appointed to a school. These principals are trained to be both expert educators and expert people managers so that they can stimulate a much higher level of performance from both teachers and students.[49]

In South Korea, Finland, and Singapore, improving student performance comes from these policies that build greater teacher and principal competency. They focus on raising teacher and student motivation.[50] But are good teaching and management worth all this effort?

The Bill and Melinda Gates Foundation launched a three-year research study aimed at measuring effective teaching, because decades of research have suggested that teachers are the most important influence on student learning. The 2013 final report found that effective teachers both produce test score gains as well as improved student performance on cognitively challenging assignments.[51]

A December 2011 value-added study by three university economists at Harvard and Columbia found that variations in teacher quality have life-long impacts on students.

Replacing a poor elementary teacher with a good teacher, these economists found, would "increase the present value of students' lifetime income by some $267,000 per classroom taught."[52] Now, multiply that by a lifetime career of poor classroom teaching. Does this help you better focus on the catastrophic impact of poor teaching on our entire society and the future direction of the U.S. economy?

A Final Word

What is the good news regarding public policy and education? We don't need another panel of experts to write a report on how to save the U.S. education system. Many good solutions are already available.

The education public policy crisis is about our culture. We have exhausted all the incremental alternatives to real systemic change. The time has finally arrived to heed Winston Churchill's prophetic words, "America always does the right thing but only after it has exhausted all the alternatives."[53] Now is the time for America to do the right thing.

Call to Action

In this second decade of the 21st century, dramatic changes in the U.S. labor economy call for major updated government policies. We have suggested where some of these changes might begin. Government agencies at all levels need to better coordinate with RETAINS in rebuilding our talent creation system.

Multiple RETAINs across a region will help each state to develop and adopt locally appropriate new education and career training mandates, business regulations, and tax policies that support an increasingly tech-driven knowledge economy. Public sector partnering with RETAINs can ensure that local education policy is more fully integrated into larger economic growth by pursuing the following goals:

#1—Institute more effective K–12 school investment policies that produce higher literacy levels, higher quality liberal arts, humanities, and career education for a larger proportion of students.

#2—Develop business career education and training investment programs and encourage all employers to participate in workplace learning.

#3—Adopt talent creation as a major component of regional economic development and as an integral part of business short-term/long-term operations.

#4—Foster a culture among families, businesses, government agencies, and the community at large that esteems and promotes education, training, reskilling, and lifelong learning.

Almost 100 years ago, a true progressive era was bold in its efforts to establish America's first system of talent development. The United States became the first nation in history ever to make that effort for all its citizens. Its reforms resulted in a great era of prosperity for most Americans.

That era is now over. Shocking talent shortcomings are now apparent across America. We need more than incremental change. Public-private policy alliances can give us something much bolder—beginning today.

Chapter 10

Falling Off
the Talent Cliff

Human history becomes more and more a race between education and catastrophe.[1]

—H. G. Wells, *The Outline of History*

In 1983, President Ronald Reagan's National Commission on Excellence in Education warned in "A Nation at Risk: The Imperative for Educational Reform" that too many Americans no longer had the right skills to get a good job. This report generated great controversy. Many condemned it as a vicious attack on the education establishment. Yet, since that time almost every occupant of the Oval Office has proclaimed himself an "Education President" and vowed to address the rising tide of mediocrity engulfing our nation's schools.

For the past three decades, an endless stream of government, business, academic, and think tank reports, white papers, surveys, and books has debated this issue and proposed solutions. Meanwhile, hundreds of billions in additional funds have been spent at every level of American education on school reform.

Unfortunately, all these efforts have not solved the U.S. employment and skills crisis. Instead, America has reached the edge of a talent cliff. We simply have run out of enough skilled people. As our high tech infrastructure starts to fall apart, the American economy faces the risk of coming to a slow grinding halt.

Today, our society's talent deficit has reached that tipping point. We must take concerted national action in all 50 states if we are to win this skill war. Unfortunately, the current American mind-set promotes sacrificing the future for the sake of the present. Short-termism is pervasive, promoting entitlement spending in government and a focus on making the quarterly numbers in business. The "have it all today" mentality has undermined our sense of obligation to future generations.

Wall Street's culture remains fixated on short-term profit taking. This translates into business boardroom fears of falling out of favor with investment gurus if a company's quarterly numbers do not meet expectations.

In the past, the United States offered many people a beacon of hope for a better future. Generations of immigrants came here willing to sacrifice some of themselves to make that American dream a reality for their children. This important focus of American culture needs renewed emphasis.[2] Working together in our local communities, we can make the sacrifices it will take to better educate all our children and provide ongoing training to all our workers for a future of good jobs in a more prosperous United States.

The Structural Revolution

John E. Silvia, chief economist at Wells Fargo, posed the question, "Is there a 21st century job for the 20th century worker?"[3] For too many workers, unemployment is becoming increasingly structural. While the unemployment rate has improved somewhat, much of this is due to the huge decline in the U.S. labor participation rate. He ominously points out that this is particularly true for prime age workers—ages 25–54—among whom the labor participation rate has fallen 1.9 percentage points since the Great Recession began. Among the causes for this decline are the departure of discouraged workers with few skills or the wrong skills, early and escalating boomer retirements, and a sharp jump in workers collecting disability insurance. However, the unemployment rate of college-educated workers has been significantly lower than that of workers who lack a high school diploma. Since 2009, there has been an average gap of 10 percentage points between these two groups.[4]

For millions of U.S. workers, the current system offers little hope for a higher paying job. The cost of continuing education; the difficulty of juggling work, study, and family life; and the low wages of many entry level jobs; all conspire to lead Americans off the talent cliff.

The world is facing a novel talent problem at a global level. New ways of dealing with all the current economic challenges are needed. As Jeffrey Sachs, director of the Earth Institute at Columbia University has asserted, "New approaches must be long-term, structural, sensitive to inequalities of skills and education, aligned with the need for more sustainable technologies, and congruent with demographic needs."[5]

This book contends that Regional Talent Innovation Networks (RETAINs) are developing new leaders and providing some of these new approaches to solving the current structural employment crisis. Unfortunately, many Americans have not yet recognized the urgency of today's economic and social challenges. "Our institutions are addicted to incrementalism," world chess champion Garry Kasparov noted recently in an article coauthored by Peter Thiel, founder of Pay Pal. "The coming generation of leaders and creators will have to rekindle the spirit of risk. Real innovation is difficult and dangerous, but living without it is impossible."[6]

Workforce 2020 and Beyond

Unless steps are taken now to prepare more workers with the skills required for 21st-century jobs, projections indicate that shortages of skilled talent will worsen in the future, both because of skill gaps and demographic declines in many developed nations, including:

- The McKinsey Global Institute predicts a worldwide shortage of up 40 million college-educated workers by 2020 while up to 95 million workers will lack the skills requisite for employment. In addition, the developing countries will face shortages of 45 million workers with secondary and vocational degrees.[7]
- The International Center for Peace and Development forecasts by 2020 a shortage of 17 million working age people in the United States.[8]
- The World Economic Forum warns that due to baby boomer retirements and talent deficits, by 2030 the United States may experience a shortage of 25 million workers and Europe may lack 45 million workers.[9]

By 2020, the U.S. job market will be sharply and unevenly divided. Seventy-five percent of the available jobs will require higher skills and offer higher pay. Approximately, 122 million workers will be needed to fill them. Fifty-five million will be qualified with another 43 million semi-qualified (if further trained) to fill these positions (i.e., 98 million workers in all).

At the same time, only about 25 percent of the available jobs will need lower skills and offer lower pay. About 41 million workers will be needed. However, 64 million Americans will possess only low skills.

Several continuing educational deficits in 2020 will have a major negative effect on workforce quality:

- Seventy-three million low-literate adults (aged 25–65)
- One million high school dropouts annually
- Over 60 percent of K–12 students testing at below basic or at basic skill levels

What is the bottom line for talent in 2020, if the predictions are accurate? The United States can expect a skilled talent shortfall of between 14 and 25 million workers to fill new and replacement jobs. Between 2020 and 2030, the Boston Consulting Group predicts high to very high talent shortages across the United States in many economic sectors, including: IT, business services, health care, public administration, education, financial services, hotels and restaurants, transport, communications, trade, construction, manufacturing, utilities, and other businesses.[10]

"Moreover, while the intensifying competition for labor will predictably boost the wages of people with readily employable skills," forecasts economist/futurist, David Pearce Snyder, "it will also fuel wage inflation and increase the costs of a wide range of professional, commercial, and consumer services."[11]

Between 2013 and 2020, falling off the talent cliff will increase the risk of triggering many detrimental socioeconomic changes across America:

1. Ten to twenty percent of small to mid-size businesses may close due to lack of key talent.
2. Product/service quality may sharply decline as talent shortages increase.
3. Technical/professional services may be rationed for consumers.
4. Vacant high-skill jobs may migrate from the United States to other nations that develop more robust talent development systems.
5. The United States may lose its current dominance in IT, aerospace, the biosciences, new materials, and other high-tech industries.
6. New tech breakthroughs may increasingly occur outside the United States.
7. More Americans may be employed by foreign-owned businesses that were formerly American owned.
8. Many additional middle-range jobs may gradually disappear.
9. There is a major risk of the United States becoming a two-class society—
   a) Professionals/Managers/Technicians
   b) Low-Skill/Low-Wage Workers
10. The U.S. standard of living may stagnate or decline.

Such a scenario will devastate the entire economy and create an expanding poverty cycle. Unless a new talent creation system is in place by 2020 that has begun to alter those conditions, major social unrest across America will become a distinct possibility.

RETAINs—Hope for the Future

Knowing a new day has to dawn is not the same as being able to work together to make it happen. Communities only now are beginning to understand that they need to collaboratively design their own economic futures. Assuring a community's economic sustainability means designing a system that works: investing in the employment base by offering ongoing training/education updates to the current workforce, while restructuring the long-term system by better educating students for many different careers or new emerging career areas.

Civic activism has long been a hallmark of American culture. Business people, educators, union leaders, government officials, and community groups and organizations are working together to form RETAINs. The United States can move beyond the current job crisis into a decade of increased opportunity for those who are willing to form partnerships focused on developing the skills and education required for employment in a 21st-century global economy. We must act now before it is too late.

In cities and states across the United States, RETAINs show how communities have already begun rebuilding their talent creation systems. These local systems are being rewired for the talent revolution occurring from Santa Ana to North Dakota to Mansfield and North Carolina and beyond.

On the local and regional levels, economic development is merging with talent development. Communities are realizing that it's not good enough to embrace IT, green energy, health care, aerospace, and so on only by lowering taxes or maintaining a good physical infrastructure. If they haven't developed a renewed talent pipeline connecting skilled people to these business sectors, they have nothing. "The only sustainable way," stated Andreas Schleicher of the OECD, "is to grow our way out by giving more people the knowledge and skills to compete, collaborate and connect."[12]

We have seen how some dynamic RETAINs have already begun this rebuilding process. It is now a question of how fast we can scale up this RETAIN movement to address the talent transition for this new labor market era.

RETAINs give us a process to build a new community consensus that overcomes social decay by forming a more objective systemic solution. This teamwork orchestrates culture change. It harmonizes partner attitudes and expectation on what is both doable and necessary for a region's better economic health.

The economic dilemma the United States faces is that to pay for its structural deficits and remain competitive, private sector job growth is critical. RETAIN partnerships can help cut through the culture war by setting up the context for private sector risk taking and public community initiatives.

Economic pundit David Wessel offers this advice, "It's clear that future prosperity depends on the U.S.—its government, business, people, universities—coalescing behind a strategy for growth and creating incentives so talent and capital flow to promising sectors where the U.S. still has an edge in an increasingly competitive global economy."[13]

I predict that the economy of the United States will return to health after the wrenching transition of this talent crisis. The jobs revolution and economic growth will continue as a new talent system addresses the turmoil of technological change and social malaise. As an optimist, I believe that American society's greater flexibility and dynamism will prevail as it has in past eras. My hope is that *Future Jobs* will inspire people in many walks of life to take a proactive role in shaping that new jobs and talent era.

Appendix I

Career Analysis Scorecard

Directions: Use the rating scale below to rank the desirability of each specific occupation you are considering based on the nine following issues:

Occupation: _____

Occupational Desirability Rating Scale

Excellent	Very Good	Good	Fair	Poor
1	2	3	4	5

ISSUES:

1. Fit for your Personality and Interests
2. Minimum Education Required
3. Current/Future Growth Outlook
4. New Job Growth
5. Replacement Jobs
6. Entry Level Salary
7. Median Salary Level
8. Regional Location of Job
9. Desirability for Job Relocation

Total Score:

Training Return-on-Investment

Human Capital ROI Worksheet Example

I. Rationale

We have developed a Human Capital Nine-Step Worksheet model for human capital investment. To make these calculations, we have formulated a worksheet compatible with Excel so that any financial manager can do the calculations.

We believe that this worksheet will allow you to accurately estimate the monetary returns both before and after most training programs. It will allow any business to better calculate training cost as a business function. Every asset has a cost. Many in senior management envision a new policy of allocating new assets to solve priority problems and seize priority opportunities. By using the Human Capital Nine-Step Return-on-Investment (ROI) Worksheet as a more accurate measurement system, we can begin to convert training and development into a new asset—human capital.

II. ROI Inputs

Before you can begin the ROI calculations, you need to determine specific performance outcomes that will be reached by the proposed training and to obtain related internal general business operating data. You will need to answer the following questions:

1. What is the employee performance area that you have targeted for improvement and for which you want a ROI measure? There are four basic business productivity issues around which you can organize your financial measurements: quality (rework), time, costs, and output.

   You must be very careful to target a productivity issue that will respond to a performance improvement program involving skills, training, or education. Too often, a business misapplies a proposed training solution to issues aligned with organizational structure, technology applications, or personal leadership issues. A good up-front management analysis of these areas can help you decide what areas will respond better to management consulting, counseling, or coaching than to the learnable aspect of performance improvement programs.

2. What is the productivity target? The skill, training, or education program provider (internal/external) needs to give you his or her best estimate on the impact the specific program will have on this productivity issues. The provider should have enough prior experience to give you this estimate or run a trial pilot program to find out.

   Not all skill, training, or education programs are equal. Some are definitely more powerful in terms of results than others. The whole purpose of running the numbers for a Human Capital ROI is to find out which program alternatives will give you the most bang for the buck. This is very healthy for your business, because it forces education providers to give you their best effort and will better direct your investment capital to seek out and use realistic performance solutions.

3. How much gross revenue do the trainees now generate from their current work (in terms of the productivity area targeted)?

4. What is the value of outsourcing work in the area trained? (How much would it cost the firm to replace the target production?)

5. What are the total work hours for all employees being trained in the unit?

6. What is the company's or business unit's profit-range percentage on sales?

7. How many hours in the training program (work hours only)?

8. How many trainees are in the training program?

9. What is the trainee's productivity rate (percent) during the training? If training is done on employee time, the rage is 100 percent. If it is done entirely on company time, the rate is 0 percent.

III. Nine Steps to Success

After you have agreed on this information within your organization, the finance person can make the ROI computations for each program alternative. What follows is an outline of the nine steps found in our Human

Capital ROI Worksheet. (You can download the worksheet free of charge at http://www.imperialcorp.com/humanCapital.html.)

Step 1: What are the training costs per trainee (excluding trainee wages)?

Calculate all the direct costs associated with the training program. These include training materials (software, books, tests), conference fees, trainer's compensation, consultant fees, travel, meals, hotel rooms, proportional capital expenditure for distance learning system, and computer hardware equipment.

Step 2: What is the trainee's lost productivity while in training?

This is an important calculation and is used instead of trainee salary, since productivity loss should be much larger than salary loss if the training is done on company time.

Step 3: What is the cost of the training program?

Compute this by adding Step 1 and Step 2.

Step 4: What is the productivity benefit of the training?

The ROI is very sensitive to this estimate of the training effect on productivity. Here, you will estimate the expected hourly, weekly, or monthly productivity benefits per trainee. We use several different methods, ranging from establishing control training groups to using a linear regression formula.

Step 5: What is the (post-training) quality benefit from the training?

Step 6: What is the lifetime quality benefit from the training?

This is determined by deciding how long the training benefit will last (employee turnover, retooling schedule for a manufacturer, and other issues) and by using a discount rate formula to estimate the duration of the training's effect.

Step 7: What is the profit for each trainee?

Step 8: What are the benefits of the total training program?

Step 9: What is the Human Capital ROI?

Comprehensive Career Academies

Listed below are leading high schools that you may contact to learn more about their specific programs. Several professional associations are also included that can be of informational assistance.

1. National Career Academy Coalition
   Professional association website offers a wealth of information on career academy programs throughout the U.S.—http://www.ncacinc.com
2. Austin Polytechnical Academy, Chicago, IL
   Pre-Engineering and advanced manufacturing—http://www.austinpolytech.com
3. Bradley Tech High School, Milwaukee, WI
   Engineering, construction, communications, arts and design, and criminal justice—http://www5.milwaukee.k12.wi.us/school/bradleytech/
4. California Academy of Mathematics and Science, Carson, CA
   STEM-related careers—http://lbcams.schoolloop.com
5. Workforce Excellence, Coachella Valley, CA
   Programs in health care, advanced technologies, arts, media, and entertainment—http://smartstudentsgreatjobs.org
6. Center for Advanced Research and Technology (CART), San Joaquin, CA
   Professional sciences, global business, advanced communications, and engineering—http://www.cart.org
7. Cristo Rey, Chicago and 21 other U.S. cities
   STEM careers and global business—http://www.cristoreynetwork.org
8. Francis Tuttle Technology Center, Oklahoma City, OK
   Career programs include health science; IT; manufacturing; science, technology, engineering and math; transportation, distribution and logistics—http://www.francistuttle.edu
9. Hawthorn High School, Los Angeles, CA
   School of Manufacturing and Engineering—http://www.hhscougars.org

10. High School Inc. Academies at Valley High School, Santa Ana, CA
    Automotive, transportation and logistics, culinary arts, engineering and manufacturing, global business, health care, and new media—http://www.sausd.us/domain/3903

11. McKenzie Center for Innovation and Technology, Indianapolis, IN
    Biomedical science, business, pre-engineering, and robotics—http://mckenzie.ltschools.org

12. Minuteman Regional High School, Lexington, MA
    Biotech and biomanufacturing—http://www.minuteman.org

13. Philadelphia Academies, Inc.—The first career-academy high school (1968)
    Academy programs include automotive and mechanical engineering, process technology, applied electrical science, biotechnology, health and life sciences, business, and technology—http://www.academiesinc.org

14. San Clemente High School, San Clemente, CA
    Automotive Technology Partnership Academy—http://www.sctritons.com/auto

15. Walker Career Center, Indianapolis, IN
    Career programs include automotive services technology, biomedical sciences, computer networking, computer-aided drafting and design, dental careers, electronics and computer technology, health science education, and pre-engineering—http://wcc.warren.k12.in.us

16. Early College High Schools Initiative
    Early college high schools are a hybrid form of career academy that accelerates the high school program to move motivated students early into college credit programs, many with a career focus. Includes over 240 schools in 28 states. For more information visit http://www.earlycolleges.org
    Two examples are:
    1) DeVry University Advantage Academy High School, Chicago, IL—http://www.high-school.devry.edu/students/get-ready/advantage-academy.jsp
    2) Bard High School Early College, Manhattan and Queens, NY—http://www.bard.edu/bhsec/manhattan/ and http://www.bhsec.bard.edu/queens/

17. New Technology High School Network
    This 15-year-old network of 62 schools operates in 14 states. Each school uses project-based learning strategies and has a specific curricular focus, including STEM, global issues, and the environment—http://www.newtechnologynetwork.org

Notes

Introduction

1. David Pratt, comp., *The Impossible Takes a Little Longer: The 1,000 Wisest Things Ever Said by Nobel Prize Laureates* (New York: Walker & Company, 2007), 39.

2. Matt Ridley, "A Key Lesson of Adulthood: The Need to Unlearn," *Wall Street Journal*, February 5, 2011, http://online.wsj.com/article/.

3. "Economic Focus, Marathon Machine," *The Economist*, November 19, 2011, 84.

4. "Global Talent Risk—Seven Responses," World Economic Forum, 2011, 35, http://www3.weforum.org/docs/PS_WEF_GlobalTalentRisk_Report_2011.pdf.

5. Jeffrey Sachs, "Death by Strangling: The Demise of State Spending," *Financial Times*, December 16, 2011, 11; James Manyika, Susan Lund, Byron Auguste, Lenny Mendonca, Tim Welsh, and Sreenivas Ramaswamy, "An Economy That Works: Job Creation and America's Future," McKinsey Global Institute, June 2011, 60, http://www.mckinsey.com/insights/mgi/research/labor_markets/an_economy_that_works_for_us_job_creation.

6. John L. Petersen, "A New End, a New Beginning," in *Innovation and Creativity in a Complex World*, ed. Cynthia G. Wagner (Bethesda, MD: World Future Society, 2009), 427.

Chapter 1

1. George Seldes, ed., *The Great Quotations* (New York: Pocket Books, 1968), 989.

2. C. Brett Lockard and Michael Wolf, "Occupational Employment Projections to 2020,"*Monthly Labor Review* 135, no. 1 (2012): 84–108; Anthony P. Carnevale, Nicole Smith, and Michelle Melton, "STEM," Georgetown University Center on Education and the Workforce, October 2011, 21–22, http://cew.georgetown.edu/stem; "A Rising Role for IT: McKinsey Global Survey Results," *McKinsey Quarterly*, December 2011, https://www.mckinseyquarterly.com/PDFDownload.aspx?ar=2900; Kyle Stock, "The Best Technology Jobs outside Tech Companies," *Fins Technology*, June 14, 2011, http://it-jobs.fins.com/Articles/SB130633935414018881/The-Best-Technology-Jobs-Outside-Tech-Companies (accessed August 30, 2012); Jon Hilsenrath and Sara Murray, "Foreign Shocks Temper America's Export-Led Rebound," *Wall Street Journal*, March 28, 2011, A2; Martin Feldstein, "A Falling Dollar Will Mean a Faster U.S. Recovery," *Wall Street Journal*, August 1, 2011, A13.

3. "The Ongoing Impact of the Recession Series," *SHRM*, http://www.shrm.org/Research/SurveyFindings/ (accessed August 15, 2012); Ann Fisher, "10 Hot Careers for

2012—and Beyond," *CNN Money*, December 27, 2011, http://management.fortune.cnn.com/2011/12/27/10-hot-careers-for-2012-and-beyond/.

4. Anthony P. Carnevale, Tamara Jayasundera, and Ban Cheah, "The College Advantage: Weathering the Economic Storm," Georgetown University Center on Education and the Workforce, August 15, 2012, 1–5, http://cew.georgetown.edu/collegeadvantage.

5. Laurence Shatkin, "Looking for a STEM Career? Try These Top Five Jobs," *JIST Publishing*, February 28, 2012, http://jist.emcpublishingllc.com/page-jist/looking-for-a-stem-career-try-these-top-five-jobs/; Keith Cline, "The 5 Hardest Jobs to Fill in 2012," Inc.com, December 19, 2011, http://www.inc.com/keith-cline/talent-shortages-in-2012.html; Claire Bradley, "7 Jobs Companies Are Desperate to Fill," *Yahoo Finance*, September 1, 2010, http://finance.yahoo.com/news/pf_article_110533.html; Joseph Walker, "What 'Big Data' Means for Your Career," *FINS Morning Coffee*, February 13, 2012, http://it-jobs.fins.com/Articles/SB0001424052970204795304577220952801376194/What-Big-Data-Means-for-Your-Career; Greg Lamm, "Average Greater Seattle Area Tech Salary Now Tops $90,000 a Year," *Puget Sound Business Journal*, January 2, 2012, http://www.bizjournals.com/seattle/blog/techflash/2012/01/seattle-tech-workers-averaged-5-raise.html; John Bedecarre and Scott Olster, "Fastest Growing Jobs in America," *CNN Money*, September 3, 2010, http://money.cnn.com/galleries/2102/pf/1009/gallery.jobs_future.fortune/index.html; Tapan Munroe, *Innovation: Key to America's Prosperity and Job Growth* (North Charleston, SC: CreateSpace, 2012), 135–138.

Chapter 2

1. Peggy Anderson, ed., *Great Quotes from Great Leaders* (Lombard, IL: Celebrating Excellence Publishing, 1990), 104.

2. Bonnie Miller, "For Young Adults, Future Interrupted," *Chicago Tribune*, July 15, 2012, 1, 13; Don Peck, *Pinched: How the Great Recession Has Narrowed Our Futures and What We Can Do about It* (New York: Crown Publishers, 2011), 70; Diane Stafford, "Historically Tough Market Takes High Toll on Teen Jobs," *Chicago Tribune*, July 2, 2012, 6; Catherine Rampell, "More Young Americans out of High School Are Also out of Work," *New York Times*, June 6, 2012, B1, B6; Nathaniel Penn, "Hello, Cruel World," *New York Times Magazine*, March 25, 2012, 45; Manuel Valdes, Travis Loller, Cristina Silva, and Sandra Chereb, "Half of New College Grads Remain Jobless or Unemployed," PJStar.com, last modified April 22, 2012, http://www.pjstar.com/free/x1364623101/Half-of-new-college-grads-are-currently-jobless-or-underemployed.

3. E.S. Browning, "Oldest Baby Boomers Face Jobs Bust," *Wall Street Journal*, December 12, 2011, A1, A16; Emy Sok, "Record Unemployment among Older Workers Does Not Keep Them out of the Job Market," *Issues in Labor Statistics*, March 2010, http://bls.gov/opub/ils/summary_10_04/older_workers.htm.

4. Andrea Coombes, "For Older Workers, Here Is Where the Jobs Will Be," *Wall Street Journal*, October 22, 2012, R4.

5. "Transitioning into Retirement: The MetLife Study of Baby Boomers at 65," April 2012, 5, https://www.metlife.com/research/transitioning-retirement.html.

6. Chardie L. Baird, Stephanie W. Burge, and John R. Reynolds, "Absurdly Ambitious? Teenagers Expectations for the Future and the Realities of Social Structure," *Sociology Compass* 2, no. 3 (2008): 947.

7. Edward E. Gordon, "Future Jobs for Gen Y: Career Planning Is Vital (What Questions to Ask)," *Encyclopaedia Britannica Blog*, May 27, 2010, http://www.britannica.com/

blogs/2010/05/future-jobs-for-gen-y-career-planning-is-vital-what-questions-to-ask; Nicholas Lore, *The Pathfinder, How to Choose or Change Your Career for a Lifetime of Satisfaction and Success* (New York: Touchstone-Simon and Schuster, 2011), 22, 229.

8. Quoted in Evans Clinchy, "Who Is out of Step with Whom?" *Education Week*, February 4, 1998, 48.

9. *Career Outlook in the US* explanation of the Interest Profiler categories:

Realistic: People with *Realistic* interests like work activities that include practical, hands-on problems, and solutions. They enjoy dealing with plants, animals, and real-world materials, such as wood, tools, and machinery. They enjoy outside work. Often, people with *Realistic* interests do not like occupations that mainly involve doing paperwork or working closely with others. **Enterprising:** People with *Enterprising* interests like work activities that have to do with starting up and carrying out projects, especially business ventures. They like persuading and leading people and making decisions. They like taking risks for profit. These people prefer action rather than thought. **Investigative:** People with *Investigative* interests like work activities that have to do with ideas and thinking more than with physical activity. They like to search for facts and figure out problems mentally rather than to persuade or lead people. **Artistic:** People with *Artistic* interests like work activities that deal with the artistic side of things, such as forms, designs, and patterns. They like self-expression in their work. They prefer settings where work can be done without following a clear set of rules. **Social:** People with *Social* interests like work activities that assist others and promote learning and personal development. They prefer to communicate more than to work with objects, machines, or data. They like to teach, to give advice, to help, or otherwise be of service to people. **Conventional:** People with *Conventional* interests like work activities that follow set procedures and routines. They prefer working with data and detail more than with ideas. They prefer work where the lines of authority are clear. Another important source of information for careers is the U.S. Department of Labor's *Occupational Outlook Handbook*, issued annually. It is available online at http://bls.gov/ooh. For each occupation, this resource includes a description of it, the education required, median pay, and the growth outlook. All this information can be accessed in a variety of ways on the website.

10. Richard Perez-Pena, "Benefits of College Degree in Recession Are Outlined," *New York Times*, January 10, 2013, A15.

11. U.S. Census Bureau, "What It's Worth: Field of Training and Economic Status in 2009," February 2012, 2.

12. U.S. Census Bureau, "*What It's Worth*," 1–13; Marjorie Connelly, Marina Stefan, and Andrea Kayda, "Is It Worth It?" *New Times Education Life*, July 22, 2012, 31; Anthony P. Carnevale, Ben Cheah, and Jeff Strohl, "Hard Times," Georgetown University Center on Education and the Workforce, January 4, 2012, 5, http://cew.georgetown.edu/unemployment.

13. Quoted in Reeve Hamilton, "Efforts Are under Way to Tie College to Job Needs," *New York Times*, January 12, 2012, http://www.nytimes.com/2012/01/13/.

14. Quoted in Adam Rodewald, "More College Grads Return for a Technical Education," *Northwestern* (Oshkosh, WI), May 12, 2012, C10.

15. Hannah Seligson, "The Jobless Young Find Their Voice," *New York Times*, May 6, 2012, 1, 6.

16. Vivek Wadhwa, "Silicon Valley Needs Humanities Students," *Washington Post*, May 17, 2012, http://www.washingtonpost.com/national/on-innovations/.

17. Rex W. Huppke, "Seeking Job That's a Calling Can Be Hang-Up," *Chicago Tribune*, May 28, 2012, 1, 5; David Brooks, "The Service Patch," *New York Times*, May 25, 2012, A25.

18. Lauren Weber, "Colleges Get Career-Minded," *Wall Street Journal*, May 22, 2012, A3; The website internships.com offers over 50,000 internships from more than 20,000 organizations located in almost 8,000 cities across all 50 states of America. Some are paid. Companies offer both full-time and part-time internships. Some internships can also include college credit.

Chapter 3

1. Ashok Divakaran, Matt Mani, and Laird Post, "Building a Global Talent Pipeline: Finding, Developing and Retaining Tomorrow's Manufacturing Workforce," Booz & Company, June 11, 2012, http://www.booz.com/global/home/what_we_think/reports_and_white_papers/ic-display/50643956.

2. Mortimer Zuckerman, "Unemployment is Still the Biggest Election Issue," *Wall Street Journal*, July 24, 2012, A15.

3. William Poundstone, "Unleashing the Power," review of *Turing's Cathedral: The Origins of the Digital Universe* by George Dyson, *New York Times* (Sunday Book Review), May 6, 2012, 21.

4. Gordon, *Winning the Global Talent Showdown*, 9.

5. Quoted in Alejandra Cancino, "Education Concerns Business Leaders," *Chicago Tribune*, August 10, 2012, 1.

6. "Global Manufacturing Outlook 2012: Fostering Growth through Innovation," KPMG Research Report, KMPG International Corporation, June 4, 2012, 3.

7. Michael S. Malone, "The Sources of the Next American Boom," *Wall Street Journal*, July 6, 2012, A13; Mark P. Mills and Julio M. Ottino, "The Coming Tech-Led Boom," *Wall Street Journal*, January 30, 2012, A15; "Tanks in the Cloud," *The Economist*, January 2, 2011, 49–50; Sruthi Ramakrishnan and Neha Alawadhi, "A Printer on the Make," *Chicago Tribune*, September 28, 2012, 3; James R. Hagerty and Mike Imada, "A New Face for Robotic Factory Workers," *Wall Street Journal*, May 31, 2012, B4; Timothy Hay, "The Robots Are Coming to Hospitals," *Wall Street Journal*, March 15, 2012, B12.

8. "Transitioning into Retirement: The MetLife Study of Baby Boomers at 65," 1–23; Monica Davey, "Many Workers in Public Service Retiring Sooner," *New York Times*, December 6, 2011, A1, A18; Joshua M. Fanzel and Paul J. Yakoboski, "2012 Retirement Confidence Survey of the State and Local Government Workforce," Center for State and Local Government Excellence and TIAA-CREF Institute, July 2012, 1–5; David Brauer, "CBO's Labor Force Projections through 2021," Congressional Budget Office, March 22, 2011, 3, http://www.cbo.gov/publication/22011; Floyd Norris, "The Number of Those Working Past 65 Is at a Record High," *New York Times*, May 19, 2012, B3.

9. Quoted in Alicia Clegg, "How to Help the Aged at Work," *Financial Times*, July 26, 2012, 10.

10. Robert I. Lerman, "Are Skills the Problem?," in A *Future of Good Jobs? America's Challenge in the Global Economy*, ed. Timothy J. Bartik and Susan N. Houseman (Kalamazoo, MI: W. E. Upjohn Institute for Employment Research, 2008), 29.

11. Anthony P. Carnevale, Nicole Smith, and Jeff Strohl, "Help Wanted: Projections of Jobs and Education Requirements through 2018," Center on Education and the Workforce, Georgetown University, 2010, 1–5, http://cew.georgetown.edu/jobs2018; Anthony P. Carnevale and Stephen J. Rose, "The Undereducated American," Center on Education and the Workforce, Georgetown University, 2011, 1, 10.http://cew.georgetown.edu/undereducated/.

12. David Neumark, Hans P. Johnson, and Marisol Cuellar Mejia, "Future Skill Shortages in the U.S. Economy?" National Bureau of Economic Research, NBER Working Paper No. 17213, 2011, 1–5, http://www.nber.org/papers/w17213.

13. Barbara Kiviat, "The Big Jobs Myth: American Workers Aren't Ready for American Jobs," *The Atlantic*, July 25, 2012, http://www.theatlantic.com/business/archive/2012/07/the-big-jobs-myth-american-workers-arent-ready-for-american-jobs/260169; R. Jason Faberman and Bhashkar Mazumder, "Is There a Skills Mismatch in the Labor Market?" *Chicago Fed Letter*, No. 300, July 2012, 1–4.

14. Carnevale, "The College Advantage," 5; David Hogberg, "Obama Approval on Economy Not Fine, as Job Woes Grow," *Investor's Business Daily*, June 12, 2012, A1.

15. John E. Silvia, "Government Spending: Three Faces of Change," *Wells Fargo Economics Group Newsletter*, March 7, 2013, 4.

16. Ben Casselman, "Help Wanted: In Unexpected Finish, Some Skilled Jobs Go Begging," *Wall Street Journal*, November 26, 2011, A1; Robert J. Samuelson, "The Great Jobs Mismatch," *Washington Post*, June 19, 2011, http://www.washingtonpost.com/opinions/.

17. Manyika et al., "An Economy that Works," 77; "Companies Worldwide Struggle to Attract and Retain Critical-Skill and High-Potential Employees, Towers Watson Survey Finds," Towers Watson, September 19, 2012, http://www.towerswatson.com/press/8012.

18. "Leading Indicators of National Employment Reports," Society for Human Resource Management (SHRM), January 2010–April 2012.

19. Jennifer Schramm, "A Growing Divide," *HR Magazine*, October 2011, 120.

20. "Risk Index 2011: Economist Intelligence Unit Executive Summary," Lloyd's of London, 8, http://www.lloyds.com/news-and-insight/risk-insight/lloyds-risk-index (accessed October 29, 2012).

21. "Global Talent Shortage Worries Multinationals," Metlife Press Releases, June 1, 2012, http://www.metlife.com/about/press-room/us-press-releases/index.html?compID=82451.

22. "Global Talent Risk—Seven Reponses, 7; Daniel Schafer, "Bosch Set to Expand Workforce by 16,500," *Financial Times*, January 27, 2011, 18; Rick Miner, "People without Jobs—Jobs without People: Canada's Labour Market Future," ABC Life Literacy Canada, March 2010, 18, http://abclifeliteracy.ca/files/People-without-jobs-Canada.pdf.

23. Manpower Group, "'Manufacturing' Talent for the Human Age," May 2011, 2, www.experis.in/Whitepaper/2011_ManufacturingTalent.pdf.

24. Manpower Group, "2012 Talent Shortage Survey Research Results," 1,10, www.manpowergroup.us/campaigns/talent-shortage-2012/.

25. Manpower Group, "Break the Crisis and Complacency Cycle and Build the Right Workforce," May 29, 2012, 2012, http://www.manpowergroup.com/investors/releasedetail.cfm?releaseid=677538 (accessed October 29).

26. Monica Mourshed, Diana Farrell, and Dominic Barton, "Education to Employment: Designing a System that Works," McKinsey & Company, December 2012, 18, http://mckinseyonsociety.com/Education-to-Employment/Report/.

27. "Young Adults Give Low Marks to High Schools," *Education Week*, April 27, 2011, 12.

28. Quoted in Alejandra Cancino, "Education Concerns Business Leaders," *Chicago Tribune*, August 10, 2012, 1.

29. Quoted in Jim Redden, "Intel Warns Business Alliance: State Must Value Education," *Portland Tribune*, April 18, 2011, http://portlandtribune.com/pt/9-news/5474-intel-warn-business-alliance-state-must-value-education.

30. "BHEF to Help Launch Business and Industry STEM Education Coalition," Business–Higher Education Forum, March 5, 2010, http://www.bhef.com/news/news releases/2010/BISEC.asp.

31. Quoted in Cancino, "Education Concerns Business Leaders," 1.

32. David Langdon, George McKittrick, David Beede, Beethika Khan, and Mark Doms, "STEM: Good Jobs Now and for the Future," (Executive Summary). U.S. Department of Commerce, Economics and Statistics Administration, ESA Issue Brief #03–11, July 2011, 1–10.

33. Anthony P. Carnevale, Nicole Smith, and Michelle Melton, "STEM: Executive Summary," Georgetown University Center on Education and the Workforce, October, 2011, 5, http://cew.georgetown.edu/stem/.

34. Christopher J. Gearon, "Jobs in Health Care on the Rise," *Chicago Tribune Business*, May 30, 2011, 21; Sarah Mann, "Addressing the Physician Shortage under Reform," Association of American Medical Colleges Reporter, April 2011, http://www.aamc.org/newsroom/reporter/april11/184178/addressing_the-physician_shortage_under_reform.html; Darrell G. Kirch, "How to Fix the Doctor Shortage," *Wall Street Journal*, January 5, 2010, A17; Suzanne Sataline and Shirley S. Wang, "Medical Schools Can't Keep Up," *Wall Street Journal*, April 13, 2010, A3; Anemona Hartocollis, "After Years of Quiet, Expecting a Surge in U.S. Medical Schools," *New York Times*, February 15, 2010, A1, A13; Annie Lawrey and Robert Pear, "Doctor Shortage Likely to Worsen with Health Law," *New York Times*, July 20, 2012, A1, A20.

35. "Nursing Shortage Fact Sheet, American Association of Colleges of Nursing," Updated August 6, 2012, http://www.aacn.nche.edu/media-relations/fact-sheets/nursing-shortage; "More Young People Are Becoming Nurses," *Rand News Report*, December 5, 2011, http://www.rand.org/news/press/2011/12/05.html.

36. Kevin Murphy, "Kansas Trying to Fill Gaping Shortage," *Chicago Tribune*, May 2, 2012, 14; "Shortage Designation: Health Professional Shortage Area & Medically Underserved Areas/Populations," HRSA Health Professions, http://bhpr.hrsa.gov/shortage/ (accessed October 29, 2012); "Millions in U.S. Lack Access to Dentists," WebMD, July 13, 2011, http://www.webmd.com/oral-health/news/20110713/millions-in-us-lack-access-to-dentists.

37. Joseph Walker, "How Google Finds New Recruits," Fins IT Jobs, June 3, 2011, http://it-jobs.fins.com/Articles/SB130642885529019387/How-Google-Finds-New-Recruits; Jessica Gwynn, "High-Tech Industry on Hiring Binge in California: Google, Facebook and Zynga Lead the Pack," *Los Angeles Times* (Business), March 25, 2011, 1; Thomas L. Friedman, "Do You Want the Good News First?" *New York Times* (Sunday Review), May 20, 2012, 1, 7; Brad Smith, "How to Reduce America's Talent Deficit," *Wall Street Journal*, October 19, 2012, A13.

38. "They're Hiring!" *CNN Money*, August 1, 2011, http://money.cnn.com/galleries/2011/fortune/1105/gallery.fortune500_most_hiring.fortune/13.html; Justin Lahart and James R. Hagerty, "Where Have America's Jobs Gone?" *Wall Street Journal*, July 12, 2011, B1.

39. Paul McDougall, "Microsoft IT Hiring Problems Bogus, Say Programmers," Information Week, August 4, 2011, http://www.informationweek.com/windows/microsoft-news/microsoft-it-hiring-problems-bogus-say-p/231300189; Jamie Eckle, "Career Watch: Misleading Government Stats on IT Employment," *Computerworld*, April 18, 2011, http://www.computerworld.com/s/article/355798/Career_Watch_Misleading_government_stats_on_IT-employment; Patrick Thibodeau, "Gartner Upbeat on Big Data Jobs," *Computerworld*, November 5, 2012, http://www.computerworld.com/s/article/9233216/Gartner_upbeat_on_big_data_jobs.

40. Christopher Drew, "Deliveries Up, Boeing Beats Forecast of Analysts," *New York Times*, July 26, 2012, B3.

41. Quoted in Hal Weitzman, "Concern as Baby-Boomers Prepare for Retirement," *Financial Times*, March 1, 2010, 21.

42. Quoted in Hal Weitzman, "Aging Workforce Creates Skills Shortages for US Manufacturers," *Financial Times*, March 1, 2010, 17.

43. Jeremy Lemer, "Manufacturing Backlog Set to Hamper Airlines' Plans to Re-Fleet," *Financial Times*, July 18, 2011, 18.

44. Edward E. Gordon, *Skill Wars: Winning the Battle for Productivity and Profit* (Boston, MA: Butterworth-Heinemann, 2000), 213–214.

45. Quoted in Jeremy Lemer, "Boeing 787 Risks Further Setbacks," *Financial Times*, November 13–14, 2010, 9.

46. Hal Weitzman, "US Skills Gap Set to Worsen with Passing of 'Baby Boomers,'" *Financial Times*, September 9, 2011, 17.

47. Quoted in Ed Crooks, "Riveting Prospects," *Financial Times*, January 7, 2011, 7.

48. "The Future of Manufacturing Opportunities to Drive Economic Growth," World Economic Forum, Deloitte Touche Tohmatsu Limited, April 2012, 4.

49. "Make: An American Manufacturing Movement," Council on Competitiveness, December 2011, 8, 9, http://www.compete.org/publications/detail/2064/make/; James R. Hagerty, "Help Wanted on Factory Floor," *Wall Street Journal*, May 6, 2011, A1, A12.

50. Adam Davidson, "Empire of the In-Between," *New York Times Magazine*, November 4, 2012, 32.

51. "Workforce Trends: Tools for Taking Control of Today's Skilled Labor Shortage," Advanced Technology Services (ATS), April 2011, 9, http://www2advancedtech.com/Portals/180468/docs/Workforce%20Trends_LR_994.pdf.

52. Joyce Gioia, "Growing Global Demand for Engineers," Herman Trend Alert, December 5, 2012, http://www.hermangroup.com/alert/archives_12-5-2012.html.

53. Tom Morrison, Bob Maciejewski, Craig Giffi, Emily Stover DeRocco, Jennifer McNelly, and Gardner Carrick, "Boiling Point? The Skills Gap in U.S. Manufacturing," Deloitte and the Manufacturing Institute, October 2011, 2, http://www.themanufacturinginstitute.org/Research/Skills-Gap-in-Manufacturing/2011-Skills-Gap-Report/2011-Skills-Gap-Report.aspx.

54. "Skills Gap in U.S. Manufacturing Is Less Pervasive Than Many Believe," Boston Consulting Group, October 14, 2012, http://www.bcg.com/media/PressReleaseDetails.aspx?id=tcm:12-118945.

55. Paul Davidson, "Tool and Die Makers Desperately Casting for Workers," *USA Today*, April 17, 2012, http://usatoday30.usatoday.com/money/economy/story/2012-04-12/

economic-recovery-manufacturing-revival/54365676/1; Linda Hall and Bobby Warren, "Scarcity of Skilled Labor: Area Manufacturers Have Difficulty Filling Positions," *Daily Record* (Wooster, OH), July 29, 2012, http://www.the-daily-record.com/local%20news/2012/07/29; Author interview with Dan Phillip, Executive Director of Transformation Network, Ashland, OH, August, 2012.

56. Adam Davidson, "Skills Don't Pay the Bills, *New York Times Magazine*, November 25, 2010, 16.

57. Emily Maltby and Sarah E. Needleman, "Small Firms Seek Skilled Workers but Can't Find Any," *Wall Street Journal*, July 26, 2012, B1.

58. Quoted in Timothy R. Homan, "Workers Lacking Skills Hinder More Factory Gains: Economy," *Bloomberg*, May 14, 2012, http://www.bloomberg.com/news/2012–05–14/workers-lacking-skills-hinder-more-u-s-factory-gains-economy.html.

59. "Workforce Trends," 7.

60. Harold L. Sirkin, Michael Zinser, Douglas Hohner, and Justin Rose, "U.S. Manufacturing Nears the Tipping Point," The Boston Consulting Group, March 2012, 12, http://www.bcgperspectives.com/Images/BCG_US_Manufacturing_Nears_the_Tipping_Point_Mar_2012_tcm80–100657.pdf; Harold L. Sirkin, Michael Zinser, and Douglas Hohner, "Made in America, Again," The Boston Consulting Group, August 2011, 3–14, http://www.bcg.com/documents/file84771.pdf.

61. Author Interview with Harry C. Moser, President, Reshoring Initiatives, August 10, 2012; Elizabeth G. Olson, "Banging the Drum to Bring Jobs Back Home," *CNN Money*, July 22, 2011, http://finance.fortune.cnn.com/2011/07/22/banging-the-drum-to-bring-jobs-back-home/.

62. Cancino, "Education Concerns Business Leaders.," 1.

63. John Ferreira and Mike Heilala, "Manufacturing's Secret Shift: Gaining Competitive Advantage by Getting Closer to the Customer," Accenture, 2011, http://www.accenture.com/SiteCollectionDocuments/PDF/Accenture_Manufacturings_Secret_Shift.pdf.

64. James R. Hagerty, "Some Firms Opt to Bring Manufacturing Back to U.S.," *Wall Street Journal*, July 18, 2012, B8.

65. "Reshoring of Some Chinese Manufacturing Jobs Becoming Likely as Cost Gap is Expected to Shrink to Just 16 Percent Next Year," The Hackett Group, May 24, 2012, http://www.thehackettgroup.com/about/research-alerts-press-releases/2012/05242012-reshoring-some-chinese-manufacturing-jobs.jsp.

66. Quoted in Edward Luce, "Why the US Is Looking to Germany for Answers," *Financial Times*, April 15, 2013, 11.

Chapter 4

1. Quoted in "Mr. Segway's Difficult Path," *The Economist*, June 10, 2010, www.economist.com/node/1695592.

2. Sam Leith, "Science Friction," *Financial Times* (Life and Arts), May 9–10, 2009, 1.

3. Brian L. Yoder, "Engineering by the Numbers," American Society for Engineering Education, http://www.asee.org/papers-and-publications/publications/college-profiles/2011-profile-engineering-statistics.pdf (accessed October 30, 2012); "Women and Information

Technology by the Numbers," National Center for Women and Information Technology, http://ncwit.org/sites/default/files/legacy/pdf/ByTheNumbers09.pdf (accessed October 30, 2010); David Beede, Tiffany Julian, David Langdon, George McKittrick, Beethika Khan, and Mark Doms, "Women in STEM: A Gender Gap to Innovation, Economics and Statistics Administration, August 3, 2011, http://www.esa.doc.gov/Reports/women-stem-gender-gap-innovation.

4. Quoted in Maija Palmer, "'Geeky' World of IT Loses Its Appeal as a Career Choice," *Financial Times*, July 6, 2011, 6.

5. Quoted in Richard Waters, "Enthusiasts Experiment on Turning Teenagers into Scientists," *Financial Times*, December 14, 2011, 6.

6. Kenneth B. Hoyt, *Career Education: History and Future* (Tulsa, OK: National Career Development Association, 2005), 148–149; Robert Reich, "General Motors Holds a Mirror Up to America," *Financial Times*, June 1, 2009, 7; Matt McGrath, "Boomers in IT: Will the Talent Shortage Affect Techies?," *Certification Magazine*, March 2008, http://www.certmag.com/read.php?in=3336.

7. Nathan Koppel, "Law School Loses Its Allure as Jobs at Firms Are Scarce," *Wall Street Journal*, March 17, 2011, A4.

8. Marissa Garff, "Focusing on Talent Trends," *T & D* (American Society for Training and Development), March 20, 2012, 18; Alice Kwan, Jeff Schwartz, and Andrew Liakopoulos, "Talent Edge 2020: Redrafting Talent Strategies for the Uneven Recovery," Deloitte University Press, January 2012, 1–14; Thomas A. Hemphill and Mark J. Perry, "U.S. Manufacturing and the Skills Crisis," *Wall Street Journal*, February 27, 2012, A13.

9. Steve Lohr, "G.E. Goes With What It Knows: Making Stuff," *New York Times* (Sunday Business), December 5, 2010, 1, 6–7.

10. Jennifer Schramm, "Undereducated," *HR Magazine* (Society for Human Resource Management), September 2011, 136.

11. "ATS Survey Underscores Critical Need for Skilled Workers at U.S. Factories as Baby Boomers Retire," Reuters, March 23, 2011, http://www.reuters.com/article/2011/03/23/idUS158451+23-Mar-2011+PRN20110323.

12. Ben Baden, "Jobs Go Unfulfilled as Skills Fall Flat," *Chicago Tribune*, December 5, 2011, 1, 4.

13. Robert Terry, "Workplaces Must Learn How to Transfer Training," *Financial Times*, December 12, 2011, 11.

14. Quoted in Jane Bird, "Skilled Staff Are Harder to Find than Ever," *Financial Times*, January 26, 2011, 3.

15. "Mid-Market Perspectives: 2012 Report on America's Economic Engine," Deloitte, 2, 40.

16. Quoted in Catherine Rampell, "Companies Spend on Equipment, Workers," *New York Times*, June 10, 2011, A1, A3.

17. John Irons, "Investments as Percentage of GDP," Economic Policy Institute, 2011, 9, http://www.epi.org/publication/11-telling-charts-about-2011-economy/; "Hard Times, Lean Firms," *The Economist*, December 31, 2011, 48; Gillian Tett, "U.S. Companies' Dash for Cash that Heralds Painful Freeze," *Financial Times*, July 13, 2012, 20.

18. Craig Barrett, "Why America Needs to Open Its Doors Wide to Foreign Talent," *Financial Times*, July 31, 2006, 15.

19. Neil G. Ruiz, Jill H. Wilson, and Shyamali Choudhury, "The Search for Skills: Demand for H-1B Immigrant Workers in U.S. Metropolitan Areas," *Brookings Institution Report*, July 18, 2012, http://www.brookings.edu/research/reports/2012/07/18-h1b-visas-labor-immigration; Miriam Jordan, "Slump Sinks Visa Program," *Wall Street Journal*, October 29, 2009, http://online.wsj.com/article/SB125677268735914549.hmtl (accessed July 5, 2011).

20. Alan Beattie, "When is a BRIC not a BRIC? When It's a Victim," *Financial Times*, January 22–23, 2011, 9.

21. John Authors, "BRIC-Like Branding is a Dangerous Path to Take," *Financial Times*, January 22–23, 2011, 18; Martin Wolf, "Big Test for the 'Great Convergence,'" *Financial Times*, October 17, 2007, 13.

22. Sundeep Tucker, "A Bidding War Makes for 'Crazy' Salaries across Asia," *Financial Times*, May 7, 2007, 7; Guy De Jonquires, "Asia Cannot Fill the World's Skills Gap," *Financial Times*, June 13, 2006, 15.

23. Martin Wolf, "How China Should Rule the World," *Financial Times*, March 23, 2010, 11; "Economic Focus-Parallel Economics," *The Economist*, January 1, 2011, 70.

24. Carl E. Walter and Fraser J. T. Howie, *Red Capitalism* (Singapore: John Wiley & Sons (Asia), 2011), 27–29; Jason Dean, Andrew Browne, and Shai Oster, "China's 'State Capitalism' Sparks a Global Backlash," *Wall Street Journal*, November 16, 2010, A1, A18.

25. Chris Patten, "The Life and Soul of the Party," *Financial Times*, May 29, 2010, 13. "Let a Million Flowers Bloom," *The Economist*, March 12, 2011, 79.

26. Robert DiCianni, "2011 Steel Industry Outlook," Paper presented at the 2011 Economic Outlook Conference, December 3, 2010, at the Federal Reserve Bank of Chicago; Robert Guy Matthews, "For Global Steel Industry, China Poses Guessing Game," *Wall Street Journal*, May 24, 2011, B1; "The Rise of the Hybrid Company," *The Economist*, December 5, 2009, 78.

27. Quoted in Todd Woody, "In the Future, Already Behind," *New York Times*, October 13, 2010, B1–B4.

28. Leslie Hook, "Beijing Raises Security Spending," *Financial Times*, March 7, 2011, 5; "China's Security State: The Truncheon Budget," *The Economist*, March 12, 2011, 48; Sharon LaFraniere and David Barboza, "China Tightens Censorship of Electronic Communications," *New York Times*, March 22, 2011, A5; Loretta Chao, "Google Objects to China's Acts," *Wall Street Journal*, March 22, 2011, B3; Michael Kan, "China Closes 130,000 Internet Cafes as It Seeks More Control," Computerworld, March 18, 2011, http://www.computerworld.com/s/article/9214762/China_closes_130_000_Internet_cafes_as_it_seeks_more_control.

29. Chris Patten, "Life and Soul of the Party," *Financial Times* (Life & Arts), May 29, 2010, 13; Michael Wines, "China Fortifies State Businesses to Find Growth," *New York Times*, August 30, 2010, A6; Robert O. Paxton, *The Anatomy of Fascism* (New York: Alfred A. Knopf, 2004), 59, 70, 137, 145, 152, 179–181, 186, 232–233.

30. Quoted in Jamil Anderlini, "Rise of China's Economy Signals Shift in Power," *Financial Times*, August 17, 2010, 2.

31. Yasheng Huang, "Reform the Private Sector," *New York Times*, December 2, 2010, http://www.nytimes.com/roomfordebate.

32. Peter Hessler, *Country Driving* (New York: Harper/Harper Collins Publishers, 2010), 92.

33. David Barboza, "From Low Cost to High Value," *New York Times*, September 16, 2010, B1; Richard Read, "As U.S. Jobs Stagger, China Deals with Labor Shortage," *The Oregonian*, March 6, 2010, http://www.oregonlive.com/business/index.ssf/2010/03/as_us_jobs_stagger.

34. Rahul Jacob and Patti Waldmeir, "Workers Call the Tune in China," *Financial Times*, February 22, 2011, 3; Keith Bradsher, "Chinese Plants Starting to Feel Labor Shortage," *New York Times*, February 27, 2010, A1; Sharon LaFraniere, "As China Ages, Birthrate Policy May Prove Difficult to Reverse," *New York Times*, April 7, 2011, A4, A9.

35. Quoted in "Lack of Talent Stifles Progress," *Eastday*, October 23, 2010, http://english.eastday.com/e/101023/u1a5508241.html.

36. "The Technology Industry: Different Strokes," *The Economist*, October 7, 2006, 72–73; Graeme Maxton, "Not Enough People in China," *The Economist: The World in 2008*, November 15, 2007, 128; Tom Mitchell, "China's 'Workshop of the World' Suffers Acute Labor Shortages," *Financial Times*, February 26, 2010, 1; Lisa Thomas, "Chinese Growth Revives War for Talent," *Financial Times*, March 9, 2010, 2.

37. "Struggle to Retain Staff in China," *Financial Times*, September 1, 2006, 2; Nicolas Timmins, "Employers Suffer Talent Shortages," *Financial Times*, October 20, 2006, 6; "Briefing Manpower—The World of Work," *The Economist*, January 6, 2007, 57–58.

38. Diana Farrell, Martha Laboissiere, Jaeson Rosenfeld, Sascha Sturze, and Fusayo Umezawa, "The Emerging Global Labor Market: Part II—The Supply of Offshore Talent in Services," McKinsey Global Institute, June 2005, 24, http://www.mckinsey.com/mgi/reports/pdfs/emerginggloballabormarket/part2/MGI_supply_fullreport.pdf.

39. Gary Gereffi and Vivek Wadhwa, "Framing the Engineering Outsourcing Debate: Placing the United States on a Level Playing Field with China and India," Duke University School of Engineering, December 2005, 2, 5, 9; Gary Gereffi, Vivek Wadhwa, and Ben Rissing, "Framing the Engineering Outsourcing Debate: Comparing the Quantity and Quality of Engineering Graduates in the United States, India, and China," Paper prepared for the SASE Conference, Trier, Germany, June 30–July 2, 2006, 13–14.

40. "Survey of the World Economy 2006," *The Economist*, 14.

41. Diana Farrell and Andrew Grant, "Addressing China's Looming Talent Shortage," McKinsey & Company, October 2005, 9.

42. Martin Wolf, "A Colossus with Feet of Clay," *Financial Times*, January 24, 2007, 6.

43. Quoted in Andrew Jacobs, "China's Army of Graduates Is Struggling," *New York Times*, December 12, 2010, A1, A12.

44. "Talent War in China Intensifies in Face of Surging Consumer Demand," Global Talent Strategy, August 10, 2012, http://globaltalentstrategy.com/en/article/talent-war-in-china-intensifies-in-face-of-surging-consumer-demand-257.

45. Jun Wang, "The Return of the 'Sea Turtles': Reverse Brain Drain to China," *China Daily*, September 27, 2005, http://www.chinadaily.com.cn/english/doc2005–09/27content_481163.htm; Don Lee, "Returning Chinese Find a Tough Market," *Los Angeles Times*, March 5, 2006, C1, C5; "Silicon Valley Deportation Order," *The Economist*, April 28, 2007, 38; "Opening the Doors: A Survey of Talent," *The Economist*, October 7, 2006, 13; "Torn Between the Claims of Two Generations," *Financial Times*, June 9, 2005, 11; Don Lee, "Research Follows Factories to China," *Los Angeles Times*, January 14, 2007, C10; Peter Cochrane, "The Reverse Brain Drain that Fuelled China's Rise," *Financial Times*, May 9, 2007, 2; Sharon LaFraniere,

"After a Long Brain Drain, China Is Luring Some Scientists Home," *New York Times*, January 7, 2010, A1, A8; Michael Pettis, "China Has Been Misread by Bulls and Bears Alike," *Financial Times*, February 26, 2010, 11; David Wessel, "China's Economy Faces Three Contradictions," *Wall Street Journal*, June 16, 2011, A15.

46. Ian Johnson, "Wary of Future, Professionals Leave China in Record Numbers," *New York Times*, November 1, 2012, A1, A3; "China Creates New Visa Category to Attract Overseas Talent," Global Talent Strategy, August 10, 2012, http://globaltalentstrategy.com/en/article/china-creates-new-visa-category-to-attract-overseas-talent-256.

47. Aaron Back and Esther Fung, "China Scraps Property Data, Clouding View," *Wall Street Journal*, February 17, 2011, A8; "Rabbit in the Headlights," *Financial Times* (The Lex Column), July 21, 2011, 12.

48. David Barboza and Kevin Drew, "Security Firm Sees Global Cyberspying," *New York Times*, August 4, 2011, A11.

49. Quoted in Elizabeth Bumiller, "US Official Warns about China's Military Buildup," *New York Times*, August 25, 2011, A12.

50. David E. Sanger, David Barboza, and Nicole Perlroth, "China's Army Seen as Tied to Hacking against U.S.," *New York Times*, February 19, 2013, A1, A9.

51. "China's Online Thieves," *Wall Street Journal*, February 20, 2013, A14.

52. Edward Wong, "Outrage Grows over Air Pollution," *New York Times*, December 11, 2011, A11; Jamil Anderlini, "Beijing 'Airpocalyse' Drives Expatriate Exodus," *Financial Times*, April 2, 2013, 5; "Leaving Asia's Shade," *The Economist*, July 24, 2010, 46; "Climate Change in Black and White," *The Economist*, February 19, 2011, 89; Shai Oster, "Floating Garbage Chokes Major Chinese Dam," *Wall Street Journal*, August 2, 2010, http://www.online.wsj.com/article; "A Golf Craze in Beijing—A Course by Any Other Name," *The Economist*, February 19, 2011, 42.

53. Kazunori Takada, "Costs, Property Rights Top Issues for U.S. Firms in China: Survey," *Reuters*, February 15, 2012, http://www.reuters.com/article/2012/02/15/.

54. Paul J. Davies, "Theft Should Not Be Part of the Deal," *Financial Times*, May 2, 2011, 4.

55. Melanie Lee, "China Retailers Also Cloning the Concept," *Chicago Tribune*, August 2, 2011, 3; Laurie Burkitt and Loretta Chao, "Made in China: Fake Stores," *Wall Street Journal*, August 3, 2011, B1.

56. Quoted in Guy Dinmore and Geoff Dyer, "Immelt Hits out at China and Obama," *Financial Times*, July 1, 2010, http://www.ft.com/intl/cms/s/0/ed654fac-8518–11df-adfa-00144feabc0.html.

57. James McGregor, "China's Drive for 'Indigenous Innovation': A Web of Industrial Policies," U.S. Chamber of Commerce, http://www.uschamber.com/reports/chinas-drive-indigenous-innovation-web-industrial-policies (accessed February 28, 2013).

58. U.S. International Trade Commission, "China: Effects of Intellectual Property, Infringement and Indigenous Innovation Policies on the U.S. Economy," May 2011, XIV, http://www.usitc.gov/publications/332/pub4226.pdf.

59. Jamie F. Metzl, "China's Threat to World Order," *Wall Street Journal*, August 17, 2011, A13/

60. "China to Nurture 7 New Strategic Industries in 2011–15," Gov.cn, October 27, 2010, http://english.gov.cn/2010–10/27/content_1731802.htm; Xu Liyan and Qiu Jing,

"Beyond Factory Floor: China's Plan to Nurture Talent," YaleGlobal Online, September 10, 2012, http://yaleglobal.yale.edu/content/beyond-factory-floor-chinas-plan-nurture-talent.

61. Geoff Dyer, "The Soap Opera of China's Housing Boom," *Financial Times*, July 7, 2010, 9; Geoff Dyer, "Slowing Property Market Tests Beijing's Nerve," *Financial Times*, July 17, 2010, 10; Martin Wolf, "How China Must Change If It Is to Sustain Its Ascent," *Financial Times*, September 22, 2010, 11; George Dyer, "Beijing Urged to Act Over Property Bubble," *Financial Times*, June 1, 2010, 1; Bob Davis, "The Great Property Bubble of China May Be Popping," *Wall Street Journal*, June 9, 2011, A1; Tom Orlik, "China Tallies Local Debt," *Wall Street Journal*, June 28, 2011, A10.

62. Quoted in Jamil Anderlini, "China Told Backlash Is Brewing on Growth," *Financial Times*, December 24, 2010, 2.

63. Quoted in Peter Marsh, "High and Dry," *Financial Times*, April 13, 2011, 7.

64. "Taming Leviathan: A Special Report on the Future of the State," *The Economist*, March 19, 2011, 10–12, 14; David Pilling, "Could China's Rulers Be Right to Be Jittery?," *Financial Times*, February 24, 2011, 9; Joseph Nye, "China's Century Is Not Yet upon Us," *Financial Times*, May 19, 2011, 11; David Barboza, "China's Inflation Poses Big Threat to Global Trade," *The New York Times*, April 18, 2011, A1, A9.

65. Jeremy Page, "China Leaders Laud 'Red' Campaign," *Wall Street Journal*, June 20, 2011, A7.

66. Quoted in Peter Stein, "Chinese Firms Need to Open Up Books," *Wall Street Journal*, June 20, 2011, C3.

67. China Merchants Bank and Bain & Company, "2011China Private Wealth Report," April 2011, 37–39, http://www.bain.com/Images/2011_China_wealth_management_report. pdf; "China's Rich People: 'So Long, and Thanks for All the Fortune!'" *Shanhaiist*, April 28, 2011, http://shanghaiist.com/2011/04/28/chinas_rich_people_so_long_and_than.php.

68. David Pilling, "China Crashes into a Middle Class Revolt," *Financial Times*, August 4, 2011, 7; Jason Dean and Jeremy Page, "Trouble on the China Express," *Wall Street Journal*, July 30–31, 2011, C1–C2; "China's Crackdown," *The Economist*, April 16, 2011, 12; Geoff Dyer and David Pilling, "Economic and Political Potholes Face a Nation Taking a Global Lead," *Financial Times*, November 23, 2010, 9; Author Interviews, 2006–2012, U.S.-China business experts in economics, finance, manufacturing, political-social growth policies, and workforce issues have been used throughout this entire review of China. For security reasons these sources will remain anonymous.

69. Quoted in Paul Beckett, "In India, Doubts Gather over Rising Giant's Course," *Wall Street Journal*, March 30, 2011, A16.

70. Tripti Lahiri, "India Passes 1.2 Billion Mark," *Wall Street Journal*, April 1, 2011, 15; Robyn Meredith, *The Elephant and the Dragon* (New York: W. W. Norton & Company, 2007), 132–133; Amy Yee, "Learning Difficulty," *Financial Times* (Special Report: The New India), May 27, 2009, 31.

71. Geeta Anand, "India Graduates Millions, but Too Few Are Fit to Hire," *Wall Street Journal*, April 5, 2011, A1; Joe Leahy, "Scarcity of U.S. Engineers behind Hiring From India, Says Jobs Group," *Financial Times*, September 2, 2010, 2.

72. "National IT/ITeS Employability Study," Aspiring Minds, August 2010, 1–4, http:// www.aspiringminds.in/docs/National_IT_ITeS_Employability_Study.pdf; "The Engineering Gap," *The Economist*, January 30, 2010, 76; NASSCOM-Kinsey Report 2005, "Extending

India's Leadership of the Global IT and BPO Industries," McKinsey Global Institute, 2005, http://www.nasscom.in/upload/10142Mckinsey_study-2005.pdf; "A Bumpier but Freer Road," *The Economist*, October 2, 2010, 76; Anand, "India Graduates Millions," A12.

73. Pratham Annual Status of Education Report, 2010, http://images2.asercentre.org/aserrepots/ASER_2010_National_highlights.pdf; Liam Julian, "Subcontinental Divide," *The Education Gadfly*, January 24, 2008, http://www.edexcellence.net/commentary/education-gadfly-weekly/2008/january-24/subcontinental-divide-1.html; Meredith, *Elephant*, 128, 156; India's illiteracy is so pervasive that Citigroup rolled out a network of biometric automatic cash machines that will recognize account holder's thumbprints and have color-coded screen instructions and voiceovers to guide illiterates through transactions. Joe Leahy, "Citigroup Gives India's Poor a Hand with Thumbprint ATMs," *Financial Times*, December 3, 2006, 1; Krishna Pokharel, "India Mandates Children Go to School," *Wall Street Journal*, April 2, 2010, A9; "Reaching the Poorest," *The Economist*, January 23, 2010, 58; James Lamont, "Roads and Teachers Crucial for Rising Star," *Financial Times* (Special Report—The World 2011), January 26, 2011, 10.

74. Vikas Bajaj, "Skipping over Rote in Indian Schools," *New York Times*, February 18, 2011, B1.

75. Yee, "Learning Difficulty," 32; Amy Kazmin, "Growing Pains as India Rushes into Business Education," *Financial Times* (Business Education Special Report), September 20, 2010, http://www.ft.com/intl/cms/s/2/189809fe-c0aa-11df-94f9–00144feab49a.html; Anjli Raval, "A Gateway of Opportunity for the Intellectual Elite of India," *Financial Times*, June 7, 2010, 10; Arlene Chang, "India Moves Ahead with Foreign-School Plan," *Wall Street Journal*, March 16, 2010, A17; K. N. Panikkar, "India: Foreign Universities Bill Needs to Be Revised," *University World News*, April 17, 2011, http://www.universityworldnews.com/article.php?story=20110415195834460; "Global Talent Risk—Seven Responses," World Economic Forum, 2011, 24; James Lamont, "Country Reaches out for Talent and Money," *Financial Times*, January 20, 2010, 4; Heather Timmons, "Some Indians Find It Tough to Go Home Again," *New York Times*, November 28, 2009, B2.

76. Quoted in Amy Kazmin, "Search for a Workable Solution," *Financial Times*, August 31, 2010, 10.

77. Quoted in Amy Kazmin, "Labour to Unlock," *Financial Times*, October 15, 2010, 11.

78. James Lamont, "Basic Services in Urban India Remain a Work in Progress," *Financial Times*, October 9, 2010, 2; Leslie Hook and Amy Kazmin, "Indian Workers Are Not Ready to Seize the Baton," *Financial Times*, September 14, 2010, 2; James Lamont, "India Struggles to Cap Wage Inflation amid Skills Shortage," *Financial Times*, May 13, 2011, 4; Patrick Barta and Krishna Pokharel, "Megacities Threaten to Choke India," *Wall Street Journal*, May 13, 2009, A1, A16; "An Elephant, Not a Tiger," *The Economist* (A Special Report on India), December 13, 2008, 11–12, 18.

79. Quoted in James Lamont and James Fontanella-Khan, "Writing Is on the Wall," *Financial Times*, March 22, 2011, 7.

80. "A Rotten State," *The Economist*, March 12, 2011, 18; Heather Timmons, "India Finds Corruption in Fast-Growing Aviation Industry," *New York Times*, April 24, 2011, 12; Banyan, "The Indian Exception," *The Economist*, April 2, 2011, 40; Gideon Rachman, "Indian Democracy Has an Ugly Side," *Financial Times*, May 9, 2009, 11; "A Million Rupees Now," *The Economist*, March 12, 2011, 47; Banyan, "The Hindu Rate of Self-Deprecation,"

The Economist, April 23, 2011, 47; Gurcharan Das, "India Says No to $80 Toilet Paper," *Wall Street Journal*, September 3–4, 2011, C2.

81. Quoted in Amol Sharma, "India's Tata Finds Home Hostile," *Wall Street Journal*, April 13, 2011, B1.

82. Amy Kazmin, "India Promises Broad Reform to Reduce Graft," *Financial Times*, February 22, 2011, 3; "Fling Wide the Gates," *The Economist*, April 16, 2011, 16.

83. Michael Spacek, "India's Enduring Naxalite Insurgency," *World Politics Review*, February 22, 2011, http://worldpoliticsreview.com/articles/7948/indias-enduring-naxalite-insurgency; Jim Yardley, "Rebels Widen Deadly Reach across India," *New York Times*, November 1, 2009, 16; James Lamont, "Premier Fine-Tunes Fight against Rebels," *Financial Times*, February 10, 2010, 4.

84. Tom Wright and Harsh Gupta, "India's Boom Bypasses Rural Poor," *Wall Street Journal*, April 30–May 1, 2011, A1, A12.

85. Quoted in Lydia Polgreen, "Turnaround of India State Could Serve as a Model," *New York Times*, April 11, 2010, 5.

86. Martin Wolf, "How India Must Change If It Is to Be an Advanced Economy," *Financial Times*, July 8, 2009, 9; "One More Push," *The Economist*, July 23, 2011, 10; "The Half-Finished Revolution," *The Economist*, July 23, 2011, 59; David Wessel, "The Shifting Demographics Driving Nation's Wealth," *Wall Street Journal*, August 12, 2010, A4; *India 2039: An Affluent Society in One Generation*, Asian Development Bank, 2009, 1–49.

87. "China Philharmonic Orchestra," *Palm Springs Friends of Philharmonic Program*, April 19, 2011, 7–8.

88. James Lamont, "India Struggles to Cap Wage Inflation amid Skills Shortage," *Financial Times*, May 13, 2011, 4; Matthew Vincent, "Big Macs and Big Wages," *Financial Times Wealth*, May 2011, 34.

89. Jamil Anderlini, "China's Army of Migrant Workers Grows Restless," *Financial Times*, June 18–19, 2011, 2.

90. David Barboza, "China's Boom is Beginning to Show Cracks, Analysts Say," *New York Times*, June 21, 2011, B8; Simon Rabinovitch, "Emphasis on Explicit Debt Hide Extent of Beijing's Local Liabilities," *Financial Times*, June 28, 2011, 3.

91. Quoted in Jamil Anderlini, "A Long Cycle Nears Its End," *Financial Times*, July 2–3, 2011, 5.

92. Michael Pettis, "China's Economy Is Headed for a Slowdown," *Wall Street Journal*, August 10, 2011, A13; David Pilling, "China Crashes into a Middle Class Revolt," *Financial Times*, August 4, 2011, 7.

93. George Magnus, "China Can Yet Avoid a Middle-Income Trap," *Financial Times*, June 30, 2011, 11.

94. *Financial Times*, June 23, 2011, 3; Joe Leahy, "A Nation Develops," *Financial Times*, January 11, 2010, 12; Schumpter, "Bamboo Innovation," *The Economist*, May 7, 2011, 23.

95. "Global Talent Risk—Seven Responses," 16.

96. Vivek Wadhwa, Anna Lee Saxenian, Richard Freeman, and Alex Salkever, "Losing the World's Best and Brightest: America's New Immigrant Entrepreneurs," Part V, Ewing Marmon Kauffman Foundation, March 2009, 7, http://www.kauffman.ord/uploadedFiles/ResearchAndPolicy/Losing_the_World's_Best_and_Brightest.pdf.

97. Xinhua News Net, March 18, 2010 and March 3, 2011.

98. Quoted in Joe Light, "Movers Pick Up China Business," *Wall Street Journal*, July 5, 2011, B8.

99. Vivek Wadhwa, Sonali Jain, AnnaLee Saxenian, Gary Gereffi, and Huiyao Wang, "The Grass Is Indeed Greener in India and China for Returnee Entrepreneurs, America's New Immigrant Entrepreneurs," Part VI, Kauffman Foundation, April 2011, 5, http://www .kauffman.org/uploaded/grass-is-greener-for-returnee-entrepreneurs.

100. "STEM," Executive Summary, 8.

101. Peter Cappelli, "Bring Back the Organization Man," *Harvard Business Review* (blog), March 15, 2012, http://blogs.hbr.org/cs/2012/03/bring_back_the_organization_ma.html.

102. Quoted in E. J. Dionne, Jr., "This Country Needs a Better Ruling Class," *Desert Sun* (Palm Springs, CA), April 18, 2011, B7.

103. Barack Obama, "Remarks by the President in Back to School Speech in Philadelphia, Pennsylvania," The White House, September 14, 2010, http://www.white house.gov/the-press-office/2010/09/14/remarks-president-back-school-speech-philadelphia-pennsylvania.

Chapter 5

1. Eric A. Hanushek, Paul E. Peterson, and Ludger Woessmann, "Achievement Growth: International and U.S. State Trends in Student Performance," Harvard Kennedy School, July 2012, x, http://www. hks.harvard.edu/pepg/PDF/Papers/PEPG12-03_CatchingUp.pdf.

2. Quoted in "Gates Says Higher Education Is Crucial to Landing Decent Job," *Chicago Tribune*, July 29, 2011, 13.

3. "The Global Competitiveness Index 2012–13: Country Profile Highlights," World Economic Forum, 3, http://www3.weforum.org/docs/CSI/2012–13/GCR_CountryHigh lights_2012–13.pdf (accessed November 30, 2012).

4. Peck, *Pinched*, 174.

5. "Education at a Glance 2012: Highlights," OECD, 13, http://www.oecd.org/edu/ highlights.pdf (accessed November 30, 2012).

6. "Rising Above the Gathering Storm: Energizing and Employing America for a Bright Economic Future," Executive Summary, National Academy of Sciences, 2007, 1, http://nap.edu/catalog/11463.html.

7. Hanushek, "Achievement Growth," 3–5.

8. Paul E. Peterson, Ludger Woessmann, Eric A. Hanushek, and Carlos X. Lastra-Anadón, "Globally Challenged: Are U.S. Students Ready to Compete?" Harvard Kennedy School, PEPG Report No. 11–03, August 2011, v-viii, http://www.hks.harvard/edu/pepg/ PDF/Papers/PEPG11–03_GloballyChallenged.pdf.

9. "Trends in International Math and Science Scores," *Straight A's*, Alliance for Excellent Education, January 14, 2013, 5, http://www.all4ed.org/publication_material/straight_ as/01142013#4; Motoko Rich, "U.S. Students Still Lag Globally in Math and Science, Tests Show," *New York Times*, December 11, 2012, A13.

10. Quoted in Erik W. Robelen, "High Achievers Scarce in Math, Science in U.S.," *Education Week*, January 12, 2011, 14.

11. Michael J. Petrilli and Janie Scull, "American Achievement in International Perspective," Thomas B. Fordham Institute, March 2011, 3–14, http://www.edexcellence.net/ publications/american-achievement-in.html.

12. "The Economic Impact of the Achievement Gap in America's Schools," McKinsey and Company, Social Sector Office, April 2009, 17, http://mckinseyonsociety.com/down loads/reports/Education/achievement_gap_report.pdf.

13. Ibid. 5.

14. "The Nation's Report Card: Mathematics 2011," National Center for Education Statistics, U.S. Department of Education, 2012, NCES 2012–458, 24, 49; "The Nation's Report Card: Reading 2011," National Center for Education Statistics, U.S. Department of Education, 2012, NCES 2012–457, 23, 52.

15. "Statement by U.S. Secretary Arne Duncan on NSEP Reading and Math 2011 Results," Ed.gov, November 1, 2011, http://www.ed.gov/news/press-releases/statement-us-secretary-education-arne-duncan-naep-reading-and-math-2011-results.

16. "The Nation's Report Card: Science 2009," National Center for Education Statistics, U.S. Department of Education, 2012, NCES 2011–451, 1; "The Nation's Report Card: Science 2011," National Center for Education Statistics, U.S. Department of Education, 2012, NCES 2012–465, 1; Sam Dillon, "Few Students Show Proficiency in Science, Federal Tests Show," *New York Times*, January 26, 2011, A13.

17. "Catching Up to College and Career Readiness," ACT, 2012, 5, http://www.act.org/research/policymakers/pdf/CatchingUpToCCR.pdf.

18. Adeshina Emmanuel, "Those 857 Desks? A Message for the Candidates," *New York Times*, June 21, 2012, A18. The one million dropout figure is based on a seven-hour school day and a 180 day school year; J. D. LaRock, "Education at a Glance: OECD Indicators 2012 United States," September 2012, http://oecd.org/education/CN-UnitedStates.pdf.

19. Lesli A. Maxwell, "States Mull Obama's Call to Raise Compulsory Attendance Age," *Education Week*, February 8, 2012, 18.

20. "Diplomas Count 2012: Trailing Behind, Moving Forward," Press Release of *Education Week*, and Education Research Center, June 7, 2012, http://www.edweek.org/go/dc12.

21. Robert Balfanz, John M. Bridgeland, Mary Bruce, and Joanna Hornig Fox, "Building a Good Nation: Progress and Challenge in Ending the High School Dropout Epidemic," America's Promise Alliance, March 2012, 1–3, http://www.americaspromise.org/our-work/grad-nation/building-a-grad-nation.aspx; George P. Shultz and Eric A. Hanushek, "Education is the Key to a Healthy Economy," *Wall Street Journal*, May 1, 2012, A15.

22. James J. Heckman and Paul A. LaFontaine, "The Declining American High School Graduation Rate: Evidence, Sources, and Consequences," *VOX*, February 13, 2008, http://www.voxeu.org/article/educated-america-college-graduates-and-high-school-dropouts.

23. Caleb Rossiter, "How Washington, D.C., Schools Cheat Their Students Twice," *Wall Street Journal*, December 1, 2012, A13.

24. Christina Theokas, "Shut out of the Military," The Education Trust, December 2010, 1–6. http://www.edtrust.org//sites/edtrust.org/files/publications/files/ASVAP_4.pdf.

25. Quoted in Christine Armario and Dorie Turner, "AP NewsBreak: Nearly 1 in 4 Fails Military Exam," *Seattle Times*, December 21, 2010, http://seattletimes.nwsource.com/html/nationworld/2013729556_apusmilitaryexam.html.

26. "The Condition of College and Career Readiness 2012," ACT, (American College Testing Service), 1–13, http:/www.act.org/research-policy/college-career-readiness-report-2012/; "A First Look at the Common Core and College and Career Readiness," ACT, 2010, 5–7, http://www.act.org/research/policymakers/pdf/FirstLook.pdf; Catherine

Gewertz, "More Students Meet ACT's College-Readiness Benchmarks," *Education Week*, August 24, 2011, 8.

27. "SAT Scores 1990–2010," National Center for Education Statistics, U.S. Department of Education, 2011, http://nces.ed.gov/fastfacts/display.asp?id=171; Stephanie Banchero, "SAT Reading, Writing Scores Hit Low," *Wall Street Journal*, September 15, 2011, A2; Lyndsey Layton and Emma Brown, "SAT Reading Scores Hit a Four-Decade Low," *Washington Post*, September 24, 2012, http://www.washingtonpost.com/local/education.

28. "SAT Report: Only 43 Percent of 2012 College-Bound Seniors Are College Ready," College Board, September 24, 2012, http://press.collegeboard.org/releases/2012/sat-report-only-43-peercent-2012-college-bound-seniors-ready.

29. "Saving Now and Saving Later: How High School Reform Can Reduce the Nation's Wasted Remediation Dollars," Alliance for Excellent Education, Issue Brief, May 2011, 1–3, http://www.all4ed.org/files/SavingNowSavingLaterRemediation.pdf.

30. Barton Kunstler, "An Educational Approach for an Era of Profound Technological Change," in *Foresight, Innovation, and Strategy: Toward a Wiser Future*, ed. Cynthia G. Wagner (Bethesda, MD: World Future Society, 2005); Lerman, "Are Skills the Problem?," 68; David Brooks, "The Cognitive Age," *New York Times*, May 2, 2008, http://www.nytimes.com/2008/05/02/opinion/02brooks.html; Gordon, *2010 Meltdown*, 231.

31. James J. Heckman and Dimitriy V. Masterov, "The Productivity Argument for Investing in Young Children," Working Paper 5, Invest in Kids Working Group, Committee for Economic Development, October 4, 2004, 1, http://jenni.uchicago.edu/Invest/.

32. Quoted in Jeremy Greenfield, "Talent Mismatch Drives Unemployment Shift," Tech Job Watch, May 19, 2011, http://it-jobs.fins.com/Articles/SB130582127624517313/Talent-Mismatch-Drives-Unemployment-Shift.

33. Scott Thurm and Pui-Wing Tam, "California's Boom Masks State's Uneven Recovery," *Wall Street Journal*, August 16, 2012, A1, A8.

34. "The Pernicious Job Gap," *Chicago Tribune*, September 3, 2012, http://articles.chicagotribune.com/2012-09-03/opinion.

35. "The State We're in 2012," *Advance Illinois*, November 2012, http://www.advanceillinois.org/filebom/swi_2012/Adv_Ill_Report_Card-Nov12.pdf.

36. Nikki Kalio, "The Softer Side of Manufacturing," *Insight on Manufacturing*, November 2012, 11.

37. Wendy Kopp, "Chicago Is a Symbol of America's Education Crisis," *Financial Times*, September 14, 2012, 9.

Chapter 6

1. Richard Melson, "Editorial Reviews: The 2010 Meltdown," Cambridge Forecast Group, December 5, 2005, http://www.cambridgeforecast.org/MIDDLEEAST/2010-MELTDOWN.html (accessed April 27, 2008).

2. Edward E. Gordon, "An Unheralded Job Success Story: North Dakota's Full Employment Strategy," *Encyclopaedia Britannica Blog*, October 13, 2011, http://www.britannica.com/blogs/2011/10/unheralded-job-success-story-north-dakotas-full-employment-strategy/.

3. Robert D. Putnam, *Bowling Alone: The Collapse and Revival of American Community* (New York: Simon and Schuster, 2000), 287; Gordon, *2010 Meltdown*, 190.

4. Putnam, *Bowling Alone*, 380, 382–384, 389, 393, 397; Fred Siegel, "Twilight of the Left," review of I *Am the Change: Barack Obama and the Crisis of Liberalism* by Charles R. Kesler, *Wall Street Journal*, September 11, 2012, A11.

5. Randall A. Yagiela, "Accelerate Community Success through Interdependent Leadership," *Solutions*, November/December 2011, http://www.gettheprofessionaledge.com

6. Robert N. Bellah, Richard Madsen, William M. Sullivan, Ann Swidler, and Steven M. Tipton, *Habits of the Heart, Individualism and Commitment in American Life* (Los Angeles: University of California Press, 1996), 38.

7. "The Tussle for Talent," *The Economist*, January 8, 2011, 68; Peter Senge, Bryan Smith, Nina Kruschwitz, Joe Laur, and Sara Schley, *The Necessary Revolution: How Individuals and Organizations Are Working Together to Create a Sustainable Workforce* (New York: Doubleday, 2008), 78.

8. Gary Paul Green, "Workforce Development Networks in Rural Areas of the United States," SR Policy Series, Southern Rural Development Center, September 2003, No. 1, 2, http://sdrc.msstate.edu/publications/other/2003_09_1-workforce.pdf; Todd Greene, "Everything Must Change: Rethinking Workforce Development," Partners Update, Federal Reserve Bank of Atlanta, March/April 2012, http://www.frbatlanta.org/pubs/partnersupdate/12no2_greene_workforce_development.cfm; Mona Mourshed, Diana Farrell, and Dominic Barton, "Education to Employment: Designing a System that Works," McKinsey & Company, December 2012, 89, 91–97, http://mckinseyonsociety.com/education-to-employment/report/.

9. Randy Yagiela, "Welcome" (Current News), *Transformation Times News*, January 2013, 1.

10. Author interview with Robert Zettler, May 1, 2012.

11. Richard Hofstadter, *The Age of Reform* (New York: Vintage Books, 1955), 16, 215.

12. Luke Johnson, "Founders: The Public Sector Needs Your Help," *Financial Times*, January 23, 2013, 10.

13. Author interview with Darcy Bucholz, Executive Director, Boone and Winnebago Counties Workforce Investment Board, May 10, 2011.

14. Author interview with Laurie Preece, Executive Director, Alignment Rockford, September 18, 2012.

15. Joel Kotkin, "The Kids Will Be Alright," *Wall Street Journal*, January 23–24, 2010, W9.

Chapter 7

1. Author interview with Robert Zettler, Workforce Consultant for the Richland County (OH) Commissioners, May 1, 2012.

2. Author interview with Cathie Olsky, March 28, 2012.

3. Author interview with Dale Ward, September 10, 2012; Dale Ward, "Voices Heard," *Santa Ana 2011 Community Guide and Business Directory*, Santa Ana Chamber of Commerce, 21–23; Gordon, *2010 Meltdown*, 109–113; Gordon, *Winning*, 151–153.

4. *OECD Territorial Reviews: The Chicago Tri-State Metropolitan Area, United States* (Paris: OEDC, 2012), 15, 18.

5. "CWICstats Dashboard Report 2nd Quarter 2012," Chicago Workforce Investment Council, 2012, 1, 3. http://www.chapinhall.org/sites/default/files/CWIC%20Quarterly%Dashboard%Report%202012%20Q2.pdf.

6. Jonathan Rothwell, "Education, Job Openings, and Unemployment in Metropolitan America," Brookings Institution, August 29, 2012, http://www.brookings.edu/research/papers/2012/08/29-education-gap-rothwell.

7. Quoted in Thomas L. Friedman, "A Progressive in the Age of Austerity," *New York Times*, October 6, 2011, 11.

8. Jeff Coen, David Heinzmann, and John Chase, "Emanuel's Push for More Charter Schools in Full Swing," *Chicago Tribune*, September 24, 2012, 1, 8; Gordon, *2010 Meltdown*, 206–207.

9. Gordon, *Winning*, 121; "Driving Innovation in Illinois by Increasing STEM Attainment," *World Business Chicago*, June 2012, http://www.worldbusinesschicago.com/news/illinois-innovation-index-june-2012; "Congratulations Class of 2012," Austin Polytechnical Academy, July 6, 2012, http://austinpolytech.org/congratulations-class-2012; "Austin Manufacturing Training Center," Austin Polytechnical Academy, http://www.austinpolytech.org/austin-manufacturing-training-center (accessed January 2, 2013); Dan Swinney, "The Polytechnical Model of Education," Center for Labor and Community Research, June 21, 2012, http://www.clcr.org/newweb/up-content/uploads/2012/10/polytech-model.pdf.

10. Quoted in "The Next (Regenerative) Industrial Age: The Story of the National Manufacturing Renaissance Campaign," Capital Institute, 2012, 109, http://www.capitalinstitute.org/sites/capitalinstitute.org/files/docs/NMRC-a%(4).pdf.

11. "Instituto Health Science Career Academy Has Grand Opening," *Hispanically Speaking News*, September 26, 2011, http://www.hispanicallyspeakingnews.com/latino-state-news/details/instituto-health-sciences-career-academy-has-grand-opening/10513/; Alex Morales, "Class Now in Session at Instituto's Health Science Career Academy," The Resurrection Project, November 14, 2011, http://www.resurrectionproject.org/news/3163.

12. Quoted in "Mayor Emanuel Announces New Partnership with Five Technology Companies to Create Early College Schools," *Cisco Newsroom*, February 28, 2012, http://newsroom.cisco.com/press-release-content?type=webcontent&articleId=675883.

13. "John Byrne, "Chicago Touts Partnership with Tech Companies," *Education Week*, March 14, 2012, 12–13; "Early College Science Technology Engineering and Mathematics Schools," Chicago Public Schools, August 29, 2012, http://cps.edu/Pages/ECSS.aspx; "Stem Pathways to College and Careers Schools: A Development Guide," IBM Corporation, 2012, 1–9; Stephanie Banchero, "New York Teams Up with IBM to Reboot a High School," *New York Times*, August 1, 2011, A3.

14. Author interview with Marie Trzupek Lynch, President and CEO, Skills for Chicagoland's Future, April 25, 2013.

15. Kathy Bergen, "Cook County, Chicago Create Jobs Program," *Chicago Tribune*, September 13, 2012, 1–2.

16. Author interview with Maria Hibbs, Workforce Consultant, August 30, 2012; Author interview with Jim Lewis, Chicago Community Trust, September 19, 2012; Author interview with Whitney Smith, Employment Program Director, Joyce Foundation, October 22, 2012.

17. *OECD Territorial Reviews, Chicago Tri-State*, 31.

18. Author interview with John Burnett, President and CEO, and Chris Beach, Director of Operations, Community Education Coalition, Columbus, Indiana, October 11, 2011; Chrissy Alspaugh, "Coalition Puts City on Track, Says Expert," *The Republic* (Columbus, IN),

June 9, 2011, A1; Chrissy Alspaugh, "Center to Fuel Local Manufacturing Economy," *The Republic* (Columbus, IN), June 9, 2011, A1; For more information on the Community Education Coalition go to: http://www.educationcoalition.com.

19. Author interview with Joe Fredkone, Instructor, Hennepin Technical College, July 29, 2010; Peter S. Goodman, "After Job Training, Still Scrambling for a Job," *New York Times*, July 19, 2010, A; Find out more about HIRED at http://www.hired.org

20. Quoted in "Jobless Rate Shows Hard Work Paying Off," *Mansfield News Journal*, September 30, 2012, 8A

21. Author interview with Robert Zettler, September 17, 2012, and March 14, 2013.

22. Quoted in Mary Beth Matzek, "Tyrannosaurus Next," *Insight*, September 2012, 28–30, http://www.insightdigital.biz/i/80745/30.

23. James Golembeski, "Workforce Paradox," *Insight on Manufacturing*, September 2012, 17, http://www.insightdigital.biz/i/82845.

24. Quoted in Matzek, "Tyrannosaurus Next," 31.

25. Author interview with Paul Rauscher, October 17, 2011.

26. Richard Ryman, "Mobile Lab Takes Manufacturing Training on the Road," *Green Bay Press—Gazette*, August 27, 2011, http://www.greenbaygazette.com/fdcp/?unique=131 4628192879

27. Rick Barrett, "Marinette Marine Struggles to Attract Young Workers," *Journal Sentinel* (Milwaukee, WI), June 16, 2012, http://www.jsonline.com/business; Author interview with Ann Franz, Strategic Partnership Manager, Northeast Wisconsin Technical College, September 18, 2012.

28. Author interview with Jerry Murphy, September 24, 2012.

29. Author interviews with Vicki Haugen, President andCEO, Vermilion Advantage, January 4, 2012, September 15, 2012, and March 27, 2013; For more information on the Vermilion Advantage, go to http://www.vermilionadvantage.com.

30. Author interview with Ross Meyer, Executive Director, Partners for a Competitive Workforce, September 13, 2012; Mike Boyer, "Factory Careers Are Where It's at," Cincinnati.Com, January 26, 2012, http://news.cincinnati.com/article; Julianna Roche, "A Changing Labor Market," CincyMagazine.Com, December 2011, http://www.cincymagazine.com/ME2/; For more information, see http://www.competitiveworkforce.com.

31. Author interview with Paul Anselmo, President, New Century Careers, September 30, 2012; For more information on New Century Careers, see http://www.ncsquared.com.

32. E-mail message from Dan Fogarty, Human Resources Manager, Schroeder Industries, October 16, 2012.

33. Author interview with Kevin Stolts, President, Talent 2025, October 19, 2012; "An Integrated Talent System for West Michigan," Talent 2025, September 12, 2011, http://talent2025.org/files/documents/misc/TALENT-2025/misc/TALENT-2025-WHITE-PAPER-FULL.pdf; George Erickcek, Brian Pittelko, Bridget Timmeney, and Brad Watts, "Talent 2025 Update Brief: Regional Workforce Demand and System Flows," Upjohn Institute for Employment Research, April 26, 2012.

34. Author interview with Fred Dedrick, Executive Director, National Fund for Workforce Solutions, October 18, 2012; For further information, see http://nfwsolutions.org.

35. Erik W. Robelen, "Funders Set New Round of Support for STEM Teaching," *Education Week*, November 7, 2012, 12.

36. For more information on the Purdue Center for Regional Development, go to http://www.pcrd.purdue.edu.

37. "What the Future Holds for Higher Education in Singapore," Knowledge@SMU (Singapore Management University, September 2011, http://ink.library.smu.edu.sg/ksmu/30; Vivien Stewart, "Singapore: Innovation in Technical Education," Asia Society, January 26, 2012, http://asiasociety.org/benchmarking/singapore-innovation-technical-education.

38. "TIMSS & PIRLS 2011," TIMSS & PIRLS International Study Center, Boston College, December 18, 2012, http://timssandpirls.bc.edu/data-release-2011/pdf/TIMMS-PIRLS-2011-International-Press-Release.pdf.

39. Francesa Froy, "Local Strategies for Developing Workforce Skills," in *Designing Local Skills Strategies*, ed. Francesca Froy, Sylvain Giguére, and Andrea Hofer (Paris: OECD, 2009), 41; "History-Penang Skills Development Centre," Penang Skills Development Centre (PSDC), 2009, http://www.psdc.org.my/html/default.aspx?ID=9&PID=155.

40. Gerrit Wiesmann, "German Companies Set Gold Standard for Apprenticeships," *Financial Times*, July 10, 2012, 4; Eric Westervelt, "The Secret to Germany's Low Youth Unemployment," NPR, April 4, 2012, http://www.npr.org/2012/04/04/149927290/the-secret-to-germanys-low-youth-unemployment; "Apprenticeship Training in Austria—The Dual System," Bundesministerium für Unterricht, Kunst and Kultur, February 23, 2007, http://www.bmukk.gv.at/enfr/school/secon/app.xml; Helena Bachmann, "Who Needs College? The Swiss Opt for Vocational School," TimeWorld, October 4, 2012, http://world.time.com/2012/10/04/who-needs-college-the-swiss-opt-for-vocational-school/; Hilary Steedman, "The State of Apprenticeship in 2010," Centre for Economic Performance, London School of Economics and Political Science, 2010, http://cep.lse.ac.uk/pubs/download/special/cepsp22.pdf.

41. Quoted in Quentin Peel, "Germany Eyes Action on Worker Shortage," *Financial Times*, April 15, 2013, 4,

42. Torben M. Andersen, Nicole Bosch, Anja Deelen, and Rob Euwais, "The Danish Flexicurity Model in the Great Recession," *VOX*, April 8, 2011, http://www.voxeu.org/article/flexicurity-danish-labour-market-model-great-recession; Gordon, *Winning*, 86–87.

43. Anna Moli and Flemming Emil Hansen, "Denmark Split on Opening Door," *Wall Street Journal*, October 11, 2012, A13.

44. Author interviews with George Darte, Walter Sendzik, and Kithio Mwanzia, St. Catharine's, Ontario, Canada, October 19, 2011.

Chapter 8

1. Robert J. Stevens, "Social Engineering," *Wall Street Journal*, April 10, 2006, A12.

2. "The CEOs' Top Priorities," *Wall Street Journal*, November 21, 2011, R2.

3. Matthew Quinn, "CFOs' Wish List," *Wall Street Journal*, June 29, 2012, C8.

4. Ibid; Michael Porter and Jan Rivkin, "What Business Should Do to Restore Competitiveness," *Fortune*, October 15, 2012, http://management.fortune.cnn.com/2012/10/15/porter-rivlin-economy-fix/.

5. Frederick M. Hess and Whitney Downs, "Partnership is a Two-Way Street: What It Takes for Business to Help Drive School Reform," U.S. Chamber of Commerce, Institute

for a Competitive Workforce, June 8, 2011, 6, http://icw.uschamber.com/publication/partnership-two-way-street-what-it-takes-business-help-drive-school-reform.

6. Robert J. Gordon, "Is U.S. Economic Growth Over? Faltering Innovation Confronts the Six Headwinds," NBER Working Paper No. 18315; Kenneth Rogoff, "Our Ignorance Will Yield More Crises in Capitalism," *Financial Times*, February 2, 2012, 9.

7. Richard Shediac, Chadi N. Moujaes, and Mazen Ramsay Najjar, "Demographics Are Not Destiny," Strategy+Business, October 31, 2011, 10, http://www.strategy-business.com/article/00091?gko=36862.

8. Andrew Hill, "Business Leaders Focus on Their Staff," *Financial Times*, January 9, 2013, 19.

9. Jennifer Schramm, "Promoting Sustainability," *HR Magazine*, March 2011, 88; Gordon, *Winning*, 131–135.

10. "2012 Talent Shortage Survey," May 2012, Manpower Group,14–15; "Manpower Group—Talent Shortage Survey," May 29, 2012, http://manpowergroup.us/campaigns/talent-shortage-2012; Hal Weitzman and Johanna Kassel, "U.S. Manufacturers Bring Training on to the Production Line," *Financial Times*, August 22, 2012, 2.

11. Lerman, "Are Skills the Problem?," 68; " 2012 Training Industry Report," *Training Magazine*, November/December 2012, 21; There are three other annual training expenditure surveys by the American Society of Training and Development (ASTD), Survey of Employer Provided Training (SEPT), and the National Employer Survey (NES); *Training Magazine* has conducted its Annual Survey for 31 years. It samples businesses with 100 or more employees. It uses a weighted survey designed to be nationally representative, while ASTD unweighted surveys are not. The *Training Magazine* survey is the only one of the four that asked firms about overall training expenditures for multiple years; Kelly S. Mikelson and Demetra Smith Nightingale, *Estimating Public and Private Expenditures on Occupational Training in the United States* (Washington, DC: U.S. Department of Labor Employment and Training Administration, 2004), 21–25; Becky Yerak, "Sitting Tight on Big Cushions," *Chicago Tribune*, September 25, 2011, 1, 3.

12. Quoted in Michael S. Malone, "How to Avoid a Bonfire of the Humanities," *Wall Street Journal*, October 25, 2012, A24.

13. "Better Skills, Better Jobs, Better Lives: A Strategic Approach to Skills Policies," OECD, May 2012, http://dx.doi.org/10.1787/9789264177338-en.

14. Simon Caulkin, "The Art of Leadership," *FT.COM/ Business Education*, January 2013, 12; Robert W. Goldfarb, "How to Bridge the Hiring Gap," *New York Times*, November 11, 2012, BU9.

15. Gordon, *2010 Meltdown*, 153–154; Gordon, *Winning*, 136–137.

16. Pat Galagan, "Disappearing Act: The Vanishing Corporate Classroom," *T & D*, March 2010, 29–31; Salaman Khan, "The Rise of the Tech-Powered Teacher," *Education Week*, October 3, 2012, 28; Mark Edmundson, "The Trouble with Online Education," *New York Times*, July 20, 2012, A19; Jennifer Hofmann, "Top 10 Challenges of Blended Learning," *Training*, March/April 2011, 12–13; Margery Weinstein, "Is Technology Fulfilling Its Promise?," *Training*, September/October 2011, 32–34; Allison Rossett and James Marshall, "E-Learning: What's Old is New Again," *T & D*, January 2010, 34–38; Edward E. Gordon, Ronald R. Morgan, and Judith A. Ponticell, *Futurework: The Revolution Reshaping American Business* (Westport, CT: Praeger, 1994), 169–192; Best practice training research that offers

the practical answers to the who, what, when, where, and how strategies and programs to improve employee training and education throughout an organization; Gordon, *2010 Meltdown*, 154–157.

17. Shaila Dewan, "Working Nonstop to Stay Relevant," *New York Times*, September 22, 2012, B1–B2.

18. Diane Stafford, "Young Achievers Often Short-Timers," *Chicago Tribune*, October 15, 2012, 4; Maria L. Kraimer, Scott E. Seibert, Sandy J. Wayne, Robert C. Liden, and Jesus Bravo, "Antecedents and Outcomes of Organizational Support for Development: The Critical Role of Career Opportunities," *Journal of Applied Psychology*, 96 (May 2011): 485–500.

19. Andrew Hill, "Rethink Required on Graduate Training, *Financial Times*, January 8, 2013, 10.

20. "The Tussle for Talent," *The Economist*, January 8, 2011, 68.

21. Edward E. Gordon, "Human Capital," in *Business: The Ultimate Resourc,* 2nd.ed. (Cambridge, MA: Basic Books, 2006), 142.

22. Jack J. Phillips and Patti P. Phillips, "Confronting CEO Expectations about the Value of Learning," *T & D*, January 2010, 53.

23. Jenny Cermak and Monica McGurk, "Putting a Value on Training," *McKinsey Quarterly*, July 2010, 4–5, http://thecreativeleadershipforum.com/storage/Putting%20 A%20Value%20on%20Training.pdf.

24. Rebecca Everett, "Tangible Return on Investment: Integrating Learning to Reach Desired Results," *T & D*, February 2009, 50–53; Gordon, *2010 Meltdown*, 174–176; Gordon, *Winning*, 138–140.

25. Gordon, *Skill Wars*, 75–83.

26. James Manyika, Susan Lund, Byron Auguste, Lenny Mendonca, Tim Welsh, and Sreenivas Ramaswamy, "An Economy that Works: Job Creation and America's Future," McKinsey Global Institute, June, 2011, 8, http://www.mckinsey.com/insights/mgi/research/labor_markets/an_economy_that_works_for_us_job_creation.

27. Peter Drucker, *Managing in Turbulent Times* (New York: Harper & Row, 1980), 44.

Chapter 9

1. *Better Skills, Better Jobs, Better Lives.*

2. "Invest in America Alliance," *Intel*, February 23, 2010, http://www.intel.com/pressroom/archive/releases/2010/20100223corp.htm.

3. Gordon, "Human Capital," 142.

4. Thomas A. Kochan, "A Jobs Compact for America's Future," *Harvard Business Review*, March 2012, 1, http://hbr.org/2012/03/a-jobs-compact-for-americas-future/ar/1.

5. Tom Peters, "Manifesto for the New Rules on Human Capital," *Financial Times*, August 27, 2012, 8.

6. Lerman, "Are Skills the Problem?," 70–71.

7. C. Torres, "The Design of Tax Systems Influence Investment in Skills Development," in *Better Skills*, 30.

8. Steven Covey, "Talks about the 8th Habit: Effective Is No Longer Enough," *Training*, February 2005, 18.

9. Carol Corrado, Dan Sichel, and Charles Hutton, "Intangible Capital and Economic Growth," National Bureau of Economic Research Working Paper No, 11948, January 2006, 32–33.

10. Quoted in Robin Harding, "How Analysts Will Add 3 Per Cent to GDP," *Financial Times*, April 22, 2013, 3.

11. Ibid.

12. Gordon, *Skill Wars*, 136–142.

13. Edward E. Gordon, "A New Talent-Investment Metric Is Needed to Advance Technological Leadership and Increase Jobs," *Employment Relations Today* 37 (Fall 2010): 9–10; David McCann, "Human Capital," *CFO Magazine*, March 2011, 34, http://www.cfo.com/article.cfm/14557286; Eric Krell, "The Global Talent Mismatch," *Human Resources*, June 2011, 4–5, http://www.shrm.org/Publications/hrmagazine/EditorialContent/2011/0611/Pages/0611krell.aspx; Edward E. Gordon, "Accounting Change Needed to Address Talent Shortfalls," Web CPA, December 22, 2009, http://www.webcpa.com/news/Accounting-Change-Needed-Address-Talent-Shortfalls-52783–1.html.

14. Corrado, "Intangible Capital," 33.

15. Jonathan Cummings, James Manyika, Lenny Mendonca, Ezra Greenberg, Steven Aronowitz, Rohit Chopra, Katy Elkin, Sreenivas Ramaswamy, Jimmy Soni, and Alllison Watson, "Growth and Competitiveness in the United States: The Role of Its Multinational Companies," McKinsey Global Institute, June 2010, 6–7, http://www.mckinsey.com/insights/americas/growth_and_competitiveness_in_us.

16. Peters, "Manifesto," 8.

17. "Female Power," *The Economist*, January 2, 2010, 49–51; Sylvia Ann Hewlett, "Focus on the Female Talent in the Backyard," *Financial Times*, May 12, 2008, 17; Sue Shellenbarger, "The Mommy Drain: Employers Beef up Perks to Lure New Mothers Back to Work," *Wall Street Journal*, September 28, 2006, D1.

18. David Wessel, "Older Staffers Get Uneasy Embrace," *Wall Street Journal*, May 15, 2008, A2; Erin White, "The New Recruits: Older Workers," *Wall Street Journal*, January 14, 2008, B3; "Retiring Baby Boomers Creating Workforce Talent Shortage," BenefitsLink, June 11, 2007, http:benefitslink.com/pr/detail.php?id=40735; Tamara Erickson, *Retire Retirement: Career Strategies for the Boomer Generation* (Boston: Harvard Business Press, 2008), 1–3, 41–47; Elizabeth Pope, "They Won't Let Me Retire," *AARP Bulletin*, March 2008, 12–13; Diana Farrell, Eric Beinhocker, Ezra Greenberg, Suruchi Shukla, Jonathan Ablett, and Geoffrey Greene, "Talkin'Bout My Generation: The Economic Impact of Aging U.S. Baby Boomers," McKinsey Global Institute, June 2008, 17–21, http://www.mckinsey.com/insights/mgi/research/americas/talkin_bout_my_generation; Experience Works is a 40-year-old national nonprofit organization that offers training and employment opportunities for older workers. For more information, see http://www.experienceworks.org or call 866–397–9757.

19. Rex W. Huppke, "Don't Be Afraid to Hire People with Disabilities," *Chicago Tribune*, December 10, 2012, 1, 4; Margery Weinstein, "An Untapped Talent Pool," *Training*, September/October, 2011, 38–40; Amy Merrick, "Erasing 'Un' from 'Unemployable,'" *Wall Street Journal*, August 2, 2007, B1; Joyce Gioia, "Hiring People with Disabilities Makes Business Sense," Herman Trend Alert, January 23, 2008, http://www.herman-group.com/alert/archive_1–23–2008.html; Kevin Hollenbeck and Jean Kimmel, "The Returns to Education and Basic Skills Training for Individuals with Poor Health or Disability," W.E. Upjohn

Institute Working Paper 01–72, August 2001, http://ssrn.com/abstract=292230; U.S. Department of Labor, Office, Occupational Health & Safety Administration, News Release, "Employers Gain Access to Database of 2,000 Job Candidates with Disabilities," March 29, 2007, 1, http://ohsonline.com/articles/2007/03/dol-database-lists-2000-job-candidates-with-disabilities.aspx.

20. Dan Bloom, "Employment-Focused Program for Ex-Prisoners," MDRC, July 7, 2006, iii, http://www.mdrc.org/employment-focused-programs-ex-prisoners; Robert K. Elder, "Beyond License Plates," *Chicago Tribune*, May 22, 2007, 1; Paul VanDeCarr, "Call to Action: How Programs in Three Cities Responded to the Prisoner Reentry Crisis," Public/Private Ventures, March, 2007, 1–2, http://ppv.issuelab.org/resource/call_to_action_how_programs_in_three_cities_responded_to_the_prisoner_reentry_crisis; Steven Greenhouse, "States Help Ex-Inmates Find Jobs," *New York Times*, January 25, 2011, B1, B4; U.S. Department of Labor, Federal Bonding Program, "A Best Practice Guide to Fidelity Bonds: The Power Tool in the Employment Toolbox." For more information, see http://www.bonds4jobs.com or call 800–233–2258; Nicole Lindahl, "Venturing beyond the Gates: Facilitating Successful Reentry with Entrepreneurship," Prisoner Reentry Institute, Summer 2007, 11, http://www.jjay.cuny.edu/VenturingBeyondtheGates.pdf; Amy L. Solomon, Jenny W. L. Osborne, Stefan F. LoBuglio, Jeff Mellow, and Debbie A. Mukamal, "Life after Lockup: Improving Reentry from Jail to the Community," May 2008. (This report features successful programs from many parts of the United States.) http://www.urban.org/UploadedPDF/411660_life_after_lockup.pdf.

21. Paul Rieckhoff, "Solving the Riddle of Veteran Unemployment," *Forbes*, June 22, 2012, http://www.forbes.com/sites/paulrieckhoff/2012/06/22/solving-the-riddle-of-veteran-employment; The website, Career One Stop, sponsored by the U.S. Department of Labor, Employment & Training Administration, offers an online "Military to Civilian Occupation Translator." It helps service members match their military skills and experience to civilian occupations. It also has links to a wide variety of information resources. See http://www.careerinfonet.org/moc/; For a review of how to expand the talent pool by better training individuals from the populations of U.S. workers cited in endnotes 14–17, see Gordon, *Winning*, 99–112.

22. Arthur Levine, "The Suburban Education Gap," *Wall Street Journal*, November 15, 2012, A19.

23. Peggy Noonan, "Look Ahead with Stoicism and Optimism," *Wall Street Journal*, January 2, 2012, 18.

24. William Bennett, "STEM-Deficient Education Holds Back Nation's Economy," *Detroit Free Press*, February 18, 2013, http://www.freep.com/apps/pbcs.dll/article?AID=2013302180009.

25. "The Great Schools Revolution," *The Economist*, September 17, 2011, 23.

26. Ibid, 24.

27. Ulrich Boser and Lindsay Rosenthal, "Do Schools Challenge Our Students," Center for American Progress, July 10, 2012, 2–4, http://www.americanprogress.org/wp-content/uploads/issues/2012/07/pdf/state_of_education.pdf.

28. "Charting a Better Course," *The Economist*, July 7, 2012, 29; "Great Schools," 25.

29. "Multiple Choice: Charter School Performance in 16 States," CREDO, June 2009, http://credo.stanford/edu/reports/MULTIPLE_CHOICE_CREDO.pdf.

30. KIPP website, http://www.kipp.org (accessed January 30, 2013).

31. Joel Klein, "New York's Charter Schools Get an A+," *Wall Street Journal*, July 27, 2012, A13.

32. Roland G. Fryer, Jr., "Learning from the Successes and Failures of Charter Schools," Hamilton Project, September 2012, 13–15, http://www.hamiltonproject.org/files/down loads_and_links/THP_Fryer_Charters_DiscPaper.pdf; Extensive research and best practices on high-quality tutoring programs can be found in Edward E. Gordon, Ronald R. Morgan, Charles O'Malley, and Judith Ponticell, *The Tutoring Revolution: Applying Research for Best Practices, Policy Implications, and Student Achievement* (New York: Rowman and Littlefield Education, 2007).

33. Quoted in Jennifer Delgado, "CPS Offers Tips on Boosting Parent Involvement," *Chicago Tribune*, November 19, 2012, 10.

34. "Up to the Challenge: The Role of Career and Technical Education and 21st Century Skills in College and Career Readiness," Association for Career and Technical Education, National Association of State Directors of Career Technical Education Consortium, and Partnership for 21st Century Skills, October 2010, 7–36, http://www.p21.org/storage/documents/CTE_Oct2010.pdf (accessed February 4, 2013); Kenneth B. Hoyt, *Career Education: History and Future* (Tulsa, OK: National Career Development Association, 2005), 23, 25, 150.

35. Philadelphia Academies Inc. website, http://www.academiesinc.org (accessed February 18, 2013); Gordon, *Winning*, 114–115.

36. Author interview with Alice Chute, CART, February 19, 2013; Gordon, *Winning*, 118–119.

37. Author interview with Sydney Rogers, Executive Director, Alignment Nashville, March 1, 2013; More information is available at http://www.alignmentnashville.org.

38. Author interviews with Thomas Flavin, CEO and President, Coachella Valley Economic Partnership, and Sheila Thornton, Council Coordinator, Coachella Valley Economic Partnership, February 20, 2013; Workforce Excellence website, http://smartstudentsgreat jobs.org (accessed February 25, 2013).

39. Don Peck, "Can the Middle Class Be Saved?" *The Atlantic*, September 2011, 72, 76; "National Career Academy Standards of Practice," December 1, 2004, http://www.career academies.net/_docs/CAGuide_APPB.pdf (accessed February 4, 2013); Lynn Olson, "Vocational Programs Earn Mixed Revenues, Face Academic Push," *Education Week*, May 24, 2006, 21; Lerman, "Are Skills the Problem?," 61–63; For additional detailed information on CCAs, see the case studies and research information in the following: Gordon, *Winning*, 113–135; Gordon, *2010 Meltdown*, 124–133; Gordon, *Skill Wars*, 213–252.

40. U.S. Department of Labor, Employment and Training Administration, http://www .doleta.gov/OA/data_statistics.cfm (accessed January 21, 2013); Nancy Hoffman, *Schooling in the Workplace* (Cambridge, MA: Harvard Education Press, 2011), 110. An excellent book on global technical education systems; Anthony P. Carnevale, Tamara Jayasundera, and Andrew R. Hanson, "Career and Technical Education: Five Ways That Pay Along the Way to the B.A.," Georgetown University Center on Education and the Workplace, September 2012, 22–26, http://cew.georgetown.edu/ctefiveways/.

41. Chris Bryant, "A German Model Goes Global," *Financial Times*, May 22, 2012, 10.

42. Ibid.

43. Ibid.

44. "Northrup Grumman Shipbuilding," Corporate Voices for Working Families, 2010, http://www.cvworkingfamilies.org/system/files/Northrup+Grumman+EL+Edits.pdf;   For more details on the Apprentice School in Newport News, see http://www.apprenticeschool.com/about.html.

45. Tony Proscio, "From Hidden Costs to High Returns," National Network of Sector Partners, 2010, 2, http://www.insightcced.org/uploads/publications/wd/HiddenCosts-HighReturns.pdf.

46. "Great Schools," 25.

47. Michael Barber and Mona Mourshed, "How the World's Best-Performing School Systems Come out on Top," McKinsey & Company, 2007, 16–23, 38, http://mckinseyonsociety.com/downloads/reports/Education/World_School_Systems_Final.pdf; "Lessons from PISA for the United States, Strong Performers and Successful Reformers in Education," (OECD Publishing, 2011), 125–126, http://dx.doi/10.1787/9789264096660-en.

48. Barber and Mourshed, "How the World's Best-Performing School Systems Come out on Top," 20–21; Nam-Hwa Kang and Miyoung Hong, "Achieving Excellence in Teacher Workforce and Equity in Learning Opportunities in South Korea," *Educational Researcher* 37 (May 2008): 202.

49. Barber and Mourshed, "How the World's Best-Performing School Systems Come out on Top," 30–31.

50. Ibid., 34–37.

51. "Ensuring Fair and Reliable Measures of Effective Teaching," MET Project, January 2013, 5, http://metproject.org/downloads/MET_Ensuring_Fair_and_Reliable_Measures_Practioner_Brief.pdf.

52. Raj Chetty, John N. Friedman, and Jonah E. Rockoff, "The Long-Term Impacts of Teachers: Teacher Value-Added and Student Outcomes in Adulthood," National Bureau of Economic Research, December 2011, 5, http://obs.rc.fas.harvard.edu/chetty/value_added.pdf; Annie Lowrey, "Study Links Good Teachers to Lasting Gains," *New York Times*, January 6, 2012, A1, A14.

53. Quoted in Sir Michael Barber, "Neither Rest nor Tranquility: Education and the American Dream in the 21st Century," WestEd Policy Perspectives, September 15, 2008, 11, http://www.wested.org/online/pubs/pp-09–02.pdf.

Chapter 10

1. H. G. Wells, *An Outline of History* (London: George Newnes, 1920), 1301.

2. David Brooks, "Carpe Diem Nation," *New York Times*, February 12, 2013, A27.

3. John E. Silvia, "Rocky Mountain Summit: July 2012," Wells Fargo Economics Group Special Commentary, August 9, 2012, 5.

4. Ibid; John E. Silvia, "Employment: Continued Hints of Structural Change," Wells Fargo Economics Group Newsletter, February 25, 2013, 1.

5. Jeffrey Sachs, "U.S. Economic Debate Must Move on from the 1930s," *Financial Times*, July 13, 2012, 9.

6. Garry Kasparov and Peter Thiel, "Our Dangerous Illusion of Technological Progress," *Financial Times*, November 9, 2012, 11.

7. Richard Dobbs, Susan Lund, and Anu Madgavkar, "Talent Tensions Ahead: A CEO Briefing," *McKinsey Quarterly*, 1, https://www.mckinseyquarterly.com/Talent_tensions_ahead_A_CEO_briefing_3033.

8. "Employment Trends in the 21st Century," International Center for Peace and Development (ICPD), http://www.icpd.org/employment/Empltrends21century.htm (accessed February 11, 2013).

9. "Global Talent Risk—Seven Responses," 7.

10. Rainer Strack, Jean-Michel Caye, Svend Lassen, Vikram Bhalla, J. Puckett, Ernesto G. Espinosa, Florent Francoeur, and Pieter Haen, "Creating People Advantage 2010," The Boston Consulting Group and World Federation of People Management Associations, September 2010, 17, http://www.aidp/ALLEGATI/FILES/2880.pdf.

11. David Pearce Snyder, "A Rendezvous with Austerity," *The Futurist*, July-August 2009, 44.

12. Quoted in Thomas L. Friedman, "Pass the Books. Hold the Oil," *New York Times*, March 10, 2012, http://www.nytimes.com/2012/03/11/opinion/.

13. David Wessel, "Desperately Seeking Blueprint for Growth," *Wall Street Journal*, August 4, 2011, A4.

Index

About the Author

EDWARD E. GORDON is an internationally recognized writer, researcher, speaker, and consultant on the future of America's and the world's workforce, educational preparation for jobs and careers, and regional economic development. His prior books include *Winning the Global Talent Showdown, The 2010 Meltdown: Solving the Impending Jobs Crisis, Skill Wars,* and *FutureWork*. He is president of Imperial Consulting in Chicago and Palm Desert, California. Imperial has served a broad range of over 300 clients from Fortune 500 companies and the Swiss government to the Federal Reserve Bank and professional associations, workforce/economic development boards, nonprofit organizations in health care, K–12, and higher education, museums, and think tanks.